Illustrated Generic CADD
Level 3

Ann W. Dunn

Wordware Publishing, Inc.

Library of Congress Cataloging-in-Publication Data

Dunn, Ann W.
    Illustrated generic CADD level 3 / by Ann W. Dunn.
        p.   cm.
    Includes index.
    ISBN 1-55622-153-3
    1. Computer graphics.   2. Computer-aided design.   I. Title.
II. Title: Illustrated generic CADD level three.
T385.D87   1989
620'.0042'0285—dc20   89-14764
                                   CIP

Copyright 1990, Wordware Publishing, Inc.
1506 Capital Avenue
Plano, Texas 75074

All Rights Reserved

Printed in the United States of America

ISBN 1-55622-153-3
10 9 8 7 6 5 4 3 2 1
9001

All inquiries for volume purchases of this book should be addressed to Wordware
Publishing, Inc., at the above address. Telephone inquiries may be made by calling:

(214) 423-0090

Contents

Contents (continued)

Recommended Learning Sequence

Recommended Learning Sequence (continued)

Module 1
ABOUT THIS BOOK

INTRODUCTION

This book describes the Generic CADD Level 3 computer aided drafting system. If you have the Level 1 or Level 2 version, just select the commands appropriate for your version, as each successive version builds on the other. Generic CADD, a product of Generic Software of Bothell, Washington, is the most widely used computerized drawing tool available for low cost. The sophisticated software is used for drawings of all types, including architectural, mechanical, circuit board layouts, manufacturing, facilities, and graphic arts.

This book is designed for the beginning computer graphic user as well as the experienced Generic CADD user. New users learn readily from the recommended learning sequence of commands, and experienced users find the text a valuable reference source, with numerous examples for full use of the commands.

The learning sequence is provided to act as a guide to learning the software. This process is similar to the way you learned to draw with pencil and paper. First the drawing size and line weights are selected, then drawing elements are created, followed by editing functions and production of the drawing on paper.

ORGANIZATION

This book is not designed to be read in page-number order. If you are just learning Generic CADD, follow the Recommended Learning Sequence found in the front of the book. After a brief introduction to the software in Modules 1 and 2, Modules 3 through 76 are arranged alphabetically by command. After you have followed the Recommended Learning Sequence through to completion, the text serves as an invaluable reference guide.

The first 15 modules in the Recommended Learning Sequence give detailed, easy-to-follow directions on entering Generic CADD, starting a drawing, and quitting the drawing. After these first modules, these explicit steps are eliminated.

For those in a hurry to actually draw with Generic CADD, Module 2, the Sample Session, employs the most commonly used commands to draw the layout of a commercial office. You quickly see that Generic CADD is highly sophisticated and capable of drawing whatever you can imagine. In addition, the Sample Session serves as a thorough overview, so you have an understanding of where you are going as you proceed through the Recommended Learning Sequence.

STYLE CONVENTIONS

Understanding a few simple conventions used in this book makes it much easier to use.

- Discussion of Generic CADD features, procedures, and applications is presented in paragraph form.
- Steps to perform the Typical Operations are numbered.
- Keys that are typed or pressed are noted in bold type.
- The notation < CR > or Return stands for the "Carriage Return" key on your computer. Depending upon your brand of computer, this key may be labeled "Return" or "Enter." There may be one of each on your keyboard. In this case, they are used interchangably. Another computer brand may use the symbol ◄┘ to denote the Return key.

HARDWARE REQUIREMENTS

Generic CADD supports a wide variety of computers, input devices, monitors, printers, and plotters. No attempt has been made to describe the procedures for configuring specific hardware. The author assumes that you or someone working with you has correctly configured Generic CADD for your particular hardware. Depending upon your hardware configuration, you may find that some of the drawings you create in the exercises extend beyond the screen boundaries. Use the ZOOM ALL (ZA) command when necessary to bring all of the graphics into view.

The minimum hardware requirements for Level 1 and 2 Generic CADD are as follows:

- An IBM PC, PC/XT, PC/AT, or compatible with 512k RAM minimum.
- 2 floppy disk drives, 360k or larger OR 1 floppy disk drive and 1 hard disk drive.
- A video graphics controller board, operating in a minimum 640 x 200 mode.

The minimum hardware requirements for Level 3 Generic CADD are as follows:

- An IBM PC, PC/XT, PC/AT, or compatible with 640k RAM.
- 2 floppy disk drives, 360k or larger OR 1 floppy disk drive and 1 hard disk drive. Note that running Level 3 on a 2-floppy drive system is not recommended.
- A video graphics controller board, operating in a minimum 640 x 200 mode.

Optional hardware includes:

- An input device, such as a mouse or a digitizer. Note that Levels 1 and 2 do not support digitizers.
- A plotter for drawing output.
- A 8087 or 80287 math coprocessor to speed performance.

Module 2
SAMPLE SESSION

INTRODUCTION

This sample session is intended to give you a quick introduction to Generic CADD. By using the power of a set of common commands, you quickly appreciate the power of this excellent design program. This session takes you through the steps necessary to create this office plan.

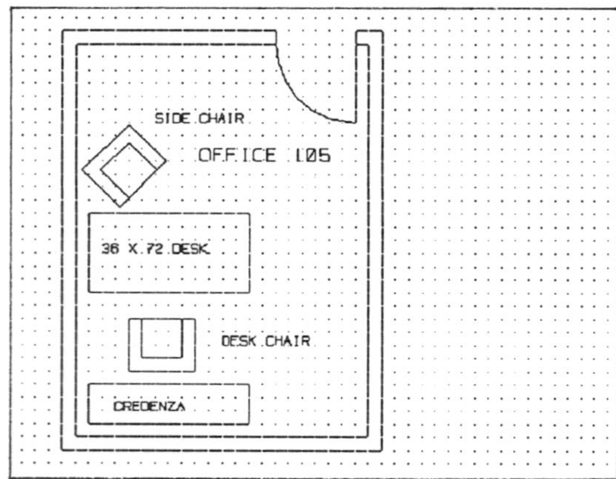

The most commonly used Generic CADD commands are used:

LIMITS (LS)	SINGLE LINE (L1)
ZOOM LIMITS (ZL)	2 POINT ARC (A2)
SIZE GRID (GS)	RECTANGLE (RE)
DOUBLE WIDTH (TH)	ZOOM WINDOW (ZW)
DOUBLE LINE (L2)	OBJECT COPY (OC)
CLEAN CORNER (KT)	ZOOM ALL (ZA)
WINDOW COPY (WC)	OBJECT BREAK (OB)
WINDOW ROTATE (WR)	REDRAW (RD)
DRAWING SAVE (DS)	TEXT PLACE (TP)
TEXT SIZE (TZ)	QUIT (QU)

Almost all of the commands in Generic CADD are accessed through the keyboard with two letters. Upper or lower case is acceptable. You can select the commands from the menu on the right of the screen with the second button of your mouse. If you do not have a mouse, use arrow keys and the PgUp and PgDn keys on your keyboard to access the full menu. If the cursor on the menu moves too fast, press Del to slow it down or Ins to speed it up. As you move the drawing screen cursor to the far right of the screen over the menu, it aligns with the rectangular menu cursor. As you move the cursor on the drawing screen, note that the menu cursor is also moving in a corresponding manner up and down the menu list. If you are using your keyboard to move on the drawing screen, use the arrow keys to move the screen cursor. Select points on the drawing screen with the first (from the left) button on your mouse. If you do not have a mouse, use the Return key on your keyboard to select points on the drawing screen. If you select the wrong command, press Esc on the keyboard to free you to select another command.

START GENERIC CADD

Perform the following steps to begin a new drawing.

1. Start Generic CADD. Type **CADD** at the DOS prompt and press **Return**. The Generic CADD title page is displayed as shown in the following illustration.

```
******   G E N E R I C  ---  C A D D   ******
                 LEVEL 3  VER. 1.11

   Configured for:

      IBM VGA  (PS/2 Models 30-286 & up) . 640 x 480     16 color

      LOGITECH LOGIMOUSE C7 (SERIAL)

      H.P. 7475A PLOTTER

      Memory Available for Drawing Data:  135230

   LICENSED TO: ANN W. DUNN, ANN W. DUNN AIA, # ILEV3 ?

         USE OF AN AUTHORIZED COPY OF THIS SOFTWARE BEYOND THIS POINT
       CONSTITUTES YOUR ACCEPTANCE OF THE ACCOMPANYING LICENSE AGREEMENT.
   Copyright(C) 1985,86,87,88,89 by GENERIC SOFTWARE,INC. All Rights Reserved.


      ******   PRESS RETURN KEY TO BEGIN - [ESC] TO QUIT   ******
```

The Level and version number of your software are listed at the top. A summary of how the software has been configured for your hardware set-up follows. Your configuration may be different from those items listed in the title page illustration. After the configuration listing is a summary statement concerning the license agreement for use of the software.

2. Press **Return** to continue. The following prompt is displayed.

ENTER A DRAWING FILE NAME

---

3. Type **SAMPLE**. Drawing names can be up to eight characters. Press **Return**. The following prompt is displayed.

DRAWING FILE NOT FOUND: SAMPLE.DWG
IS THIS A NEW DRAWING (Y OR N)

Generic CADD has not found a drawing by that name, and it is asking you to verify that this is a new drawing.

4. Type **Y** to confirm. No Return is necessary. Now, the drawing screen and menu are displayed. You are ready to begin a drawing.

```
                                                    DRAW
                                                    COMPONENT
                                                    TEXT
                                                    HATCH/FILL
                                                    ZOOMS
                                                    LINES
                                                    OBJECTS
                                                    WINDOWS
                                                    LAYERS
                                                    DRAWING
                                                    DIMENSION
                                                    CONTROLS
                                                    GRIDS
                                                    DISPLAY
                                                    UNITS
                                                    UTILITIES
                                                    MEASURE
                                                    OUTPUT



                                                    ██████████


   ENTER A COMMAND >
   DRAWING NAME: SAMPLE,  LAYER: 0, ALL LAYERS: OFF,  ZOOM 1: 4.30
   MEMORY USED:   0.000%, LINE TYPE: 0, LINE COLOR: 1
```

SET UP THE DRAWING

5. Set the drawing dimensions.

ENTER A COMMAND > **LS**
CHANGE HEIGHT LIMIT (24.000) IN. > **18'**

CHANGE WIDTH LIMIT (36.000) IN. > **14'**

---

6. Now ZOOM to show the full extents of the drawing area just defined.

```
ENTER A COMMAND > ZL
```

7. Set the grid size.

```
ENTER A COMMAND > GS
CHANGE GRID SIZE (1.000) IN. > 6  <CR>
```

DRAW THE FLOOR PLAN

8. Set the thickness of the wall.

```
ENTER A COMMAND > TH
CHANGE DOUBLE LINE OFFSET 1 (1.000) > 0 <CR>
CHANGE DOUBLE LINE OFFSET 2 (0.000) > 6 <CR>
```

9. Set grid snap. This snap mode remains in effect until issued again.

```
ENTER A COMMAND > SG
SNAP TO GRID IS ON
```

10. Draw the wall lines, beginning in the upper left corner.

```
ENTER A COMMAND > L2
ENTER START POINT > > 1',17'  <CR>
```

11. Prepare to enter wall distance. Set coordinate entry to relative mode.

```
ENTER NEXT POINT > MR
MANUAL ENTRY/LAST POINT
```

12. Enter length of wall line by entering the X and Y coordinates.

NOTE
Unless the foot notation mark is given in a distance, Generic CADD assumes the distance is in inches.

```
ENTER A POINT OR COMMAND > 13',0  <CR>
ESCAPE OR PEN UP TO STOP
```

13. Enter remaining wall distances.

```
ENTER NEXT POINT >  0,-16'  <CR>
ENTER NEXT POINT >  -12',0  <CR>
ENTER NEXT POINT >  0,17' <CR>
```

14. The four walls are complete. Discontinue wall line.

```
ENTER NEXT POINT >  PU
```

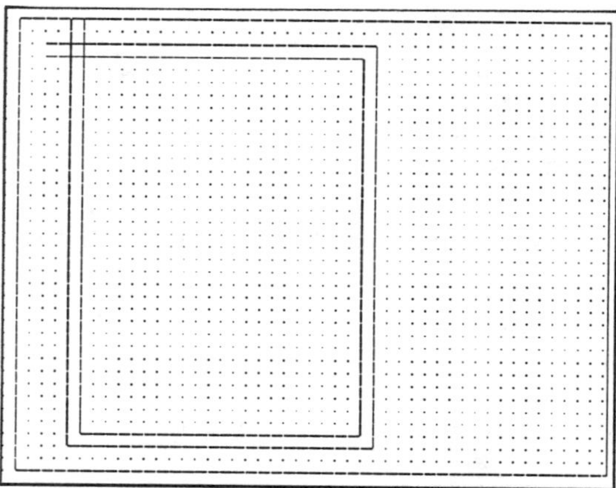

15. Set the coordinate entry mode to offset from the drawing origin.

```
ENTER A COMMAND >  MO
MANUAL ENTRY/ORIGIN
```

16. Clean up the intersecting lines in the upper left corner.

```
ENTER A COMMAND >  KT
ENTER A POINT ON THE OBJECT TO CORNER CLEAN >  2'2,16'8 <CR>
ENTER A POINT OUTSIDE CORNER >  1'6,17'6  <CR>
```

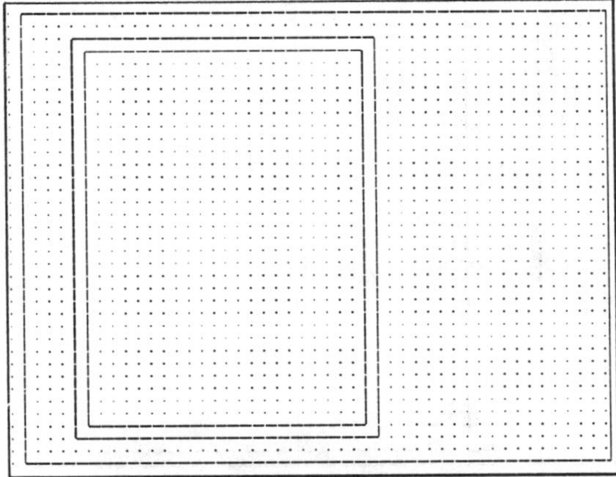

17. Now break an opening in the wall for the doorway. Break each wall line, beginning with the outside line.

```
ENTER A COMMAND>  OB
ENTER A POINT ON THE OBJECT TO BREAK>  13',17'  <CR>
ENTER BREAK POINT>  13',17'  <CR>
ENTER SECOND BREAK POINT>  10',17'  <CR>
```

18. Repeat to break the inside line of the wall.

NOTE

To repeat the previous command, you may press the Spacebar or enter the two letter command designation again. If no command is given, Generic CADD assumes you are drawing straight lines with the L1 command.

```
ENTER A COMMAND>  <Spacebar>
```

Pressing the Spacebar repeats the Object Break command.

```
ENTER A POINT ON THE OBJECT TO BREAK>  13',16'6  <CR>
ENTER BREAK POINT>  13',16'6  <CR>
ENTER SECOND BREAK POINT>  10',16'6  <CR>
```

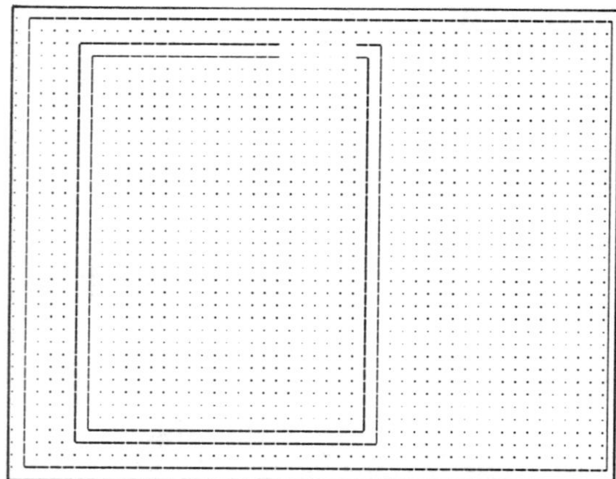

19. Redraw the drawing screen to have all the grid points reappear.

> ENTER A COMMAND> **RD**

20. Add two 6" lines to close the wall gaps.

> ENTER A COMMAND> **L1**
> ENTER START POINT> > **10',16'6 <CR>**
> ENTER NEXT POINT> **10',17' <CR>**
> ENTER NEXT POINT> **PU**

NOTE

The PEN UP command is also invoked by pressing the Esc key.

21. Repeat to close the remaining gap.

> ENTER A COMMAND> **L1**
> ENTER START POINT> > **13',16'6 <CR>**
> ENTER NEXT POINT> **13',17' <CR>**
> ENTER NEXT POINT> **PU**

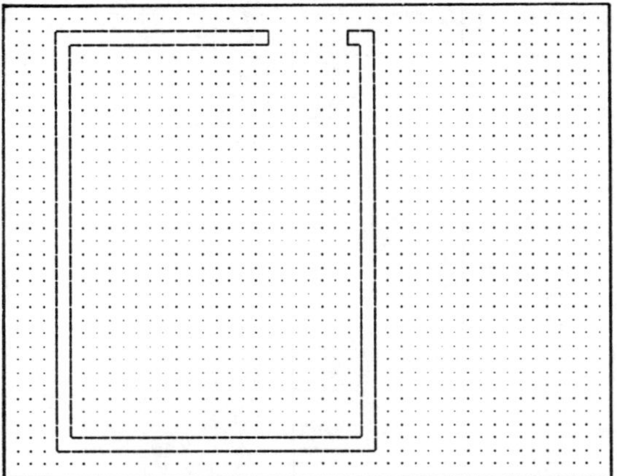

22. Add the door.

```
ENTER A COMMAND > L1
ENTER START POINT > > 13',16'6  <CR>
ENTER NEXT POINT > 13',13'6  <CR>
ENTER NEXT POINT > PU
```

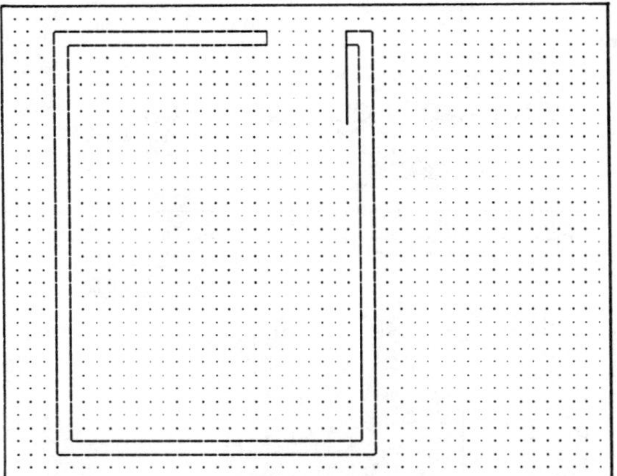

23. Add the arc to represent the door swing.

```
ENTER A COMMAND > A2
ENTER THE CENTER OF THE ARC > 13',16'6  <CR>
ENTER START OF ARC > 10',16'6  <CR>
ENTER THE END OF THE ARC > 13',13'6  <CR>
```

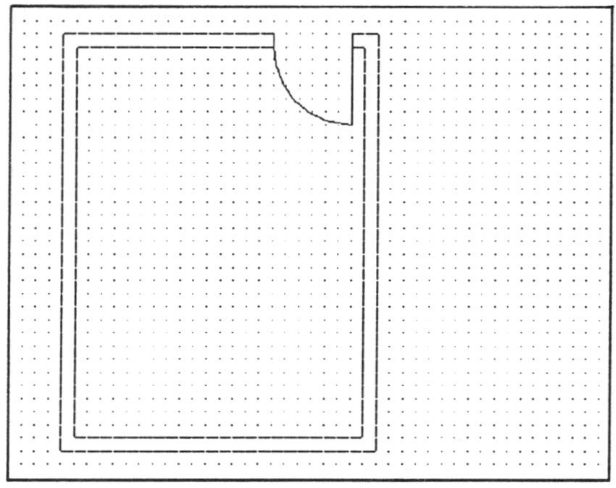

NOTE

If you make a mistake at any time, type EL or select Objects-Erase Last to remove each line drawn in the reverse order of placement.

24. Draw a rectangle to create the desk.

```
ENTER A COMMAND > RE
ENTER A CORNER OF RECTANGLE > 3',7'  <CR>
ENTER NEXT CORNER OF RECTANGLE > 9',10' <CR>
```

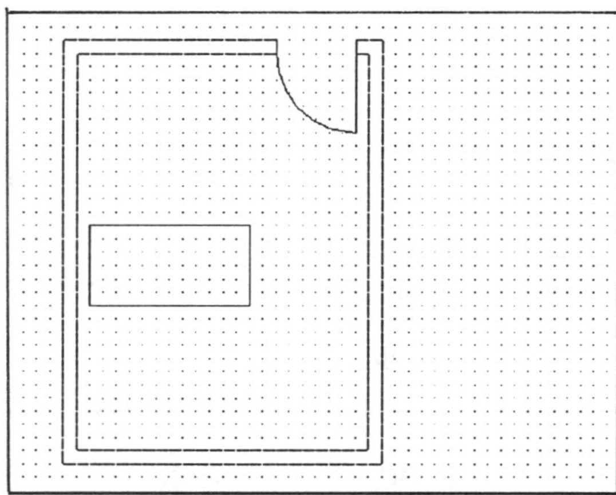

25. Draw the credenza as a rectangle.

```
ENTER A COMMAND> RE
ENTER A CORNER OF RECTANGLE> 3',2'  <CR>
ENTER NEXT CORNER OF RECTANGLE> 9',3'6  <CR>
```

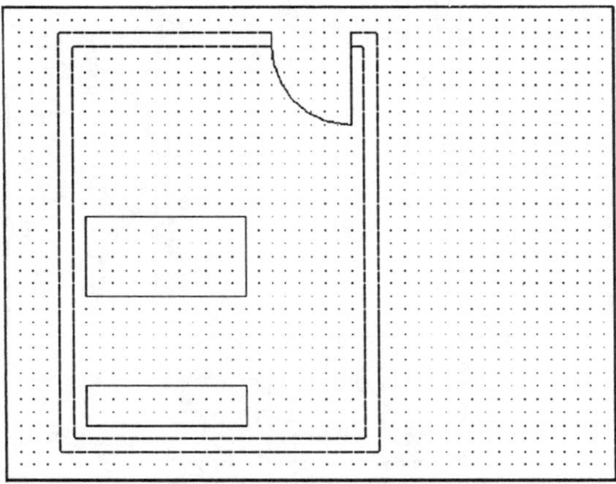

26. Draw the desk chair. Enlarge the screen viewing area to see the chair to be drawn more easily.

```
ENTER A COMMAND> ZW
PLACE WINDOW> (Select two diagonal points that will create a windowed viewing area around the desk/credenza area.)
ENTER A COMMAND> RE
ENTER A CORNER OF RECTANGLE> 4'6,4'  <CR>
ENTER NEXT CORNER OF RECTANGLE> 7',6'  <CR>
```

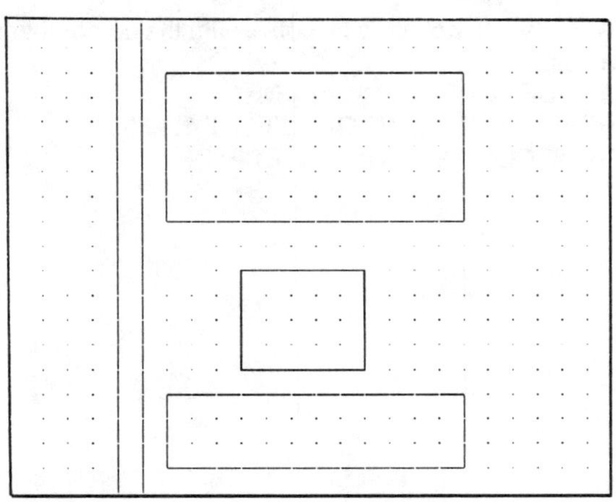

27. Create the chair arms and back by drawing lines.

```
ENTER A COMMAND> L1
ENTER START POINT>> 5',6'  <CR>
ENTER NEXT POINT> 5',4'6  <CR>
ENTER NEXT POINT> 6'6,4'6  <CR>
ENTER NEXT POINT> 6'6,6'  <CR>
ENTER NEXT POINT> PU
```

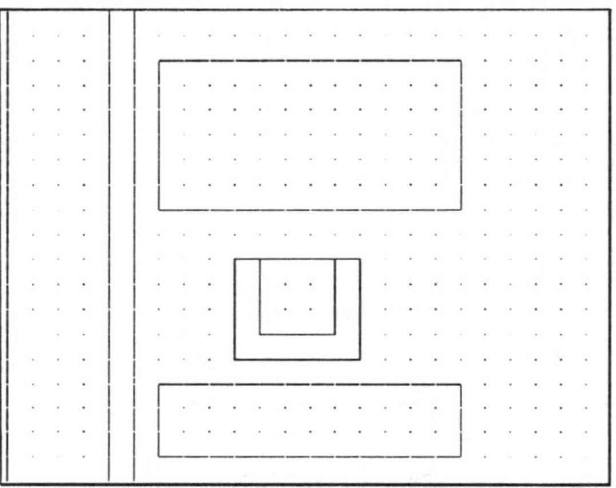

28. View entire drawing.

```
ENTER A COMMAND> ZA
```

29. Create the side chair by copying the desk chair.

```
ENTER A COMMAND> WC
PLACE WINDOW> (Select two diagonal points with the cursor that create a window to
contain the desk chair.)
ENTER A REFERENCE POINT> 5',5'  <CR>
ENTER A NEW REFERENCE POINT OR OFFSET 4',12'  <CR>
ENTER NUMBER OF COPIES (1-99)> 1  <CR>
```

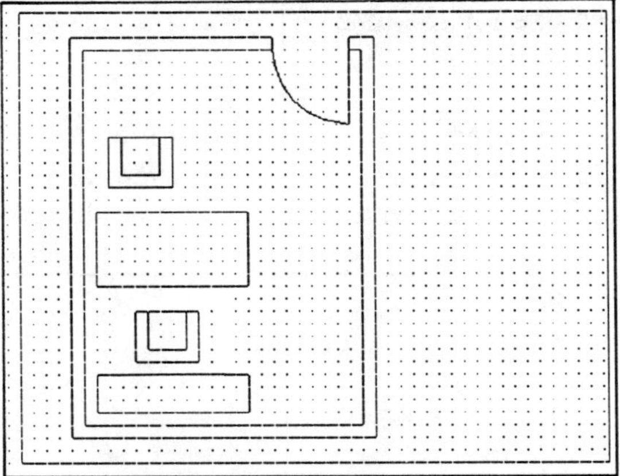

30. Rotate the side chair into position as shown.

```
ENTER A COMMAND> WR
PLACE WINDOW> (Select two points to define a window around the side chair.)
ENTER AN AXIS POINT> 4'6,12' <CR>
ENTER THE ANGLE> 225 <CR>
```

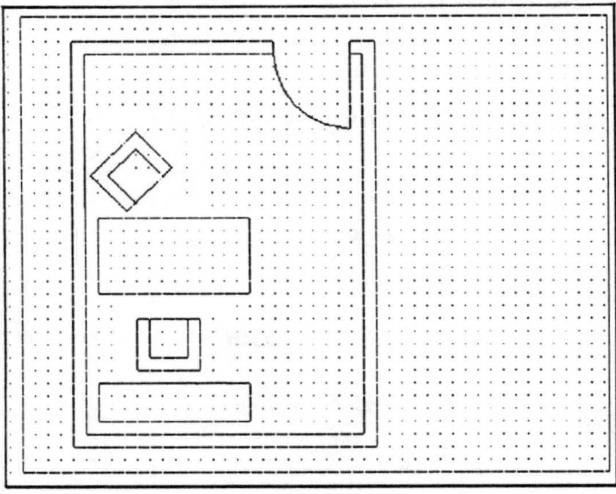

31. Redraw the screen to re-establish the visibility of the grid points.

```
ENTER A COMMAND> RD
```

32. Select the proper size for the text.

NOTE

When sizing text, think of its size when plotted. Because you are drawing at actual size, you must overscale the text to obtain the right height when the drawing is plotted.

```
ENTER A COMMAND > TZ
CHANGE TEXT SIZE (1.0000 in.) >  6 <CR>
```

33. Place the text on the drawing.

NOTE

When placing text, do not use the PU command to exit the TP command. Generic CADD only prints PU on your drawing. Use Esc instead.

```
ENTER A COMMAND > TP
SELECTED FONT IS: MAIN
ENTER TEXT STARTING POINT > (Select the point on the screen to   begin the Office 105
label.)
ENTER A CHARACTER > OFFICE 105 <CR>
ENTER A CHARACTER >
```

34. Select a smaller text size and label the furniture text.

```
ENTER A COMMAND > TZ
CHANGE TEXT SIZE (6.000) > 4  <CR>
ENTER A COMMAND > TP
FONT IS: MAIN
SELECT TEXT STARTING POINT > (Select the point on the screen to begin the desk
label.)
ENTER A CHARACTER > 36 X 72 DESK  <CR>
ENTER A CHARACTER >
```

35. Repeat for the remaining labels shown on the illustration.

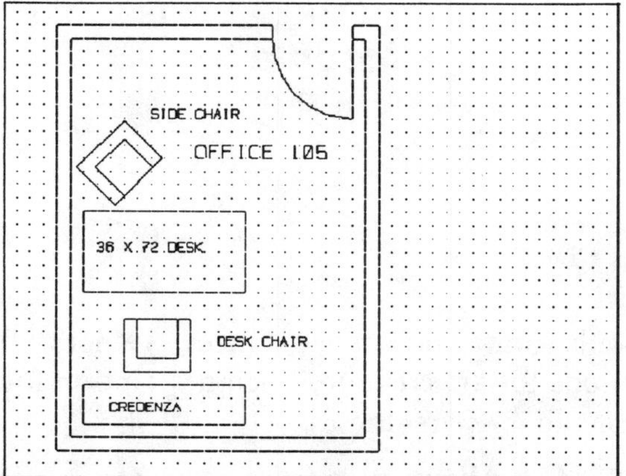

SAVE AND CONTINUE

36. Save your drawing.

```
ENTER A COMMAND > DS
SAVE FILE (SAMPLE.DWG)
```

The drawing is saved as SAMPLE.DWG.

37. Turn to Module 53 to continue the learning sequence.

Module 3
ARC

DESCRIPTION

The ARC commands draw incomplete circles. Generic CADD offers three different input methods for arc creation. Each description follows, complete with the two-letter command in parentheses.

TWO POINT ARC (A2) Allows specification of the center of an arc and an endpoint to create the arc. The arc is attached to the screen cursor, rubber banding as the cursor moves. This feature enables visual selection of the remaining endpoint of the arc.

THREE POINT ARC (A3) Allows specification of one endpoint, a midpoint on the arc itself, and the remaining endpoint to create the arc. The point selected on the arc determines the arc's curve and does not need to be the midpoint between the two selected endpoints.

FOUR POINT ARC (A4)Allows selection of the arc center, start point, a midpoint indicating direction, and an endpoint.

APPLICATIONS

As basic drawing elements, arcs become the simple building components of larger, more complex drawings. The ability to define an arc in a variety of ways means greater ease and flexibility of drawing creation.

TYPICAL OPERATION

In this activity you draw three arcs using each of the three available input methods.

1. Begin a new drawing called "ARC."

2. Draw the first arc by selecting two points and the center.

```
ENTER A COMMAND >  A2
ENTER THE CENTER OF THE ARC >  8,8 <CR>

ENTER START OF THE ARC >  6,10 <CR>
Note the rubber banding line connecting the arc center to the arc start point.

ENTER THE END OF THE ARC >  (Move the screen cursor clockwise approximately 180
degrees and select the point on the screen to end the arc with the mouse or by pressing
Return.)
```

NOTE

The arc endpoint is not exactly where the screen cursor is located. Instead, the endpoint is on the rubber banding line at the radius distance established when the center point and the arc start point are selected.

3. Draw the second arc using three points.

```
ENTER A COMMAND >  A3
ENTER START OF THE ARC >  15,12 <CR>
ENTER A MIDPOINT VERY ACCURATELY >  20,15 <CR>
ENTER THE END OF THE ARC >  18,10 <CR>
```

4. Draw the third arc by specifying four points.

```
ENTER A COMMAND >  A4
ENTER THE CENTER OF THE ARC > 32,19 <CR>
ENTER START OF THE ARC >  29,14 <CR>
ENTER DIRECTION OF ARC >  20,14 <CR>
ENTER THE END OF THE ARC >  20,20 <CR>
```

5. Zoom to bring all the arcs into full view.

```
ENTER A COMMAND >  ZA
```

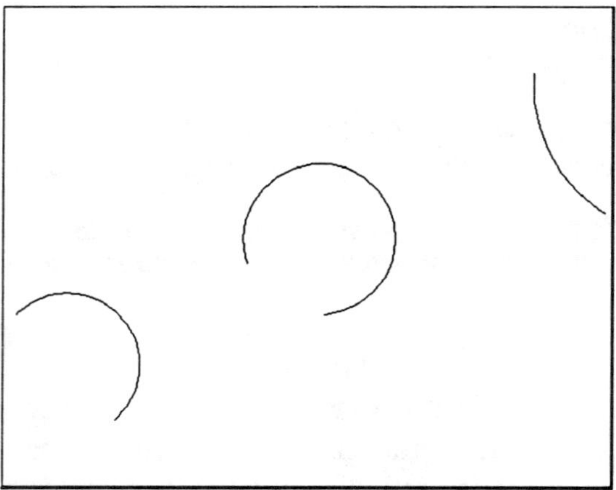

6. Quit the drawing without saving.

7. Turn to Module 27 to continue the learning sequence.

Module 4
AUTOFILLET

DESCRIPTION

AUTOFILLET (AF) automatically creates fillets between lines and double lines as they are being drawn. This command is a toggle. When toggled on, all lines and double lines drawn are filleted according to the current radius value set in FILLET RADIUS. When AUTOFILLET is toggled off, lines and double lines are drawn normally. The default setting is AUTOFILLET off.

AUTOFILLET coupled with DOUBLE LINES allow you to draw continuous flowing double lines which are automatically trimmed. When using ERASE LAST to delete portions of autofillet double lines, realize that the first EL commands entered erase a line, arc, and another line on one side of the double line. Then the same pieces of the autofilleted double line on the opposite side are removed.

APPLICATIONS

Autofilleting is useful for site design to show walkways, roads, etc. This command makes quickly drawn heating and ventilating ductwork plans, also.

When many fillets are needed on a series of single or double lines, AUTOFILLET is considerably faster than using the FILLET command to fillet each one.

TYPICAL OPERATION

In this session you draw a series of automatically filleted double lines.

1. Start a new drawing called "AUTOFILL."

2. Set the fillet radius.

```
ENTER A COMMAND > RF
CHANGE FILLET RADIUS (0.500) in > 2 < CR >
```

3. Toggle on AUTOFILLET.

```
ENTER A COMMAND> AF
AUTO FILLET IS ON
```

4. Draw a line series.

```
ENTER A COMMAND> L2
ENTER START POINT> >2,2  <CR>
ENTER NEXT POINT> 4,6  <CR>
ENTER NEXT POINT> 10,4  <CR>
ENTER NEXT POINT> 18,9  <CR>
ENTER NEXT POINT> 4,15  <CR>
ENTER NEXT POINT> 7,20  <CR>
ENTER NEXT POINT> 24,12  <CR>
ENTER NEXT POINT> 18,3  <CR>
ENTER NEXT POINT> 17,20  <CR>
ENTER NEXT POINT> PU  <CR>
```

5. Clean up the crossing intersection.

NOTE

The CLEAN CORNER command cleans intersections created in DOUBLE LINES with AUTOFILLET.

```
ENTER A COMMAND> KT
ENTER A POINT ON THE OBJECT TO CORNER CLEAN> 17,16  <CR>
ENTER A POINT OUTSIDE CORNER> 17,16  <CR>
```

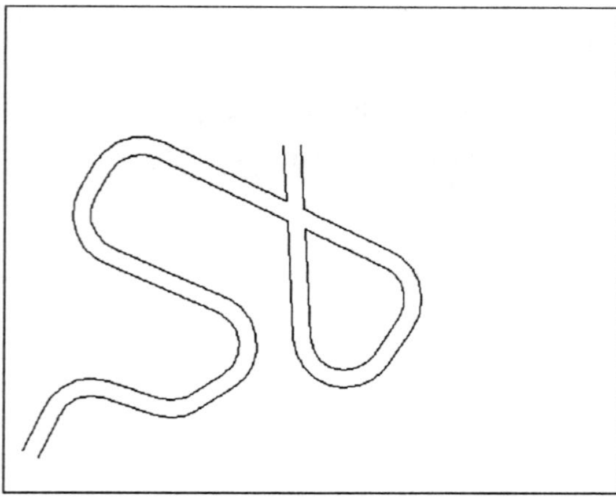

6. Toggle AUTOFILLET off.

```
ENTER A COMMAND>  AF
AUTO FILLET IS OFF
```

7. Quit the drawing without saving.

8. Turn to Module 68 to continue the learning sequence.

BASEPOINT/MANUAL ENTRY OFFSET BASEPOINT

DESCRIPTION

The basepoint acts as a temporary origin point for your drawing. When MANUAL ENTRY OFFSET BASEPOINT (MB) is selected, all coordinate points entered are referenced from the basepoint. Your input remains in this mode until you change it or exit Generic CADD. The BASEPOINT (BP) command allows you to select the coordinates for the basepoint. The basepoint is also used for aligning a digitizer in the TRACE MODE command. At the basepoint prompt, enter the coordinates for the new basepoint in relation to the current origin.

APPLICATIONS

MANUAL ENTRY OFFSET BASEPOINT is used when you want to set a temporary origin on your drawing. When creating a drawing using existing dimensions, setting basepoints as you move around the drawing is usually easier than working from the (0,0) original drawing origin.

TYPICAL OPERATION

In this activity you draw lines using both the original drawing origin and an origin identified with a basepoint.

1. Start a new drawing called "BASE."

2. Display the default grid for easy reference.

```
ENTER A COMMAND >  GR
DISPLAY GRID IS ON
```

3. Draw a line.

NOTE

The default entry mode is MANUAL ENTRY OFFSET ORIGIN. Note that the coordinates given are in reference to the drawing origin.

```
ENTER A COMMAND > L1
ENTER START POINT > > 5,5   <CR>
ENTER NEXT POINT > 10,5   <CR>
ENTER NEXT POINT > PU
```

4. Set a new origin point by defining a basepoint.

```
ENTER A COMMAND > BP
CURRENT BASE POINT: X 0"  0.00"  Y  0"   0.00"
SET A NEW BASEPOINT > 10,10   <CR>
```

5. Change to basepoint entry mode.

```
ENTER A COMMAND > MB
MANUAL ENTRY/BASEPOINT
```

6. Draw a line using the new origin.

```
ENTER A COMMAND > L1
ENTER START POINT > > 5,5   <CR>
ENTER NEXT POINT > 10,5   <CR>
ENTER NEXT POINT > PU
```

7. Quit the drawing without saving.

8. Turn to Module 14 to continue the learning sequence.

Module 6
BEZIER EDIT

DESCRIPTION

BEZIER EDIT (BE) allows you to edit two adjacent Bezier curve sections at once. If you have toggled RUBBER BANDING to ON, you see the points move as you locate them in the new position.

APPLICATIONS

This command allows you to change a portion of a previously drawn Bezier curve without having to draw the curve over entirely. This capability is an excellent tool for manipulating topographical contour lines that change due to drainage or new building requirements.

TYPICAL OPERATION

In this session you draw a Bezier curve and edit two portions.

1. Begin a new drawing called "BEZIER."

2. Toggle construction points on to see the points you select.

```
ENTER A COMMAND >  PC
DISPLAY CONSTRUCTION POINTS IS ON
```

3. Draw a Bezier curve.

```
ENTER A COMMAND >  BV
ENTER FIRST POINT >  4,5
ENTER NEXT POINT (ESC OR PENUP TO QUIT) > 8,15   <CR>
ENTER NEXT POINT (ESC OR PENUP TO QUIT) >  22,6   <CR>
ENTER NEXT POINT (ESC OR PENUP TO QUIT) >  28,10   <CR>
ENTER NEXT POINT (ESC OR PENUP TO QUIT) >  PU
```

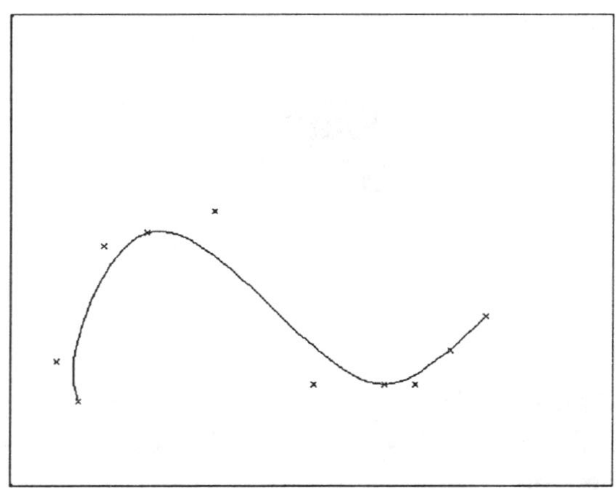

4. Edit the curve.

```
ENTER A COMMAND >  BE
ENTER A POINT ON THE OBJECT TO BEZIER EDIT >  4.3,10  <CR>
ENTER A POINT ON THE OBJECT TO BEZIER EDIT >  14,12  <CR>
ENTER POINT TO BE MOVED >  6.5,3  <CR>
```

NOTE

Bezier editing is dynamic. After the point to be moved is selected, move the cursor on the screen to observe the changing shape of the curve.

```
ENTER NEW LOCATION 21,17 <CR>
```

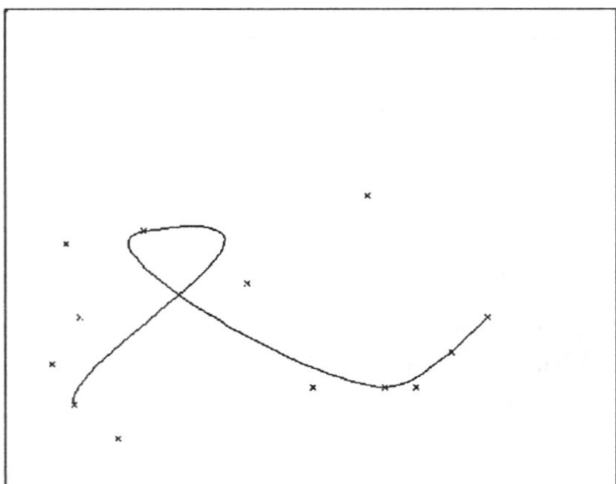

5. Quit the drawing without saving.

6. Turn to Module 44 to continue the learning sequence.

Module 7
CHAMFER/CHAMFER DISTANCE

DESCRIPTION

The CHAMFER (CH) command creates a line between two selected non-parallel lines which appears as a cut off corner. The lines may cross each other or not quite meet. The distance from the intersection of the two lines to the point where each line is chamfered is set in the CHAMFER DISTANCE (CA) command. To chamfer a pair of lines, select a point on each line at the prompt. The chamfer is then inserted according to the radius in CHAMFER DISTANCE.

The CHAMFER DISTANCE (CA) command actually sets two distances. The chamfer itself is determined by the distance between the intersection of the two lines and a point on the first line and the intersection of the two lines and a point on the second line. Once entered, these values remain in effect until changed. Chamfers already on your drawing are not changed. The default chamfer distance is 0. When the chamfer distances are set to 0, the two selected lines meet at a single point, similar to the FILLET command if FILLET RADIUS is set to 0.

APPLICATIONS

Chamfers are used in many details from architectural woodworking to countertop edge details.

TYPICAL OPERATION

In this sesion you draw two lines and complete a chamfer.

  1. Start a new drawing called "CHAMFER."

2. Draw two lines.

```
ENTER A COMMAND> L1
ENTER START POINT>> 3,6  <CR>
ENTER NEXT POINT> 9,14  <CR>
ENTER NEXT POINT> PU
ENTER A COMMAND>L1
ENTER START POINT>> 12,12  <CR>
ENTER NEXT POINT> 18,6  <CR>
ENTER NEXT POINT> PU
```

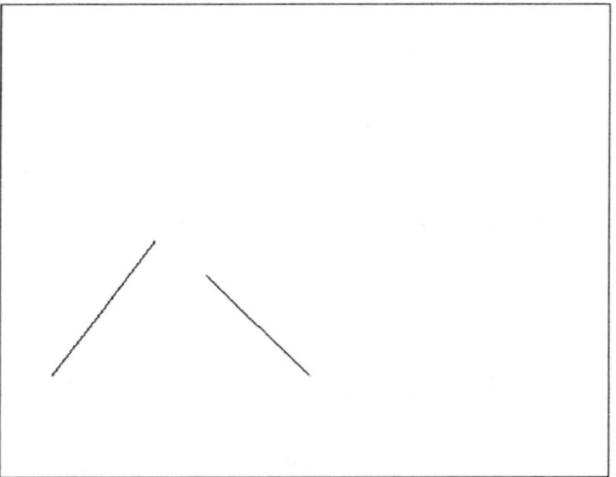

3. Set the chamfer distances.

```
ENTER A COMMAND> CA
CHANGE CHAMFER DIST 1 (0.000) IN> 2  <CR>
CHANGE CHAMFER DIST 2 (0.000) IN> 2  <CR>
```

4. Create the chamfer.

```
ENTER A COMMAND> CH
ENTER A POINT ON THE OBJECT TO CHAMFER> 8,13  <CR>
SECOND OBJECT> 15,9  <CR>
```

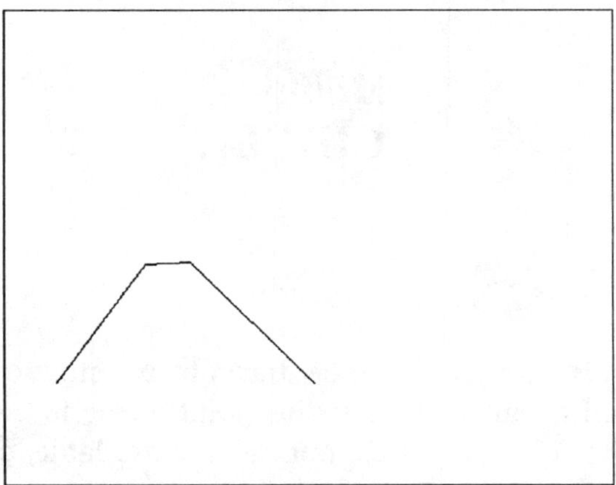

5. Quit the drawing without saving.

6. Turn to Module 36 to continue the learning sequence.

Module 8
CIRCLE

DESCRIPTION

The circle commands allow circles to be drawn by selection of three points on the circle or selection of a center and a radius point. Generic CADD sees a circle as a single object. The following circle options are available, each shown with the two-letter command in parentheses.

TWO POINT CIRCLE (C2)   Allows creation of a circle with selection of a center point and a point on the circle circumference.

THREE POINT CIRCLE (C3)   Three point specifies a circle by three points on the circle circumference.

APPLICATIONS

A circle is a basic drawing component, often used in mechanical design as well as architectural and engineering work. The ability to define a circle with three points or a center and radius point means greater ease of creating accurate drawing elements.

TYPICAL OPERATION

In this session you create two circles using a different creation method for each.

1. Begin a new drawing named "CIRCLE."

2. Draw a circle by defining the center point and a radius point.

```
ENTER A COMMAND >  C2
ENTER CENTER OF CIRCLE >  8,8   <CR>
ENTER A POINT ON CIRCLE >  12,8   <CR>
```

3. Now draw another circle by selecting three circumference points.

```
ENTER A COMMAND>  C3
ENTER FIRST POINT ON CIRCLE>  20,8  <CR>
ENTER SECOND POINT ON CIRCLE>  24,11  <CR>
ENTER THIRD POINT ON CIRCLE>  18,10  <CR>
```

Your drawing should look like the following screen view.

4. Quit the drawing without saving.

5. Turn to Module 55 to continue the learning sequence.

Module 9
CLEAN CORNER

DESCRIPTION

CLEAN CORNER (KT) automatically trims all lines in an intersection originally created with two sets of parallel lines. This command completes the cleaning of T shaped intersections, L shaped or corner intersections, and cross or X shaped intersections. Parallel lines eligible for automatic cleanup with CLEAN CORNER are usually created in the DOUBLE LINE command, but can be created with STRAIGHT LINE also. The two sets of parallel lines may intersect at any angle, but must cross one another for CLEAN CORNER to function properly. To perform the cleanup, select a point inside the intersection you want to clean. Then select a point outside the intersection. This outside point directs Generic CADD to the type of intersection you want to clean up. Use the following summary to help select the point you want.

Cross or X type intersections	Select a point within the intersection.
T type intersections	Select a point inside the two lines you want removed, but outside of the actual intersection.
Corner or L type intersections	Select a point outside the intersection and outside the corner desired in the cleanup.

APPLICATIONS

CLEAN CORNER is used extensively with the DOUBLE LINE command, just as an erasing shield and eraser are used when drawing walls in manual drafting. This Generic CADD capability enables you to be fast with drawing entry, not worrying about the neatness of the drawing. You know CLEAN CORNER corrects most of the defects.

TYPICAL OPERATION

In this activity you create a number of double line intersections and clean them up.

1. Begin a new drawing called "CLEAN."

2. Set the wall thickness to 2" total width.

```
ENTER A COMMAND> TH
CHANGE DOUBLE LINE OFFSET1 (1.000)> 1   <CR>
CHANGE DOUBLE LINE OFFSET2 (0.000)> 1   <CR>
```

3. Draw an parallel wall intersection.

```
ENTER A COMMAND> L2
ENTER START POINT> > 6,4  <CR>
ENTER NEXT POINT> 6,22   <CR>
ENTER NEXT POINT> PU
ENTER A COMMAND> L2
ENTER START POINT> > 2,15  <CR>
ENTER NEXT POINT> 11,15  <CR>
ENTER NEXT POINT> PU
```

4. Copy the intersecting walls.

```
ENTER A COMMAND> WC
PLACE WINDOW> (Place a window around both sets of parallel lines.)
ENTER A REFERENCE POINT> 6,15  <CR>
ENTER NEW REFERENCE POINT OR OFFSET> 18,15  <CR>
ENTER NUMBER OF COPIES (1-99)> 2 <CR>
```

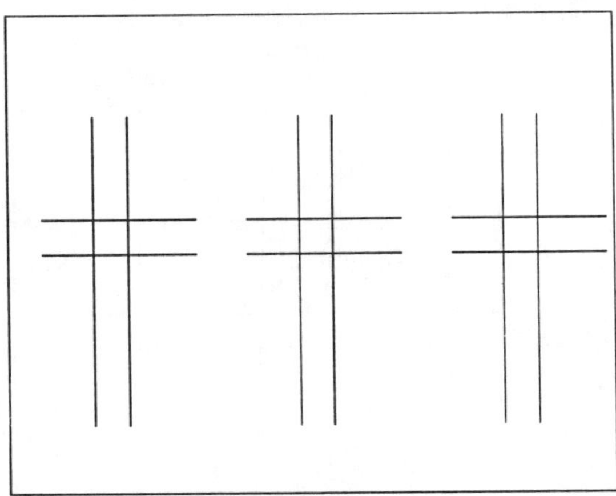

5. Clean the first intersection as a cross.

```
ENTER A COMMAND> KT
ENTER A POINT ON THE OBJECT TO CORNER CLEAN> 6,15  <CR>
```

NOTE

When you select points to define a cross intersection to be cleaned, choose the second point also within the intersection.

```
ENTER A POINT OUTSIDE CORNER> 6,15  <CR>
```

6. Clean the center intersection as a T intersection.

```
ENTER A COMMAND> KT
ENTER A POINT ON THE OBJECT TO CORNER CLEAN> 18,15  <CR>
ENTER A POINT OUTSIDE CORNER> 16,15  <CR>
```

7. Clean the remaining intersection as a corner.

```
ENTER A COMMAND> KT
ENTER A POINT ON THE OBJECT TO CORNER CLEAN> 30,15  <CR>
ENTER A POINT OUTSIDE CORNER> 32,17  <CR>
```

NOTE

Sometimes you may receive an error message "Object not found" when selecting a point. In this case, zoom back to get all four intersecting lines within the search area of the cursor or increase the tolerance factor (TO).

8. Quit the drawing without saving.

9. Turn to Module 61 to continue the learning sequence.

Module 10
COMPONENTS

DESCRIPTION

Components are groups of objects that are assigned a name and an origin point. A component acts as a single object, with the reference point, also known as the origin, basepoint, or handle, used to place the component on the drawing. Any item that you place many times on one or more drawings should be defined as a component. Examples of components include doors and windows, north arrows and graphic scales, furniture, and title blocks. The size of a component is limited only by your computer's memory.

Generic CADD offers a number of commands which aid in the creation and manipulation of components. Each available option is described below, with the corresponding two-letter command in parentheses.

COMPONENT CREATE (CC) Allows you to create components from objects you draw on the screen. The objects must be visible. ALL LAYERS EDIT must be on if the objects are created on more than one layer. Select a window to completely enclose the objects you want to become a component, enter the name of the component, press and select the reference or origin point. The component name can be up to twelve characters, but only the first eight characters are saved if the component is saved to disk. The group of objects used to define the component is not a component in itself. To become a component, the objects must be erased and the component placed in the same location. Once defined, the component can be placed in other locations only within the same drawing. If you want to use the component on other drawings, it must be first saved to disk with the COMPONENT SAVE command. To see that the component was defined properly, check the COMPONENT LIST. This command also appears in the windows menu as WINDOW COMPONENT (CC).

COMPONENT EXPLODE (CE) Allows you to turn a component back into the objects from which it was originally defined. A component acts as a single object on your drawing, regardless of the number of objects used to create it originally. COMPONENT EXPLODE returns only the individually selected component to its original graphic status, including returning all the objects to their original layers. No other components are affected. The definition of the component is also not affected.

COMPONENT REPLACE (CN) Allows you to replace all placed locations of one component with another component. Enter the name of the component you want to be replaced, then the name of the component you want to appear in its place. All reference points are aligned, and the placed characteristics of the original component (rotation, scale etc.) are also associated with the new component. Replacement occurs over the entire drawing.

COMPONENT REMOVE (CX) Allows you to remove all placements of a specified component from a drawing. This command also removes the component definition from the drawing file. COMPONENT REMOVE is used for major editing only, as once initiated, the component no longer exists. To remove a single component from a drawing, use the **OBJECT ERASE** or **WINDOW ERASE** commands.

COMPONENT SAVE (CS) Allows you to save the definition of a component to a disk to use in additional drawings. The Generic CADD subdirectory is the default storage location, unless you specify another location. The component name is restricted to a maximum of eight characters. The .CMP extension designation is automatically added. When saving a component definition to disk, although Generic CADD allows you to save it under a name different from the one under which the component was originally defined, this procedure is not suggested.

COMPONENT LOAD (CL) Allows you to bring up a previously saved component to a drawing file for placement on the drawing with the COMPONENT PLACE command. When placing a component on a drawing using COMPONENT PLACE, Generic CADD looks for the component only in the default directory location. If the component is saved in a different location, COMPONENT LOAD must be used first to bring the component to the drawing. To load the component, enter only the component name, with no extension added. Precede the component name with the complete path location if the component is saved in other than the default directory.

COMPONENT PLACE (CP) Allows you to place a previously created or saved component on your drawing. After entering the component name, select the point on the drawing you want to align with the chosen reference or origin point on the component. Generic CADD places the component, using the current scale and rotation settings. A reference point is shown at the component origin point. Another way to select a component to place is to select it from the component menu using the COMPONENT LIST command. A component may also be dragged onto the screen using the COMPONENT DRAG command toggled to the on position.

COMPONENT DRAG (CG) Allows you to see ghosted images of a component as it is placed on the screen with the COMPONENT PLACE command or selected from the COMPONENT LIST command. COMPONENT DRAG is a toggle, with the default set to ON, allowing you to see the images of components as they are placed. The more complex the component the more time it takes to drag it into position, therefore it may be beneficial to toggle COMPONENT DRAG off by selecting the command again. The current setting of the toggle remains in effect until you change it or exit Generic CADD.

COMPONENT SCALE (CZ) Allows you to alter the scale of a placed component to change its size and/or shape to be different from the dimensions of the originally defined component. Generic CADD lets you change the scale in both the X and Y direction. The scale value may be greater or less than one, which is the value at which the component is originally created. A negative value of X or Y mirrors the component either horizontally (X) or vertically (Y). Scale values remain in effect until changed. The scale of components already placed on your drawing is not altered. After placing a component, if needed, use WINDOW RE-SCALE to alter the scale value.

COMPONENT ROTATION (CR) Allows you to define the angle at which a component is placed on your drawing. At the prompt, three options for entering the angle are available. You can enter the desired angle, if known; type A for angle to define the angle on the screen with a basepoint and a ray point; or type V for vertex to define the angle on the screen with a basepoint and two ray points. Generic CADD measures angles from the horizontal position in a counterclockwise rotation, beginning with the first ray selected and ending with the second ray selected. The resulting angle is displayed on the prompt line. COMPONENT ROTATION is used before the COMPONENT PLACE command to define the desired rotation. The values set in this command remain in effect until they are changed. Angles between −360 and 360 degrees are accepted. Positive angles are calculated from horizontal, moving in a counterclockwise direction. Use the WINDOW ROTATE command to alter the rotation of a component already placed on the drawing.

COMPONENT LIST Allows you to select a component for placement on your drawing from a list on the screen menu. This list is all the components currently defined in your drawing from which you can choose. There is no corresponding two-letter command for COMPONENT LIST. After selecting the command from the menu, the screen menu is replaced by the component list. When the list is too lengthy to fit in total on the screen, you may page down by selecting the appropriate keys on the menu or the keyboard. Page up operates accordingly. Select with the cursor the name of the desired component, then select a reference point on the screen for placement. To end COMPONENT LIST, select page down to return to the main menu.

COMPONENT LIST ON/OFF (CO) Allows you to turn off the component list so that it does not appear on the menu. This command is a toggle. Each time it is selected, the status changes to the opposite of the current setting.

COMPONENT IMAGE (CI) Allows the graphics used to create a component to be placed on the drawing without having the status of a component. The object or objects look like the component, but act like the individual objects. This command is a toggle and the current status remains in effect until changed. Images are placed on your drawing using the COMPONENT PLACE command. No reference points are shown to correspond to the image origin point, as the object is not a component. Generic CAD recognizes all the construction points of the objects used in the image.

COMPONENT SNAP (GC) Allows you to use the Generic CADD snap modes to snap to any construction points in the graphics composing the component. Generic CADD sees a component as only a single point, the reference or origin point. The available snap modes, such as NEAREST POINT and SNAP CLOSEST, do not work with components until COMPONENT SNAP is toggled on. Without using COMPONENT SNAP, the alternative is to explode the component using COMPONENT EXPLODE or place an image. In either case, the graphic is no longer a component. The toggle setting of this command remains in effect until you change it or exit Generic CADD. The default is COMPONENT SNAP to an off position.

COMPONENT PATH (P2) Allows you to change the disk and directory where components are stored. When loading a component, Generic CADD looks in this location for the component. This location setting remains in effect until you change it or exit Generic CADD. If your path includes a directory, remember to end the directory with a backslash to provide a separation from the component name which Generic CADD adds.

COMPONENT DUMP (CD) Allows you to save to disk all at once all the components currently defined on your drawing. Much faster than a series of COMPONENT SAVE commands, COMPONENT DUMP combines these operations.

APPLICATIONS

Components allow you to create graphic elements only once and use them on many different drawings. A consistency of appearance is maintained from drawing to drawing as well as increased drawing creation speed. Occasionally, you use a component on a drawing similar to a special item needed. The component is placed, then exploded and modified accordingly. This process is faster than creating a new item from scratch.

COMPONENT REPLACE is useful when clients (or you) change their mind about a product to use, as a quick swap can be made. It is important to keep the reference point of similar component types in the same relative position, as when a replacement occurs, Generic CADD aligns the reference points. Most importantly, every occurrence of a particular component on a single drawing is swapped, and there is no risk in missing an object as often occurs when drafting manually.

COMPONENT REMOVE lets you remove a component from a drawing as well as from its storage location on disk. This aspect saves the time it would take to exit and erase the component in DOS.

COMPONENT DRAG is helpful when visually placing symbols, especially to make sure a placed component will not cover other graphics in the drawing.

The scale and rotation capabilities allow you to create a set of basic symbols that become quite varied when altered by scale and/or rotation.

COMPONENT LIST lets those of you who do not type well avoid typing the component name and instead select it from the menu list.

The COMPONENT SNAP capability lets you align components to other components or to other objects by points other than the reference or origin points. This capability enhances the accuracy of all component placements.

TYPICAL OPERATION

In this activity you draw two rectangles to represent a desk, make them a component, and manipulate the component using the various component commands.

1. Start a new drawing called "COMP."

2. Draw two rectangles.

```
ENTER A COMMAND> RE
ENTER A CORNER OF RECTANGLE> 6,19  <CR>
ENTER NEXT CORNER OF RECTANGLE> 12,22  <CR>
ENTER A COMMAND> RE
ENTER A CORNER OF RECTANGLE> 6,19  <CR>
ENTER NEXT CORNER OF RECTANGLE> 8,16  <CR>
```

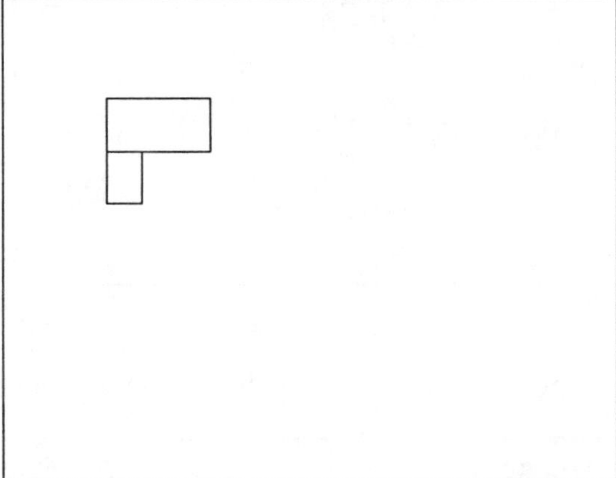

3. Toggle reference points to the on position.

```
ENTER A COMMAND> PR
DISPLAY REFERENCE POINT IS ON
```

4. Make the desk a component.

```
ENTER A COMMAND> CC
PLACE WINDOW (Select two diagonal points to surround the rectangles completely.)
ENTER COMPONENT NAME> DESK1  <CR>
ENTER THE COMPONENT REFERENCE POINT> 6,22  <CR>
```

5. Place the component on the drawing.

```
ENTER A COMMAND> CP
ENTER COMPONENT NAME> DESK1 <CR>
```

NOTE

COMPONENT DRAG in the on position is the Generic CADD default. Note the ghosted image of the component and how it is attached to the cursor at the defined origin point.

```
ENTER PLACEMENT LOCATION> 15,22  <CR>
```

6. Place another component, snapping to the first component placed.

```
ENTER A COMMAND> GC
COMPONENT SNAP IS ON
ENTER A COMMAND> CP
ENTER COMPONENT NAME> DESK1  <CR>
ENTER PLACEMENT LOCATION> SC
CLOSEST POINT TO (Select the lower left corner of the smaller rectangle of the first
placed component.)
```

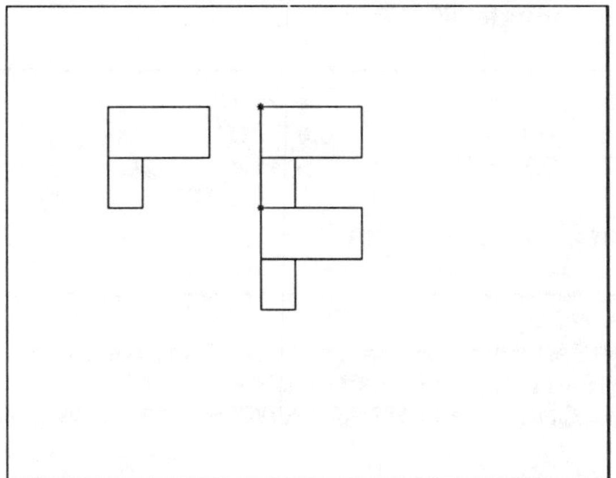

7. Change the component rotation value.

```
ENTER A COMMAND > CR
ENTER COMPONENT ROTATION (0.000) LIMITS: ( − 360.000 TO 360.000) > 45   <CR>
```

8. Change the component scale value.

```
ENTER A COMMAND > CZ
ENTER NEW X SCALE(1.000) > .5  <CR>
ENTER NEW Y SCALE (0.500) >   <CR>
```

9. Place a component with the new rotation and scale values.

```
ENTER A COMMAND > CP
ENTER COMPONENT NAME > DESK1  <CR>
ENTER PLACEMENT LOCATION > 20,10  <CR>
```

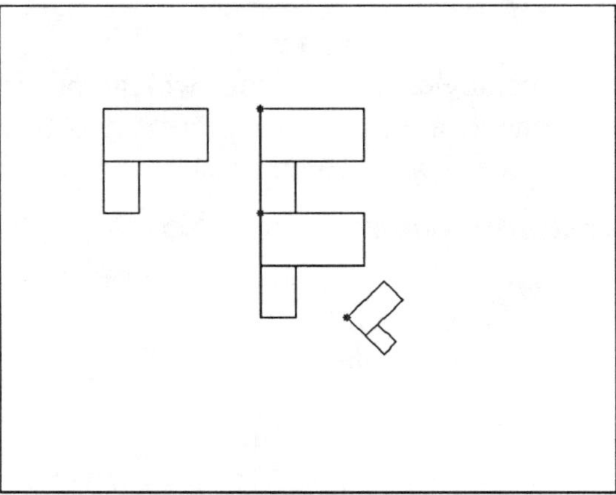

10. Draw another rectangle.

```
ENTER A COMMAND> RE
ENTER A CORNER OF RECTANGLE> 5,8  <CR>
ENTER NEXT CORNER OF RECTANGLE> 11,11  <CR>
```

11. Make the rectangle a component.

```
ENTER A COMMAND> CC
PLACE WINDOW (Select two diagonal points to create a window to contain the rectangle.)
ENTER COMPONENT NAME> DESK2  <CR>
ENTER THE COMPONENT REFERENCE POINT> 5,11  <CR>
```

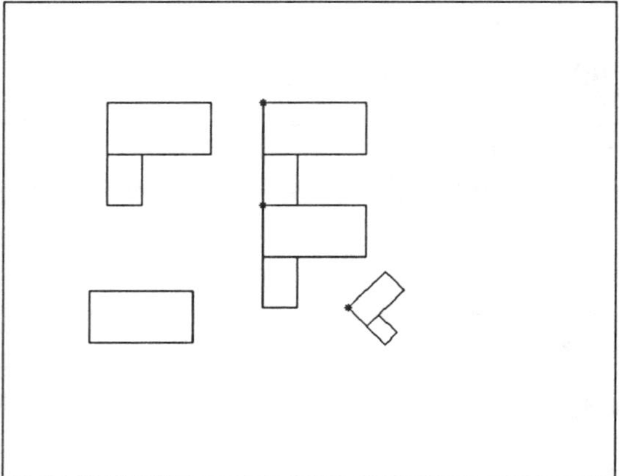

12. Replace one desk for another throughout the drawing.

```
ENTER A COMMAND> CN
ENTER COMPONENT NAME> DESK1  <CR>
```

NOTE

The first two rectangles drawn, from which you defined the
DESK1 component, are not a component and therefore are
not affected by the replace command.

```
NAME OF REPLACING COMPONENT> DESK2  <CR>
```

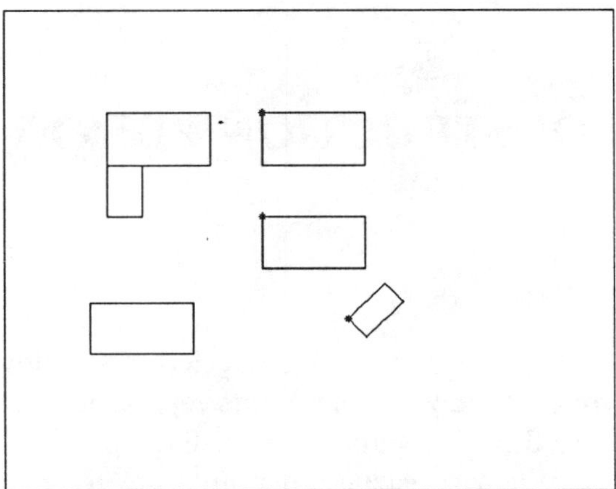

13. Place additional desk components by using the list.

ENTER A COMMAND > (Select COMPONENT from the ROOT menu on the screen.)
ENTER A COMMAND > (Select COMP LIST from the COMPONENT submenu on the screen.)
ENTER A COMMAND > (Select DESK1 from the list with the cursor bar.)
ENTER PLACEMENT LOCATION > **25,22** **<CR>**

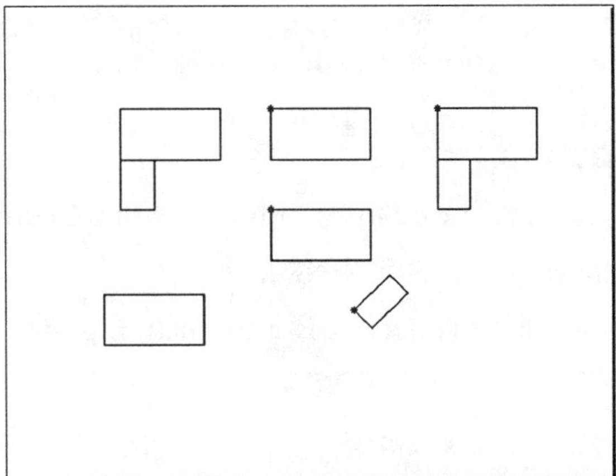

14. Quit and save the drawing for use in Module 56.

15. Turn to Module 56 to continue the learning sequence.

Module 11
CONSTRUCTION POINTS

DESCRIPTION

CONSTRUCTION POINTS (PC), when toggled on, allows small x-shaped graphics to appear while drawing. These points represent the points you selected on the drawing screen to draw lines and objects. Each point is essentially a vertex or endpoint of a line. When construction points are toggled on, the x-shaped points also show on lines you drew when the command was toggled off. When toggled off, the construction points are not visible. The Generic CADD default is construction points off. Construction points never plot, so you do not need to remember to turn them off to plot.

APPLICATIONS

Sometimes when drawing it is useful to see how your linework is created, particularly for future reference or attachment of other lines. Construction points on allows you to leave tracks behind you as you draw. Of course, these points are not needed at all times, so they can easily be toggled off.

TYPICAL OPERATION

In this practice exercise you create lines with and without construction points.

1. Start a new drawing called "CONPT."

2. Draw a line. Note that the default is construction points off.

```
ENTER A COMMAND >  L1
ENTER START POINT > >  3,3  <CR>
ESC OR PEN UP TO STOP
ENTER NEXT POINT >  4,12  <CR>
ESC OR PEN UP TO STOP
ENTER NEXT POINT >  PU
```

3. Toggle construction points on.

```
ENTER A COMMAND> PC
DISPLAY CONSTRUCTION POINTS IS ON
```

4. Draw a line series.

```
ENTER A COMMAND> L1
ENTER START POINT>> 6,6  <CR>
ESC OR PEN UP TO STOP
ENTER NEXT POINT> 12,12  <CR>
ESC OR PEN UP TO STOP
ENTER NEXT POINT> 20,12  <CR>
ESC OR PEN UP TO STOP
ENTER NEXT POINT> PU
```

5. Toggle construction points off.

```
ENTER A COMMAND> PC
DISPLAY CONSTRUCTION POINTS IS OFF
```

6. Redraw the screen to remove the construction points visually.

```
ENTER A COMMAND> RD
```

7. Toggle the construction points on again.

```
ENTER A COMMAND> PC
DISPLAY CONSTRUCTION POINTS IS ON
ENTER A COMMAND> RD
```

NOTE

Notice that all lines show construction points, even those
created when construction points were off.

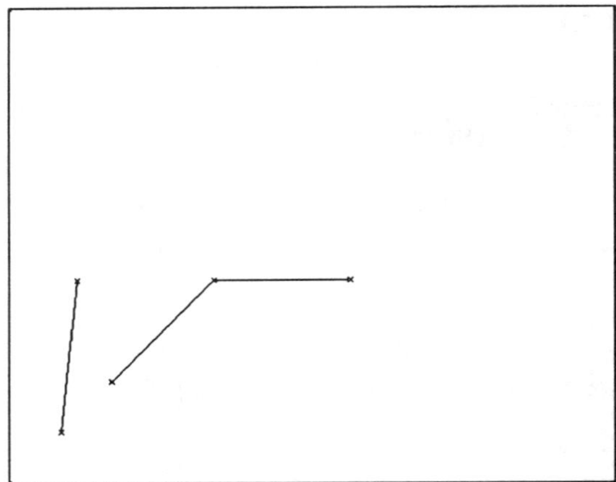

8. Quit without saving the drawing.

9. Turn to Module 62 to continue the learning sequence.

Module 12
CURSOR COLOR/CURSOR SIZE
/CURSOR MOVEMENT

DESCRIPTION

The cursor commands control the size, color, and the movement of the drawing screen cursor. The cursor commands are described below, with each corresponding two-letter command in parentheses.

CURSOR COLOR (CK) allows you to set the color of the drawing cursor on the video screen. This command also controls the color of the rectangular box surrounding the drawing area of the screen. As with all commands involving color selection, the available colors range from 0 to 255. The corresponding screen color representing each of these color values depends upon the graphics card you are using. At the command prompt, enter the color number desired and the cursor and drawing screen box show the new values.

CURSOR SIZE (CU) allows you to change the size of the drawing screen cursor. The default is a value of 32. The maximum allowable value is 639. The size is selected by entering a positive value which corresponds to the number of pixels used to display the cursor. Pixels are the points of light used to dislay the screen images and are dependent upon the resolution of the monitor and the graphics card you are using. The larger the value entered at the prompt, the larger the cursor appears on the screen. A value of zero creates a cursor that spans the full screen.

CURSOR MOVEMENT (CM) is a toggle command used only when you use the arrow keys as a pointing device. The default is the off position. If CURSOR MOVEMENT is toggled to the on position, the cursor snaps to each grid point only if the grid snap mode is in the on position. If SNAP TO GRID is in the off position, the cursor movement increment is controlled by the Insert and Delete keys. Pressing the Insert key causes the cursor to move in progressively larger increments. After seven selections, the increment cycle begins again. Each press of the Delete key causes the cursor to move in progressively smaller increments. The increment cycle begins again after seven selections. The CURSOR MOVEMENT command has no effect if you use a mouse or a digitizer as a pointing device.

APPLICATIONS

The color option for the cursor allows you to select a color specifically for your drawing type. You may want to choose a color that you do not use for graphic creation to easily distinguish the cursor, even in a dense drawing. Changing the cursor size allows you to use a small cursor for most of your work, yet enlarge it when you need to visually align objects, for instance. The color and size of the cursor are largely personal decisions. The movement control command option means when using the keyboard as a pointing device, you have more control over the cursor speed as it moves on the drawing screen.

TYPICAL OPERATION

In this exercise you change the cursor color and the cursor size and toggle the cursor movement.

1. Start a new drawing called "CURSOR."

2. Note the default size and color of your drawing cursor.

3. Change the cursor color.

```
ENTER A COMMAND >  CK
```

NOTE
Generic CADD also allows you to select a color from the color bars in the menu area.

```
CHANGE COLOR NUMBER (12) LIMITS: 0 TO 255 >  9   <CR>
```

4. Change the cursor size.

```
ENTER A COMMAND >  CU
CHANGE CURS SIZE (32) LIMITS: 0 TO 639 >  100   <CR>
```

The cursor should now be approximately one half the drawing screen height.

5. Change the cursor size again.

```
ENTER A COMMAND> CU
CHANGE CURS SIZE (100) LIMITS: 0 TO 639> 500   <CR>
```

Now you have a full screen drawing cursor.

6. Display the default grid.

```
ENTER A COMMAND> GR
DISPLAY GRID IS ON
```

7. Snap to the grid.

```
ENTER A COMMAND> SG
SNAP TO GRID IS ON
```

8. Toggle the cursor movement to the on position.

```
ENTER A COMMAND> CM
CURSOR MOVEMENT DISTANCE - ONE GRID POINT IS ON
```

Use the keyboard arrow keys to move the cursor on the screen. Note that the cursor snaps to every grid point.

9. Toggle the cursor movement to the off position.

```
ENTER A COMMAND> CM
CURSOR MOVEMENT DISTANCE - ONE GRID POINT IS OFF
```

Use the keyboard keys to move the cursor on the drawing screen. Note that the cursor now snaps to every other grid point.

10. Quit the drawing.

11. Turn to Module 59 to continue the learning sequence.

Module 13
CURVES

DESCRIPTION

Curves are basic drawing elements. They are created by selecting points, which Generic CADD then connects to create a curve. A minimum of three points must be selected. The available curve options are described below, with each two-letter command in parentheses.

COMPLEX CURVE (CV) Allows creation of a smooth curve by selection of a minimum of three points, through which Generic CADD fits a smooth curve. Also known as a B-spline curve, the complex curve is fitted through each point selected. As you select the points on the screen, line segments are drawn to approximate the curve. Once you finish point selection, Generic CADD redraws a curve to fit through each point.

BEZIER CURVE (BV) Allows creation of a smooth curve by selection of a minimum of three points. Generic CADD uses these points to create a curve defined by a number of tangent lines that control the direction and curvature of the curve at each endpoint. The endpoints of the tangent lines are called control points.

APPLICATIONS

As basic drawing elements, curves usually become a part of a larger drawing, combining with lines and arcs to create a more complex figure. Often they are used to represent topographical contours on a site plan.

TYPICAL OPERATION

In this activity you draw a single curve of each type.

1. Start a new drawing called "CURVES."

2. Toggle construction points on to see the points you select.

```
ENTER A COMMAND >  PC
DISPLAY CONSTRUCTION POINTS IS ON.
```

3. Draw a complex curve.

```
ENTER A COMMAND >  CV
ENTER A PENUP TO COMPLETE CURVE
ENTER A POINT ON CURVE >  2,2   <CR>
ENTER A POINT ON CURVE >  6,6   <CR>
ENTER A POINT ON CURVE >  8,12 <CR>
ENTER A POINT ON CURVE >  3,14   <CR>
ENTER A POINT ON CURVE >  7,16   <CR>
ENTER A POINT ON CURVE >  PU
```

Once the last point is selected, the curve is drawn.

4. Draw a Bezier curve.

```
ENTER A COMMAND >  BV
ENTER FIRST POINT >  10,4   <CR>
ENTER NEXT POINT(ESC OR PENUP TO QUIT) >  16,14   <CR>
ENTER NEXT POINT(ESC OR PENUP TO QUIT) >  20,15   <CR>
ENTER NEXT POINT(ESC OR PENUP TO QUIT) >  25,18   <CR>
ENTER NEXT POINT(ESC OR PENUP TO QUIT) >  20,20 <CR>
ENTER NEXT POINT(ESC OR PENUP TO QUIT) >  PU
```

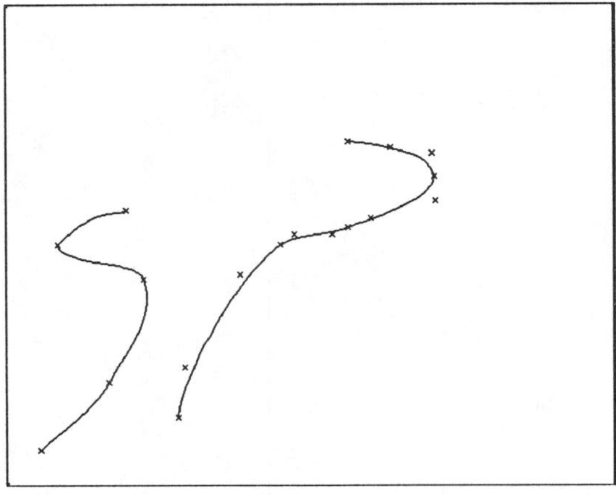

5. Use the ERASE LAST command to observe how each curve reacts to modification.

```
ENTER A COMMAND > EL
```

Notice that the last section in the Bezier curve is erased.

```
ENTER A COMMAND > EL
ENTER A COMMAND > EL
```

Now the entire Bezier curve is erased.

6. Continue with ERASE LAST to erase the complex curve.

```
ENTER A COMMAND > EL
```

The entire complex curve is erased all at once.

7. Quit the drawing without saving.

8. Turn to Module 6 to continue the learning sequence.

Module 14
DIGITIZER

DESCRIPTION

Generic CADD allows you to specify a pointing device from several available options. Among the options is the digitizer. A number of commands are used to set up the area on the digitizer for pointing on the screen and to define and load a menu to be used on the digitizer. Each command option is described below with the corresponding two-letter command in parentheses.

DIGITIZER ACTIVE AREA (PM) allows you to define the specific area on a digitizer to use in pointing on the drawing screen. This command functions only if you are using a digitizer for a pointing device. After entering the command, select the lower left corner of the area on the digitizer you want to be active by pressing the first button on the digitizer puck. Then select the upper right corner using the same technique.

LOAD DIGITIZER MENU (LD) allows you to load a digitizer menu file. Each printed digitizer menu that you lay on your digitizer must have a loaded corresponding digitizer menu file. At the prompt, enter the name of the file you want Generic CADD to load. Also include the full path designation if the menu is not in the default location. Generic CADD automatically adds the .MNU extension to the filename. When you load a digitizer menu, the video menu is lost. If needed, load the video menu again with the LOAD VIDEO MENU command.

SELECT DIGITIZER MENU (SD) allows you to have up to ten active digitizer menus at once. At the prompt, respond with yes if you want all menus to be active, or respond no tc activate a single menu at a time. More than one menu can be placed on the same digitizer area.

APPLICATIONS

Special menus on your digitizer can help you tailor Generic CADD specifically for your needs. Customization is a plus, as it increases your productive speed and also reduces the chances of error. Use the DIGITIZER ACTIVE AREA command to define a smaller area for the digitizer puck to move around on if you need space for a digitizer menu you want to access. Use the SELECT DIGITIZER MENU command to have several menus active simultaneously. When working on several projects during a work session, this command is helpful.

TYPICAL OPERATION

No exercise is included.

Turn to Module 67 to continue the learning sequence.

Module 15
DIMENSIONS

DESCRIPTION

The dimensioning commands allow you to add dimensions to your drawing. Generic CADD offers a variety of commands for creating and manipulating dimensions. In Generic CADD, as in most CAD programs, all drawing is done in actual size, so the dimensioning task is similar to pulling out the tape measure to measure what you have drawn. Generic CADD does this for you automatically. Each dimensioning option is described below with the corresponding two-letter command in parentheses. Some of the options control the placement of the dimension itself, while a large number control the parameters used to determine exactly how the dimension looks. Once these options are set, they remain in effect until you change them or exit Generic CADD. Refer to Module 16 for information on the text associated with dimensioning.

DIMENSION MODE (UM) Allows you to choose between three modes of dimensioning. These are used in both linear and angular dimensions. After selecting DIMENSION MODE, choose number 1 for single mode, 2 for partitioned, or 3 for cumulative mode. The Generic CADD default is single mode.

SINGLE MODE allows you to select two points to dimension, then the dimension is placed. To place another dimension, select two additional points.

PARTITIONED MODE allows you to string a series of dimensions in succession, the last point of one dimension becoming the first point of the next dimension.

CUMULATIVE MODE allows you to complete a series of dimensions, each building upon the dimension of the previously selected one. The first point selected for the first dimension becomes the first point for the second dimension. Each successive dimension line is automatically offset from the previous line for easy readibility.

LINEAR DIMENSIONING (LX) Allows you to dimension horizontal, vertical, and angled lines on your drawing. Selected line terminators, text, and extension lines are added automatically. At the prompt, select the two points between which you want to dimension. Snap modes are important to insure accuracy. Then choose the point where you want the dimension to be located and the dimension is automatically placed on your drawing.

ANGULAR DIMENSIONING (AX) Allows you to dimension the angle between two selected lines. Select the center point, usually at which the two lines intersect, then identify each angled line. The points to select these lines must be identified in a counterclockwise manner. After you choose a location for the arched dimension line, select a location for the text dimension. Selected line terminators, text, and extension lines are added automatically.

DIMENSION DIRECTION (UD) Allows you to select the direction of the dimension. The options are HORIZONTAL, VERTICAL, or ALIGNED. HORIZONTAL and VERTICAL insure perfectly straight horizontal or vertical dimension lines, while ALIGNED allows the dimension to be parallel to the angled object you are measuring. Select the desired direction by entering the corresponding number at the prompt. The default is (1) Aligned. The direction selected remains in effect until you change the value or exit Generic CADD.

DIMENSION LAYER (UL) Allows you to select any of the layers 0 through 255 on which to place the dimension. When choosing a layer, Generic CADD makes that layer the active layer. Check that ALL LAYERS EDIT is toggled to the on position, or Generic CADD cannot find the points you are dimensioning, as they are on another layer. Layer 0 is the default. The selected dimension layer remains in effect until you change the layer or exit Generic CADD. Dimensions already on the drawing are not changed.

DIMENSION COLOR (SK) Allows you to choose the color used for dimension lines, line terminators, and text. Color number 1 is the default. The selected dimension color remains in effect until you change it or exit Generic CADD. Dimensions already placed on the drawing are not affected.

ERASE LAST DIMENSION (ED) Allows you to remove a single dimension from your drawing. Acting like an instant eraser, this command erases the entire dimension line, extension lines, text, and line terminators. Unlike ERASE LAST, ERASE LAST DIMENSION can be used only once. It does not erase several dimensions placed in succession.

ARROW TYPE (AT) Allows you to select among six different line terminators. Slashes, circles, and arrowheads of various angles are available. After selecting the command, choose the number corresponding to the desired line terminator. The length of the arrowhead lines and the diameter of the circle option are set in the LETTER SIZE command. The default is type (2), a 30 degree arrowhead. The selected type remains in effect until you change the selection or exit Generic CADD. Line terminators already placed on the drawing are not changed.

ARROW MODE (AW) Allows you to toggle between closed or open arrowheads. If the arrowheads are closed, a line is drawn to connect and close the two angled lines of the arrowheads. If open, only the two angled lines composing the arrowhead appear. If the current setting is to the on position and arrowheads are closed, entering the command toggles the mode to off, causing future placed arrowheads to be open. Likewise, if the current position is set to off and arrowheads are open, entering the command toggles the arrow mode to on, causing future placed arrowheads to be closed. Arrow closed on is the default position. Once changed, the mode remains in effect until you change it or exit Generic CADD. Arrowheads already placed on the drawing are not affected.

EXTENSION OFFSET (XO) Allows control of the distance between the dimension extension lines and the points being dimensioned. The default is .5 inches or whatever unit you are using. Once specified, the offset remains in effect until you change it or exit Generic CADD. Existing dimension lines are not affected.

EXTENSION LENGTH (XL) Allows you to determine the extension line length by specifing the distance above and below the dimension line. The default is .5 inches or whatever unit you are using. Once specified, the extension line length remains in effect until you change it or exit Generic CADD. Dimensions already placed on the drawing are not affected.

EXTENSION STRETCH (XS) Allows you to toggle between variable length extension lines or extension lines that are fixed in all dimensioning cases by the length set in the EXTENSION LENGTH command. As a toggle, if EXTENSION STRETCH is on and extension lines are stretched to meet the object being dimensioned, entering the command toggles it to the off position, and extension lines are drawn as specified in the EXTENSION LENGTH command. Extension line stretch is toggled to the off position as the Generic CAD default.

PROXIMITY FIXED (PF) Allows you to determine where the dimension lines are placed in relation to the points on the object being dimensioned. This command is a toggle. PROXIMITY FIXED ON, the default setting, locates the dimension lines away from the closest point dimensioned by the distance specified in the EXTENSION OFFSET command. PROXIMITY FIXED OFF allows you to choose the dimension line location.

APPLICATIONS

Dimensions are used to portray accurate measurements of the objects in your drawing. The dimension options offered by Generic CADD give a wide range of versatility, covering all object types to be dimensioned.

DIMENSION COLOR allows you to control the color and therefore the line weight of the dimension linework, as Generic CADD plots by associating plotter pen to color. DIMENSION LAYER allows you to separate the dimensions from other parts of the drawing, therefore making it possible to turn the dimension layers off for viewing or plotting.

EXTENSION LENGTH and OFFSET allow adjustment to be appropriately sized to the plotted scale of the drawn object, whether a site plan or a small detail.

EXTENSION STRETCH allows you to place a dimension line in exactly the desired location or save time by having Generic CADD position the line automatically.

ARROW TYPE and ARROW MODE allow you to create a variety of line terminator types, depending upon the type of drawings you design. ERASE LAST DIMENSION saves time by allowing you to quickly erase the last dimension if it is incorrect. A mistake occurs usually because you forget to change a dimension variable or text size.

TYPICAL OPERATION

In this activity you draw and dimension a line figure.

1. Start a new drawing called "DIM."

2. Change the drawing limits.

```
ENTER A COMMAND> LS
CHANGE HEIGHT LIMIT (24.00) IN> 24'  <CR>
CHANGE WIDTH LIMIT (36.000) IN >24'  <CR>
```

3. View the drawing limits.

```
ENTER A COMMAND> ZL
```

4. Set the grid size.

```
ENTER A COMMAND> GS
CHANGE GRID SIZE (1.000) IN> 12  <CR>
```

5. Draw a line series.

```
ENTER A COMMAND> L1
ENTER START POINT> > 8',17'  <CR>
ESC OR PEN UP TO STOP
ENTER NEXT POINT> 17',17'  <CR>
ENTER NEXT POINT> 17',10'  <CR>
ENTER NEXT POINT> 24',10'  <CR>
ENTER NEXT POINT> 24',2'  <CR>
ENTER NEXT POINT> 8',2'  <CR>
ENTER NEXT POINT> 8',17'  <CR>
ENTER NEXT POINT> PU
```

6. Set the text height.

```
ENTER A COMMAND> LH
CHANGE LETTER HEIGHT (1.000) IN> 6  <CR>
```

7. Set the extension line length.

```
ENTER A COMMAND> XL
CHANGE OUTSIDE FIXED EXTENSION (WITNESS) LINE LENGTH (0.500) IN> 6  <CR>
CHANGE OFFSET BETWEEN EXTENSION (WITNESS) AND ITEM (0.500) IN> 6 <CR>
```

8. Set the extension offset.

```
ENTER A COMMAND> XO
CHANGE OFFSET BETWEEN EXTENSION (WITNESS) LINE LENGTH AND ITEM (0.500)
IN> 6  <CR>
```

9. Change the dimension layer.

```
ENTER A COMMAND> UL
0 = CURRENT LAYER
CHANGE SET DIMENSION LAYER (0) LIMITS: 0 TO 255> 5  <CR>
```

10. Toggle PROXIMITY FIXED to the off position.

```
ENTER A COMMAND> PF
PROXIMITY FIXED IS OFF
```

11. Dimension the top horizontal line.

```
ENTER A COMMAND> LX
```

NOTE

Generic CADD accepts points identifying objects to be dimensioned in any order.

```
ENTER FIRST POINT> 8',17'  <CR>
HIT (ESC) TO QUIT
ENTER NEXT POINT> 17',17'  <CR>
```

NOTE

PROXIMITY FIXED is in the off position, so the dimension line is placed exactly where you locate the cursor at the prompt.

```
ENTER LOCATION OF DIMENSION> 12',19'  <CR>
ENTER FIRST POINT> <ESC>
```

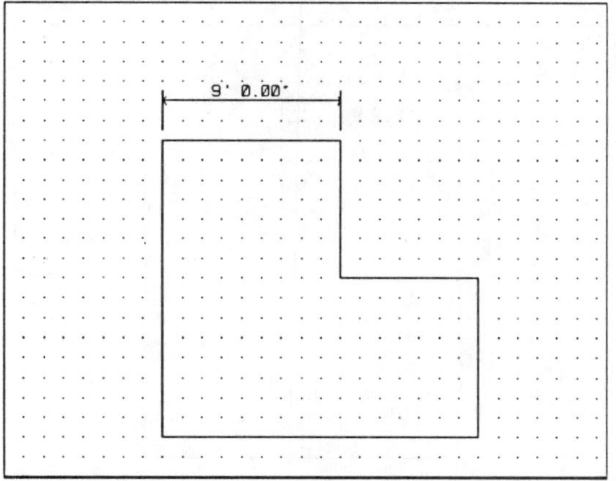

12. Reset the dimension mode to cumulative.

```
ENTER A COMMAND> UM
1 = SINGLE, 2 = PARTITIONED, 3 = CUMULATIVE
CHANGE DIMENSION MODE (1) LIMITS:1 TO 3  3<CR>
```

13. Specify the dimension direction.

```
ENTER A COMMAND> UD
1 = ALIGNED, 2 = HORIZONTAL, 3 = VERTICAL
CHANGE DIMENSION DIRECTION (1) LIMITS: 1 TO 3 2  <CR>
```

14. Toggle EXTENSION STRETCH to the on position.

```
ENTER A COMMAND> XS
EXTENSION STRETCH IS ON
```

15. Dimension both top horizontal lines.

```
ENTER A COMMAND> LX
ENTER FIRST POINT> 8',17' <CR>
HIT  <ESC> TO QUIT!
ENTER NEXT POINT> 17',17'  <CR>
ENTER LOCATION OF DIMENSION> 12',21'  <CR>
ENTER NEXT POINT> 24',10'  <CR>
ENTER NEXT POINT>
```

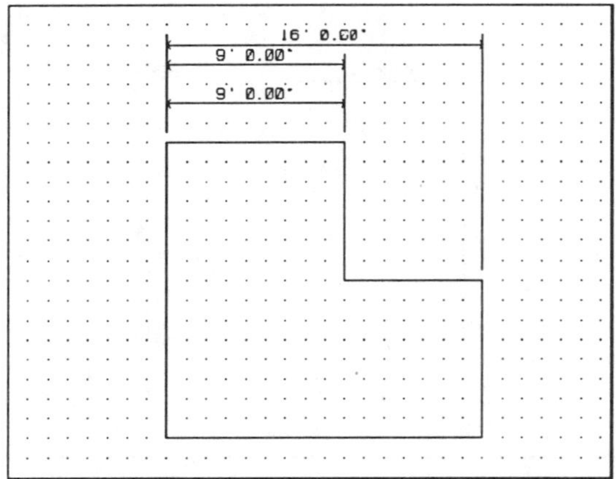

16. Change dimensional mode.

```
ENTER A COMMAND >  UM
1 = SINGLE, 2 = PARTITIONED, 3 = CUMULATIVE
CHANGE DIMENSION MODE (3) LIMITS: 1 TO 3 >  1   <CR>
```

17. Specify the dimension direction.

```
ENTER A COMMAND >  UD
1 = ALIGNED, 2 = HORIZONTAL, 3 = VERTICAL
CHANGE DIMENSION DIRECTION (2) LIMITS: 1 TO 3 >  3   <CR>
```

18. Dimension the left vertical line.

```
ENTER A COMMAND >  LX
```

NOTE

If you are in horizontal mode and try to dimension a vertical
line or vice versa, Generic CADD gives an error message that
it cannot dimension a zero length.

```
ENTER FIRST POINT >  8',2'   <CR>
HIT (ESC) TO QUIT!
ENTER NEXT POINT > >  8',17'   <CR>
ENTER LOCATION OF DIMENSION >  5',5'   <CR>
ENTER FIRST POINT >  <ESC>
```

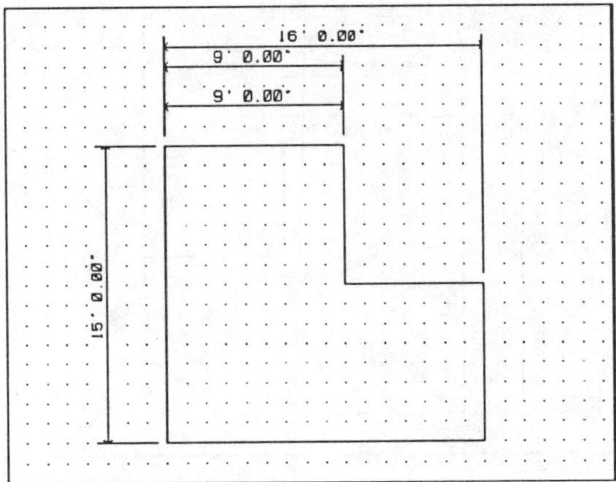

19. Change the arrowhead type.

```
ENTER A COMMAND> AT
1 = 15 DEG, 2 = 30 DEG, 3 = 45 DEG, 4 = 60 DEG, 5 = CIRCLE, 6 = SLASH
CHANGE ARROWHEAD TYPE (2) LIMITS: 1 TO 6> 4  <CR>
```

20. Change the arrowhead mode.

```
ENTER A COMMAND> AW
ARROW CLOSED IS OFF
```

21. Change the dimension direction.

```
ENTER A COMMAND> UD
1 = ALIGNED, 2 = HORIZONTAL, 3 = VERTICAL
CHANGE DIMENSION DIRECTION (3) LIMITS: 1 TO 3> 1  <CR>
```

22. Create an angled dimension between two selected corner points.

```
ENTER A COMMAND> LX
ENTER FIRST POINT> 17',17'  <CR>
HIT <ESC) TO QUIT!
ENTER NEXT POINT> 24',10'  <CR>
ENTER LOCATION OF DIMENSION >23',18'  <CR>
ENTER FIRST POINT> <ESC>
```

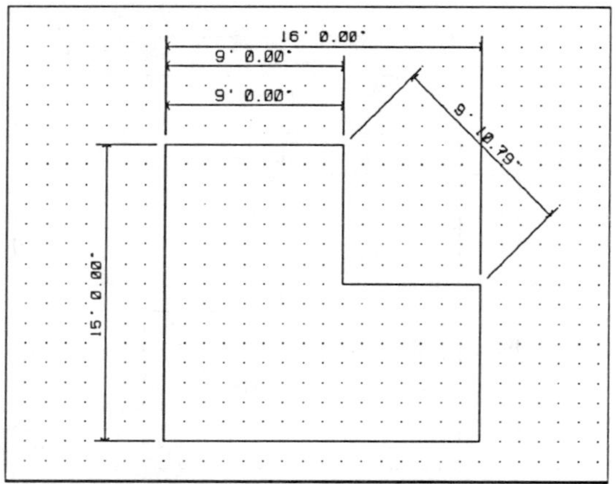

23. Add an angled line to the figure.

```
ENTER A COMMAND> L1
ENTER START POINT>> 24',10'  <CR>
ENTER NEXT POINT> 18',2'  <CR>
ENTER NEXT POINT> PU
```

24. Dimension the angle.

```
ENTER A COMMAND> AX
ENTER CENTER POINT> 18',2'  <CR>
HIT   (ESC) TO QUIT!
SPECIFY IN COUNTER CLOCKWISE ORDER
ENTER POINT ON FIRST RADIUS> 23',2'  <CR>
ENTER POINT ON NEXT RADIUS> 24',10'  <CR>
ENTER LOCATION OF DIMENSION> 22',5'  <CR>
ENTER TEXT PLACEMENT> 19',3'  <CR>
ENTER CENTER POINT>  <ESC>
```

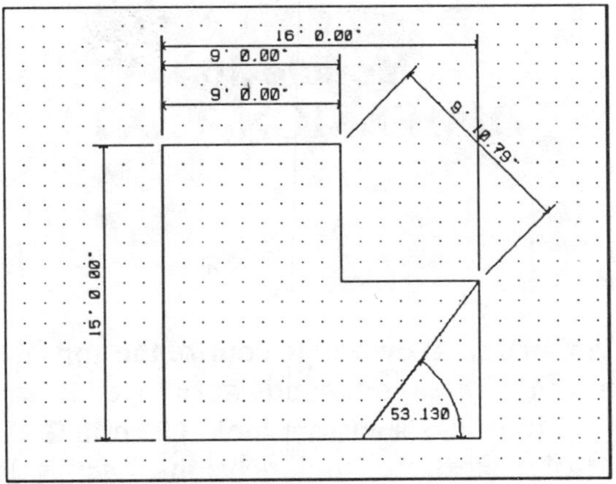

25. Delete the last dimension drawn.

> ENTER A COMMAND > **ED**

26. Redraw the screen.

> ENTER A COMMAND > **RD**

27. Quit the drawing without saving.

28. Turn to Module 16 to continue the learning sequence.

Module 16
DIMENSION TEXT

DESCRIPTION

The dimension text commands allow you to control the appearance of dimensional text added to your drawing. These commands work together with the dimensioning commands to give your drawings a custom look. Generic CADD offers a number of commands to control the text used in dimensions. Each is described below with the appropriate two-letter command in parentheses.

LETTER SIZE (LH) Allows you to set the size or height of the text that is placed automatically in the dimensioning commands. The Generic CADD default is one. The selected text height remains in effect until you change it or exit Generic CADD. Text already on the drawing is not changed.

LETTER FONT (LF) Allows you to select the lettering style or font for dimension text. Seven fonts are available, and the default is Main font. When choosing an alternative font, the font must be in the Generic CADD subdirectory. Upon selection, you are asked if you want to load the font at the current time. If you choose no, when you place a dimension, each character is loaded as needed. The selected font remains in effect until you change it or exit Generic CADD. Fonts already on the drawing are not changed.

LETTER PLACEMENT (LP) Allows you to choose whether the dimension text is placed above the dimension line or set into the dimension line, thus gapping the line. Select number 1 for placement in the dimension line and number 2 for placement above the dimension line. Placement above the dimension line is the default. Once a placement mode is chosen, it remains in effect until you change it or exit Generic CADD. Dimensional text already placed on the drawing is not affected.

LETTER DIRECTION (LR) Allows you to select how the text is aligned in relation to the dimension line. The two options are horizontal, regardless of the direction of the dimension line, or aligned, the default, which creates text in the direction of the dimension line, whether horizontal, vertical, or angled. Once a letter direction is set, it remains in effect until you change it or exit Generic CADD. Dimensional text already placed on the drawing is not changed.

OVERRIDE TEXT (OT) Allows you to toggle between the automatic creation of dimension text by Generic CADD or manual entry of the text, in which Generic CADD gives you the opportunity to enter the text to appear with the dimension line. OVERRIDE TEXT OFF is the default position. This toggle command setting remains in effect until you change it or exit Generic CADD.

APPLICATIONS

The dimension text commands allow you to create varied yet specific dimensions on your drawing. LETTER SIZE and LETTER FONT easily adjust the text to a height and lettering style appropriate to the scale and type of drawing you are creating. OVERRIDE TEXT allows you to enter dimensions different from what Generic CADD actually measures, appropriate if the length dimensioned varies or covers a range of lengths, depending upon the application. LETTER PLACEMENT also allows you to adjust the text placement in relation to the dimension line, depending upon the accepted convention for your drawing type.

TYPICAL OPERATION

In this exercise, you draw and dimension a simple figure, changing the text variables.

1. Start a new drawing called "DIMTEXT."

2. Draw a line figure.

```
ENTER A COMMAND> L1
ENTER START POINT>> 4,6  <CR>
ENTER NEXT POINT> 4,20  <CR>
ENTER NEXT POINT> 14,20  <CR>
ENTER NEXT POINT> 14,15  <CR>
ENTER NEXT POINT> 22,15  <CR>
ENTER NEXT POINT> 22,20  <CR>
ENTER NEXT POINT> 31,20  <CR>
ENTER NEXT POINT> 31,6  <CR>
ENTER NEXT POINT> 4,6  <CR>
ENTER NEXT POINT> PU
```

3. Choose a dimension font.

```
ENTER A COMMAND> LF
ENTER THE FONT NAME> DECO  <CR>
FONT DECO IS SELECTED
LOAD FONT NOW? (Y,N)> Y
SELECTED FONT IS:DECO
```

4. Change the text placement in the dimension line.

```
ENTER A COMMAND> LP
(1 = IN DIMENSION LINE, 2 = ABOVE DIMENSION LINE)
CHANGE LETTERING PLACEMENT (2) LIMITS: 1 TO 2> 1  <CR>
```

5. Change letter size.

```
ENTER A COMMAND> LH
CHANGE LETTER HEIGHT (1.000) IN.> .5  <CR>
```

6. Dimension the figure.

```
ENTER A COMMAND> LX
ENTER FIRST POINT> 4,20  <CR>
HIT  <ESC> TO QUIT!
ENTER NEXT POINT> 14,20  <CR>
ENTER LOCATION OF DIMENSION> 8,20  <CR>
ENTER FIRST POINT> <ESC>
```

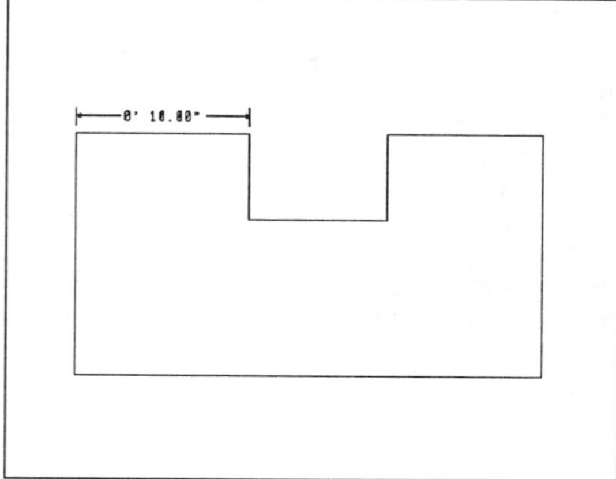

7. Change the letter direction.

```
ENTER A COMMAND> LR
(1 = HORIZONTAL, 2 = ALIGNED)
CHANGE LETTERING DIRECTION (2) LIMITS: 1 TO 2> 1  <CR>
```

8. Dimension the vertical left side of the figure.

```
ENTER A COMMAND> LX
ENTER FIRST POINT> 31,6  <CR>
HIT  <ESC> TO QUIT
ENTER NEXT POINT> 31,20  <CR>
ENTER LOCATION OF DIMENSION> 33,12  <CR>
ENTER FIRST POINT>  <ESC>
```

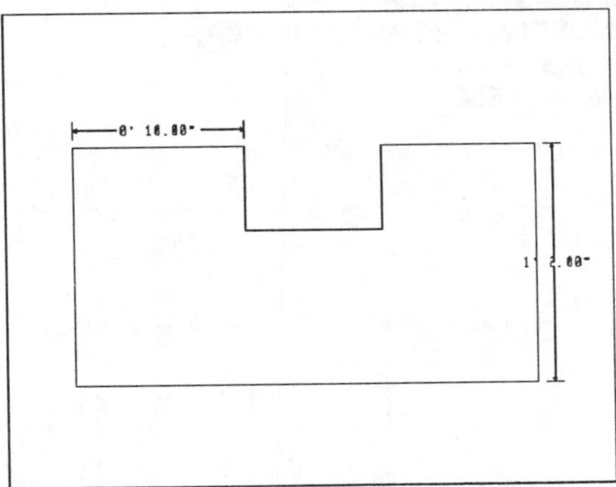

9. Reset the letter direction.

```
ENTER A COMMAND> LR
(1 = HORIZONTAL, 2 = ALIGNED)
CHANGE LETTERING DIRECTION (1) LIMITS: 1 TO 2> 2  <CR>
```

10. Override the text dimension.

```
ENTER A COMMAND >  OT
DIMENSION TEXT OVERRIDE IS ON
```

11. Change the text placement in the dimension line.

```
ENTER A COMMAND >  LP
(1 = IN DIMENSION LINE, 2 = ABOVE DIMENSION LINE >
CHANGE LETTERING PLACEMENT (1) LIMITS: 1 TO 2 >  2   < CR >
```

12. Dimension the top horizontal line.

```
ENTER A COMMAND >  LX
ENTER FIRST POINT >  22,20   < CR >
HIT   < ESC > TO QUIT!
ENTER NEXT POINT >  31,20   < CR >
ENTER LOCATION OF DIMENSION >  27,21   < CR >
ENTER TEXT VARIES >   < CR >
ENTER FIRST POINT >  < ESC >
```

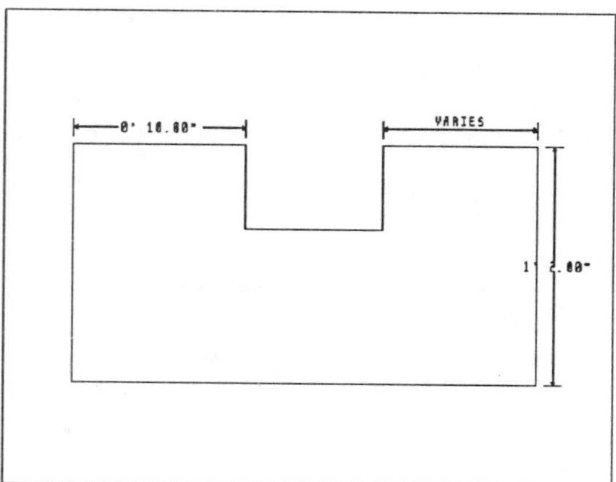

13. Quit the drawing without saving.

14. Turn to Module 30 to continue the learning sequence.

DISPLAY COLOR

DESCRIPTION

DISPLAY COLOR (DK) sets the color of the text on your screen menu, the prompt line at the bottom of the screen, and the information at the top of the screen. This command also controls the color of the displayed grid. As with all commands involving color selection, the available color values range from 0 to 255. The corresponding color representing each of these color values depends upon the graphics card you are using. At the command prompt, enter a new value and press Return. If you prefer, choose the color from the color bars shown in the menu area. Once selected, the screen text changes.

APPLICATIONS

DISPLAY COLOR allows you to choose colors that best suit your environment and personal taste. Rooms with bright lighting need brighter screen menu colors to distinguish them when the menu cursor is placed on the commands. Similarly, displayed grids are easer to read in brighter colors. Practice changing the colors until you find a combination that works well for your work.

TYPICAL OPERATION

In this activity you change the color of the grid and screen menu from the default values.

1. Start a new drawing called "COLOR."

2. Display the default grid.

```
ENTER A COMMAND > GR
DISPLAY GRID IS ON
```

3. Change the display color.

```
ENTER A COMMAND > DK
CHANGE COLOR NUMBER (11) LIMITS: 0 TO 255 > 14 <CR>
```

NOTE

When the display color is changed, the screen text changes immediately. You must redraw the screen to see the effect on the grid points.

```
ENTER A COMMAND > RD
```

4. Change the display grid to another color.

```
ENTER A COMMAND > DK
CHANGE COLOR NUMBER (14) LIMITS: 0 TO 255 > 10 <CR>
ENTER A COMMAND > RD
```

5. Continue to change color values until you find a color that functions well for you.

6. Quit the drawing.

7. Turn to Module 12 to continue the learning sequence.

Module 18
DISPLAY COORDINATES

DESCRIPTION

The coordinates that appear at the top of the drawing screen reflect each selected point on the drawing screen. Generic CADD offers three ways that coordinates are calculated and displayed. Each coordinate mode is described below, with the corresponding two-letter command in parentheses.

ABSOLUTE COORDINATES (AC) displays the coordinate location of the cursor as an X and Y distance from the drawing origin. The format for the coordinates, whether inches, feet, meters, etc., is controlled with the units commands. This command is a toggle, turning the display at the top of the screen on or off with each selection. The default is ABSOLUTE COORDINATES in the on position. To see the absolute coordinates after selecting the command, you must redraw the screen.

DELTA COORDINATES (DC) displays the coordinates of the cursor as an X and Y distance in relation to the previously selected point. The format of the coordinates, whether inches, feet, meters, etc., is controlled with the units commands. This command is a toggle, turning the display at the top of the drawing screen on or off with each selection. When drawing a line, after you select the first point, as you move the cursor away to select the second point, the coordinates displayed are in relation to the first point. Thus you know the length of the line you are drawing. To see the delta coordinates after selecting the command, you must redraw the screen.

POLAR COORDINATES (PT) displays coordinates of the cursor in the delta format, but as a distance and an angle, rather than an X and Y coordinate. Each coordinate is displayed in relation to the previously selected point. This command is a toggle, turning the polar mode on or off.

APPLICATIONS

Depending upon the objects you are drawing, different coordinate modes are needed. Absolute mode is needed for creating maps or any drawing in which all points are measured from the same point, such as a benchmark. Delta coordinates are used in architectural drawings, where the lengths of individual building parts are needed. In architectural work, occasionally polar mode is needed to create angled partitions and placing of parts on an angle. In any drawing type, polar is used when angles and lengths along the angles are involved.

TYPICAL OPERATION

In this activity you draw several objects while toggling between the three coordinate modes.

1. Start a new drawing called "COORD."

2. Draw a line using the default of ABSOLUTE COORDINATES.

```
ENTER A COMMAND > L1
ENTER START POINT > >  5,5  <CR>
```

NOTE

Notice that the coordinate display reflects the coordinates entered.

```
ESC OR PEN UP TO STOP
ENTER NEXT POINT > 20,20  <CR>
ENTER NEXT POINT > 24,15  <CR>
ENTER NEXT POINT > PU
```

3. Change to DELTA COORDINATE display mode.

```
ENTER A COMMAND > DC
DELTA DISPLAY COORDINATES IS ON
```

4. Draw a line while observing the delta coordinates.

```
ENTER A COMMAND > L1
```

NOTE
Although the cursor is still located at the last point drawn
using absolute coordinates (24,15), in DELTA
COORDINATES the display now indicates that point as (0,0).

ENTER START POINT > > **6,6** <**CR**>

NOTE
Even though delta coordinates are displayed, the entry mode
is the manual entry offset origin default.

ENTER NEXT POINT > **18,9** <**CR**>

NOTE
Once a point is selected, the delta display displays the point
as (0,0).

ENTER NEXT POINT > (Move your cursor away from the previously selected point to
observe the changing coordinates on the screen display.)
ENTER NEXT POINT > **PU**

---

5. Change the display to polar coordinates.

ENTER A COMMAND > **PT**
POLAR COORDS DISPLAY IS ON

---

6. Observe the changing coordinates as you move the cursor.

ENTER A COMMAND > **L1**
ENTER START POINT > > **10,10** <**CR**>
ENTER NEXT POINT (Pull the cursor out away from the point just selected and move it in
a slow counterclockwise direction. Observe the changing distances and angles in the
display.)
ENTER NEXT POINT > **PU**

---

7. Toggle polar coordinates display to off.

ENTER A COMMAND > **PT**
POLAR COORDS DISPLAY IS OFF

Note that now the delta coordinates appear on the display.

8. Toggle delta coordinates to off.

```
ENTER A COMMAND > DC
DISPLAY DELTA COORDINATES IS OFF
```

Now no coordinates appear in the display.

9. Quit the drawing.

10. Turn to Module 17 to continue the learning sequence.

Module 19
DOUBLE LINE/DOUBLE WIDTH

DESCRIPTION

The DOUBLE LINE (L2) and DOUBLE WIDTH (TH) commands work together
to automatically draw parallel lines. DOUBLE LINE is used to draw the parallel
lines, while DOUBLE WIDTH controls the distance between the two parallel lines.
A complete description of each follows.

DOUBLE LINE (L2) Allows you to draw parallel lines automatically. You draw
a single line on the screen as you do in the STRAIGHT LINE
command, and Generic CADD replaces it with parallel lines
simultaneously. The lines are cleaned up at the corners as you draw
them.

DOUBLE WIDTH (TH) Allows you to set the distance parallel lines are apart in
the DOUBLE LINE command. The default setting is 1 for offset
1 and 0 for offset 2. Actually the lines that Generic CADD draws
are offset a specified distance to either side of the line defined by
the points you select on the screen. When drawing in Generic
CADD, left and right are determined by the direction in which the
line is being created. Imagine that you are walking on the line in
the direction in which it is being created, and you can easily
visualize which side is left and which is right, even if you draw a
vertical line. When entering the width factor for a double line, you
are asked for two offset values. The total of these values equals
the width of the parallel lines. Offset 1 is the side of the wall which
is to the left of the single line you draw on the screen. Likewise,
offset 2 is to the right of the line you draw on the screen. You can
also enter the width by showing Generic CADD on the screen.
Type D for distance and select two points on the screen to represent
the desired line width.

APPLICATIONS

Double lines are commonly used to draw walls of varying thicknesses. They may also be used to denote roads or walkways, mechanical ductwork, or cabling layouts. The uses for these valuable Generic CADD capabilities are endless.

TYPICAL OPERATION

In this exercise you draw several double lines of varying widths.

1. Start a new drawing called "DLINE."

2. Set the double line width to 4."

```
ENTER A COMMAND >  TH
CHANGE DOUBLE LINE OFFSET1 (1.000) IN >  2   <CR>
CHANGE DOUBLE LINE OFFSET2 (0.000) IN >  2   <CR>
```

3. Draw a double line.

```
ENTER A COMMAND >  L2
ENTER START POINT > >  2,2   <CR>
ESC OR PEN UP TO STOP
```

NOTE

In this example, each offset value is equal. The points selected on the screen represent the centerline of the wall, but are not actually drawn on the screen. Note the cursor position in relation to the lines drawn as each coordinate set is entered.

```
ENTER NEXT POINT >  8,10   <CR>
ENTER NEXT POINT >  15,10   <CR>
ENTER NEXT POINT >  20,20   <CR>
ENTER NEXT POINT >  PU
```

4. Reset the parallel wall thickness.

```
ENTER A COMMAND >  TH
CHANGE DOUBLE LINE OFFSET1 (2.000) > 1   <CR>
CHANGE DOUBLE LINE OFFSET2 (2.000) > 3   <CR>
```

5. Draw another parallel line series.

```
ENTER A COMMAND>  L2
ENTER START POINT> >  30,22  <CR>
ESC OR PEN UP TO STOP
ENTER NEXT POINT>  28,10  <CR>
ENTER NEXT POINT>  20,5  <CR>
ENTER NEXT POINT>  PU
```

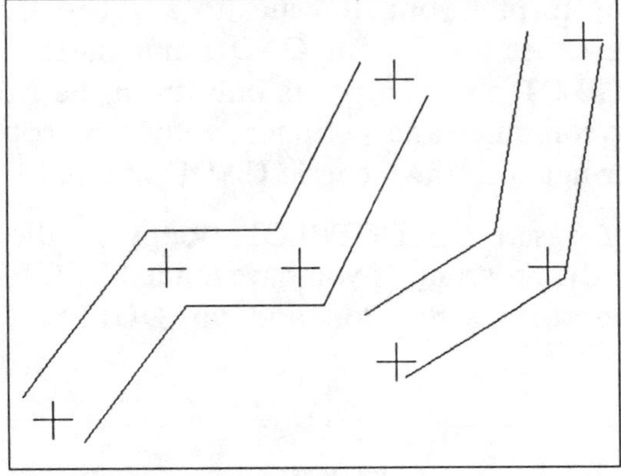

6. Quit the drawing without saving.

7. Turn to Module 9 to continue the learning sequence.

Module 20
DOTPLOT

DESCRIPTION

DOTPLOT allows you to plot your drawings to a dot matrix printer, including laser and color printers. See the Generic CADD manual for the printers that are supported. The DOTPLOT program prints only from the LPT1 parallel port of your computer. Your computer and peripherals must be configured properly to run DOTPLOT. Refer again to the Generic CADD manual.

To access DOTPLOT insert the DOTPLOT floppy in the A drive and type DOTPLOT to initiate the program. If you have loaded DOTPLOT onto your hard drive, change to the appropriate directory and type DOTPLOT. The following title page appears:

```
                        Level 3  Version 1.10

     Configured for:

          IBM VGA  (PS/2 Models 30-286 & up) . 640 x 480     16 color

          LOGITECH LOGIMOUSE C7 (SERIAL)

          IBM GRAPHICS PRINTER - LOW RES

          Memory Available for Drawing Data:     195110




          USE OF AN AUTHORIZED COPY OF THIS SOFTWARE BEYOND THIS POINT
          CONSTIIUTES YOUR ACCEPTANCE OF THE ACCOMPANYING LICENSE AGREEMENT.
     Copyright(C) 1985,86,87,88,89 by GENERIC SOFTWARE,INC. All Rights Reserved.


               **********  PRESS RETURN KEY TO BEGIN  **********
```

The current configuration is displayed, along with the Generic CADD license agreement. Your configuration may differ from the illustration shown. If you are using DOTPLOT for the first time you must configure DOTPLOT at this time by selecting the configuration option on the next menu screen. Press Return and the following menu appears:

```
                    Level 3   Version 1.10

                         MAIN MENU

        1)  CONFIGURE DOTPLOT
        2)  DISPLAY DIRECTORY FILES
        3)  LOAD A DRAWING
        4)  DISPLAY DRAWING STATUS
        5)  LIST OBJECTS IN CURRENT WINDOW
        6)  SELECT VIEW & DISPLAY OPTIONS
        7)  PLOT THE DRAWING
        8)  QUIT DOTPLOT
        9)  DISPLAY PRINTER LOOKUP TABLE



        ENTER SELECTION >
```

Each of the menu items is described below:

1) CONFIGURE DOTPLOT

This option allows you to select the current hardware in use with DOTPLOT. This option must be completed before DOTPLOT will work. A video graphics card, a pointing device, and a printer must be selected. The other items on the menu are optional. The menu appears as follows:

```
        * * *    C O N F I G U R A T I O N   M E N U    * * *


        1) Select a Video Graphics Display
        2) Select a Pointing Device
        3) Select a Printer
        4) Change the Default Drawing Parameters
        5) Set Default Paths
        6) Set Keyboard Function Key Commands
        7) Set Drawing Size (limits)
        8) Set Screen Ratio
        9) Return to MAIN MENU



        Enter a selection number >>>
```

2) DISPLAY DIRECTORY FILES

This option allows you to list the specified files in a particular directory location. Press Return to list the files in the default path that you may have set in option 5 of the CONFIGURATION menu. If you have not set the default path, enter the complete path location of the files you want to view.

3) LOAD A DRAWING

To begin plotting a drawing, you must first load it to the screen. This option allows you to load a drawing created previously in Generic CADD. Type in the filename at the prompt. Remember to include the full path location if the file is not located in the default directory. You may also load a drawing at the same time you enter DOTPLOT by typing DOTPLOT FILENAME at the DOS prompt, where FILENAME is the name of the drawing you want to load. Adding the drawing name extension is not necessary. If you want to perform these two steps simultaneously, be sure that the drawing is in the same directory as DOTPLOT or that you have set the default paths in option 5 of the CONFIGURATION menu to the same location as the drawing you want to load. Otherwise, DOTPLOT will not find the drawing to load.

4) DISPLAY DRAWING STATUS

This option displays various types of information about the loaded drawing. The drawing name is at the top of the screen display. Information includes the number of points, lines, characters, and components; memory used and available; grid size and grid display, reference points, and construction points on or off; layers displayed and layers with data. The screen for the SAMPLE.DWG is shown below:

```
                    DISPLAY DRAWING STATUS1.10


       DRAWING NAME IS:  SAMPLE

   POINTS:      928 , LINES:    259  , CHARACTERS:      0  , COMPONENTS:      0

   MEMORY AVAILABLE:  195110
   MEMORY USED:      9280
   MEMORY REMAINING:  185830

   GRID SIZE IS:  1.0000 ,  GRID DISPLAY IS:
   REFERENCE POINTS ARE:
   CONSTRUCTION POINTS ARE:

   ALL LAYERS ARE DISPLAYED
   LAYERS WITH DATA:                  1

   HIT RETURN TO CONTINUE >>>
```

5) LIST OBJECTS IN CURRENT WINDOW

This option generates an on-screen list of the displayed objects on the loaded drawing. A drawing must first be loaded before this option will work. The object type, line type, color, and layer are listed. Press Return to view the entire list, screen page by screen page. A single screen view of objects in the SAMPLE.DWG is shown below:

```
                    LIST OBJECTS IN CURRENT VIEW

      LINE   TYPE:0, WIDTH:0,   COLOR:1,   LAYER:0
      LINE   TYPE:0, WIDTH:0,   COLOR:1,   LAYER:0
      LINE   TYPE:0, WIDTH:0,   COLOR:1,   LAYER:0
      LINE   TYPE:0, WIDTH:0,   COLOR:1,   LAYER:0
      LINE   TYPE:0, WIDTH:0,   COLOR:1,   LAYER:0
      LINE   TYPE:0, WIDTH:0,   COLOR:1,   LAYER:0
      LINE   TYPE:0, WIDTH:0,   COLOR:1,   LAYER:0
      LINE   TYPE:0, WIDTH:0,   COLOR:1,   LAYER:0
      LINE   TYPE:0, WIDTH:0,   COLOR:1,   LAYER:0
      LINE   TYPE:0, WIDTH:0,   COLOR:1,   LAYER:0
      LINE   TYPE:0, WIDTH:0,   COLOR:1,   LAYER:0
      LINE   TYPE:0, WIDTH:0,   COLOR:1,   LAYER:0
      LINE   TYPE:0, WIDTH:0,   COLOR:1,   LAYER:0


      HIT RETURN TO CONTINUE OR [ESC] TO EXIT >
```

6) SELECT VIEW & DISPLAY OPTIONS

This option allows you to adjust the display of the loaded drawing. When you select this option, the loaded drawing immediately appears on the screen. DOTPLOT assumes you want to make modifications to the drawing display before plotting. You must have a drawing loaded before this option will function. A number of Generic CADD commands pertaining to display are available for your use, either from the screen menu or through keyboard commands. These commands include all of the ZOOM commands, including pan and redraw; the UNITS commands; a number of the DISPLAY commands; and drawing load, plot, erase; plus QUIT and MAIN MENU (SF) to return you to the DOTPLOT main menu.

7) PLOT THE DRAWING

This option begins the plotting process. You must have a drawing loaded. You may also begin the plotting process by selecting DRAWING PLOT from the on-screen menu or by typing DP from the keyboard. It is also possible to enter DOTPLOT directly from the Generic CADD menu by entering the XD command. Think of these letters as representing an Exit to DOTPLOT. Your drawing is already loaded and on the screen, so you proceed immediately into the plotting process. Once in DOTPLOT, type RT to return to Generic CADD. DOTPLOT takes you through a number of prompted commands, each of which ask for specific information needed to plot the drawing to your specifications. Each option is described below:

    A.   PAPER SIZE allows you to specify the size of paper on which the drawing is printed. The X dimension or width of the paper is displayed first, with a default of 8.000 inches. The default and the limits displayed may vary depending upon the printer you have configured with DOTPLOT. Press Return to accept the default or enter the desired width. Remember even most wide carriage printers are limited to 13-1/2" width. The Y dimension or length is prompted next, with a default of 10.000 inches. Again, press Return to accept or enter the desired length. As in plotting with a pen plotter, allow some space around the edges of the paper for a border. DOTPLOT plots the entire sheet size if desired, so you may want to make the X and Y dimensions slightly smaller than the actual paper size you are using.

B.   PLOT TYPES allows you to choose among three types:

1.   PLOT CURRENT VIEW plots the current drawing screen view to fit on the specified paper size, regardless of the scale. Type V to access this option. The paper size is not necessarily the actual paper size, but the total area you want the plotted drawing to occupy. You are then prompted for a FAST REDRAW. If you select Y for yes, DOTPLOT redraws the loaded drawing view as a dotted rectangle with a dotted X through it. The rectangle represents the overall boundary of the drawing. On large drawings it is faster to redraw in this manner. If you select N for no, the drawing is displayed in the normal manner. DOTPLOT then rotates the drawing 90 degrees if it fits better on the sheet when turned. DOTPLOT then asks for confirmation to plot the drawing.

2.   PLOT FULL DRAWING plots the entire drawing fitted to the specified paper size. Type F to access this option. The paper size is not necessarily the actual paper size, but the total area you want the plotted drawing to occupy. You are then prompted for a FAST REDRAW. If you select Y for yes, DOTPLOT redraws the loaded drawing view as a dotted rectangle with a dotted X through it. The rectangle represents the overall boundary of the drawing. On large drawings it is faster to redraw in this manner. If you select N for no, the drawing is displayed in the normal manner. DOTPLOT then rotates the drawing 90 degrees if it fits better on the sheet when turned. DOTPLOT then asks for confirmation to plot the drawing.

3.   PLOT AT USER SCALE allows you to specify the desired plotted scale, origin, and rotation. Type S to access this option. You are then prompted for a FAST REDRAW. If you select Y for yes, DOTPLOT redraws the loaded drawing view as a dotted rectangle with a dotted X through it. The rectangle represents the overall

boundary of the drawing. On large drawings it is faster to redraw in this manner. If you select N for no, the drawing is displayed in the normal manner. Then you are asked for the drawing scale, expressed in a ratio of 1 to the desired scale. To set the scale, enter the desired ratio and press Return. The first number in the ratio is assumed to be a value of one. A drawing one quarter the actual size is 1:4 scale. Twice the actual size is 1:1/2. If you are using architectural or engineering scales, the conversion from feet to inches is necessary. For example, 1/8" = 1'0"scale is the same as 1/8" = 12, which is the same as 1" = 96. The scale ratio is thus 1:96. Using this example, 1/4"scale becomes 1:48; 1/2" scale becomes 1:24; and 3/4"scale becomes 1:16. You are then asked if you want to turn the drawing 90 degrees. Answer Y for yes if it helps fit the drawing on the sheet. When a drawing is turned 90 degrees, the default origin is in the upper left corner. The DOTPLOT displays the drawing at the specified scale within a rectangle representing the sheet size. You are asked if the plot scale is correct. If you answer N for no, you are again asked for a scale value. You can proceed through these steps as many times as necessary until you are satisfied. If the scale is acceptable, enter Y for yes. and you are asked if the plot origin is correct. Responding N for no allows you to move the sheet border rectangle, which is now attached to your screen cursor, over the drawing to reposition the origin. You can also enter the origin coordinates through the keyboard if you want. You are again asked if the plot origin is correct. Once you answer Y for yes, you are asked if you want to plot the drawing. If you enter Y for yes, the drawing is printed. Make sure your printer is turned on. If you answer N for no, you are returned to the drawing display.

8) QUIT DOTPLOT

This option exits you from the DOTPLOT program to your previous location before entering DOTPLOT.

9) DISPLAY PRINTER LOOKUP TABLE

This option displays a list of printer equivalents for printers not listed in the DOTPLOT configuration menu. Use this list when configuring your software if your specific printer is not one of those listed. The first page of the list is shown below:

```
If your printer does not appear on the DotPlot configuration
menu, try locating your printer in the following table.

If your printer is not listed in the configuration menu or
the table below, then try:

   For dot-matrix printers - EPSON or IBM
   For laser printers - Hewlett Packard or Canon



                                   Choose This From The
Your Printer                       DotPlot Configuration Menu
-------------                      --------------------------

ANADEX                             OTHER GRAPHICS PRINTERS
ANTEX DATA SYTEMS                  EPSON
AT&I 475                           C. ITOH
BROTHER                            EPSON and COMPATIBLES
CAL-ABCO (LEGEND, CP VII)          EPSON
CANON PW-1156A                     EPSON

Press any key for more, ESC to Quit.
```

APPLICATIONS

DOTPLOT is used to generate quick plots for initial review. The commands are as varied as those in the PLOT command, so a variety of plot types is easily obtained. DOTPLOT also provides a low cost option to get drawings on paper for those who do not own a more expensive pen plotter. By changing the configuration, you can get quick, low resolution prints or high resolution prints to paper, depending upon the need. Small areas of larger sheets can also be printed to the printer, making sure that all the parts of the drawing are correct before plotting to a pen plotter.

TYPICAL OPERATION

In this activity you load the SAMPLE.DWG drawing and print using DOTPLOT.

1. Begin Generic CADD by loading the SAMPLE.DWG drawing created in Module 2.

2. Enter DOTPLOT from Generic CADD.

NOTE

If you have an older version of Generic CADD, you must enter DOTPLOT from the DOS prompt.

```
ENTER A COMMAND > XD
```

NOTE
When in the DOTPLOT program, the screen format remains
the same as Generic CADD, but the screen menu is limited.

```
SWITCHING TO DOTPLOT........
YOU ARE NOW IN DOTPLOT, TYPE [DP] TO PRINT.
TYPE [RT] TO RETURN TO CADD.
```

3. Begin the plotting process.

```
ENTER A COMMAND> DP
CHANGE PAPER WIDTH (8.000IN) LIMITS:2.000IN TO 24.000IN>   <CR>
CHANGE PAPER LENGTH (10.000IN) LIMITS:2.000IN TO 120.000IN> <CR>
ENTER "V" TO PLOT CURRENT VIEW
ENTER "F" TO PLOT FULL DRAWING
ENTER "S" TO PLOT USER SCALE> S
FAST REDRAW? (Y/N)> N
CURRENT PLOT SCALE: (1:1.00)
ENTER NEW PLOT SCALE: 1:??> 48   <CR>
ROTATE 90 DEGREES? (Y/N)> N
IS THE PLOT SCALE CORRECT? (Y/N)> Y
IS THE PLOT ORIGIN CORRECT? (Y/N)> N
ENTER NEW PLOT ORIGIN (Move the sheet size box attached to the cursor so the
drawing is roughly centered on the sheet and locate in position.)
IS THE PLOT ORIGIN CORRECT? (Y/N)> Y
PLOT THIS DRAWING? (Y/N)> Y
```

The drawing is printed.

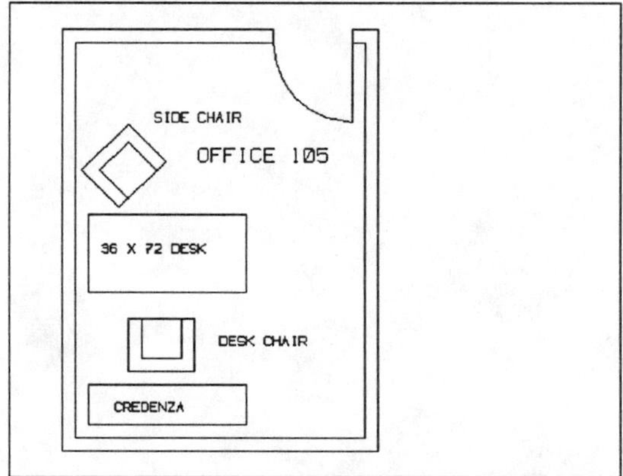

4. Return to Generic CADD.

```
ENTER A COMMAND> RT
RETURNING TO CADD......
```

5. Quit the drawing.

6. Turn to Module 21 to continue the learning sequence.

DRAWING CHANGE/ROTATE /RESCALE/REORIGIN

DESCRIPTION

Generic CADD has a number of commands that allow you to make changes to your entire drawing. These generate fast editing and modification. Each command is described below with the corresponding two-letter command in parentheses.

DRAWING CHANGE (DG) Allows you to alter several features of objects that are already drawn on the drawing. These include the line type, line color, line width, and layer. At the prompt, enter the kind of object to change from the submenu of options, then enter the line type to change, followed by the color of objects to change, the line width to change, and the layer to change. Then you enter the new values for the line type, line color, line width, and layer. The selected objects are then redrawn on the screen with the new values.

DRAWING ROTATE (DR) Allows you to rotate all the objects within an entire drawing to a specified angle. At the prompt, select an origin or axis point. This point remains in the same location during the rotation. Then enter the angle to rotate around the axis. Three options for entering the angle are available. You can enter the desired angle, if known; type A for angle to define the angle on the screen with a basepoint and a ray point; or type V for vertex to define the angle on the screen with a basepoint and two ray points. Generic CADD measures angles from the horizontal position in a counterclockwise rotation, beginning with the first ray selected and ending with the second ray selected. Every point in the drawing rotates. The grid goes not, however, and the X axis and the Y axis are still horizontal and vertical respectively.

DRAWING RESCALE (DZ) Allows you to change the scale of all objects on your drawing. At the command prompt, enter the X scale, then the Y scale. All drawing objects are then scaled accordingly, using the origin as a reference point. The drawing limits and grids as well as other drawing parameters remain the same.

DRAWING REORIGIN (DO) Allows you to change the drawing origin. Care should be exercised when using this command, as all points are measured from the origin. In addition, the plot commands use the origin as a reference and the zoom commands use the origin as the lower left corner. Even the DRAWING REORIGIN command uses the origin as a reference, making it nearly impossible to put the origin back where it was originally. At the prompt, enter the new X origin and the new Y origin.

APPLICATIONS

DRAWING CHANGE, DRAWING ROTATE, DRAWING RESCALE, AND DRAWING REORIGIN further enhance the editing capabilities of Generic CADD. Manipulating an entire drawing at once saves valuable time and insures that all objects to be changed are found and changed.

TYPICAL OPERATION

In this session you create a drawing, modify several objects, and rotate and rescale the entire drawing.

1. Start a new drawing called "DCHANGE."

2. Draw several objects in the default values.

```
ENTER A COMMAND> RE
ENTER A CORNER OF RECTANGLE> 5,5  <CR>
ENTER NEXT CORNER OF RECTANGLE> 2'7,1'3  <CR>
ENTER A COMMAND> RE
ENTER A CORNER OF RECTANGLE> 6,6  <CR>
ENTER NEXT CORNER OF RECTANGLE> 14,14  <CR>
ENTER A COMMAND> C2
ENTER CENTER OF CIRCLE> 1'10,10  <CR>
ENTER A POINT ON CIRCLE> 1'10,1'2  <CR>
```

3. Change the default line color.

```
ENTER A COMMAND> LK
CHANGE LINE COLOR NUMBER (1) LIMITS: 0 TO 255> 5  <CR>
```

4. Change line type.

```
ENTER A COMMAND > LT
CHANGE LINE TYPE (0) LIMITS: 0 TO 255 > 7   <CR>
```

5. Draw more objects with the new values.

```
ENTER A COMMAND > RE
ENTER A CORNER OF RECTANGLE > 1'4,6  <CR>
ENTER NEXT CORNER OF RECTANGLE > 2'6,1'2  <CR>
ENTER A COMMAND > C2
ENTER CENTER OF CIRCLE > 1'10,10   <CR>
ENTER A POINT ON CIRCLE > 1'10,1'1   <CR>
```

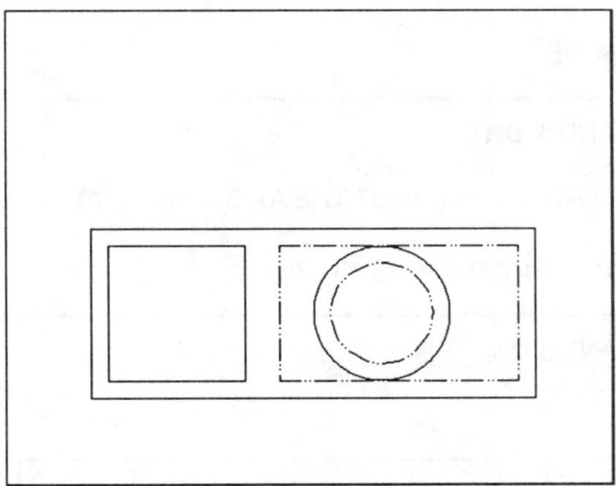

6. Change all the rectangles with linetype 0 and color 1 in the drawing.

```
ENTER A COMMAND > DG
(1)POINT (2)LINE (3)CIRCLE (4)ARC (5)ELLIPS (6)CURV (7)TXT (8)CMP
ENTER TYPE OF OBJECT FROM ABOVE (RETURN FOR ALL) > 2  <CR>
ENTER PARAMETERS TO CHANGE
LINETYPE (0-255) RETURN FOR ALL > 0  <CR>
LINE WIDTH (0-255) RETURN FOR ALL > <CR>
COLOR (0-255) RETURN FOR ALL > 1  <CR>
LAYER (0-255) RETURN FOR ALL > <CR>
CHANGE THEM TO >
LINE TYPE (0-255) RETURN FOR NO CHANGE > 5  <CR>
LINE WIDTH (0-255) RETURN FOR NO CHANGE > <CR>
COLOR (0-255) RETURN FOR NO CHANGE > 3  <CR>
LAYER (0-255) RETURN FOR NO CHANGE > <CR>
CHANGE LINES, OF LINETYPE: 0, ALL WIDTHS, OF COLOR: 1, ALL LAYERS
TO NEW LINETYPE: 5 SAME WIDTHS, NEW COLOR: 3, SAME LAYERS (Y,N) > Y
```

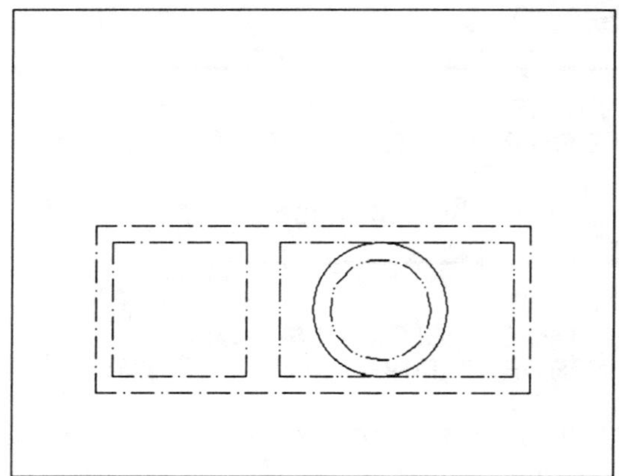

7. Rotate the drawing.

```
ENTER A COMMAND> DR
ENTER AN AXIS POINT> 3,3  <CR>
ENTER ANGLE OF ROTATION ABOUT THE AXIS> 45  <CR>
```

8. Zoom to get the entire drawing in view.

```
ENTER A COMMAND> ZA
```

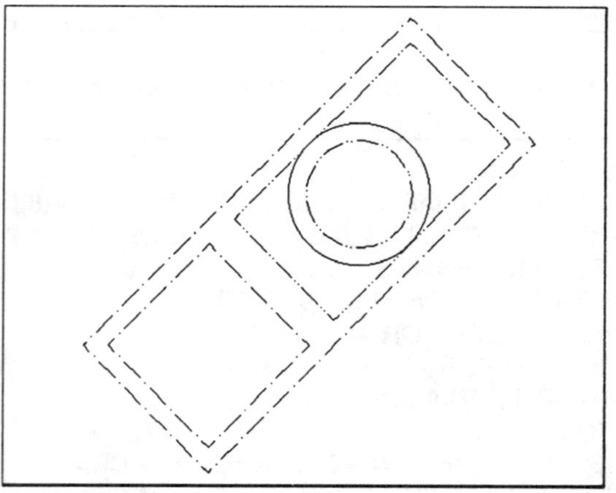

9. Scale the drawing to half size.

```
ENTER A COMMAND > DZ
ENTER NEW X SCALE (1.000) > .5  <CR>
ENTER NEW Y SCALE (0.50) >  <CR>
```

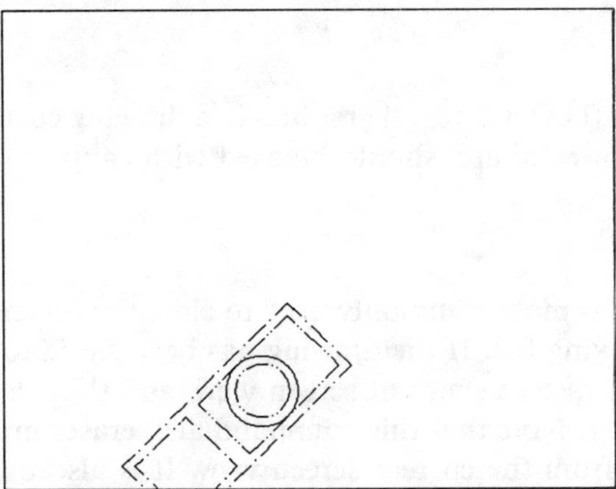

10. Zoom to bring entire drawing into view.

```
ENTER A COMMAND > ZA
```

11. Quit the drawing without saving.

12. Turn to Module 15 to continue the learning sequence.

Module 22
DRAWING ERASE

DESCRIPTION

DRAWING ERASE (DX) deletes all graphics in a drawing currently on the screen. This command is powerful and should be used with caution.

APPLICATIONS

DRAWING ERASE is most commonly used to clear the screen in preparation for loading another drawing file. If the drawing has been saved to the hard disk, this command will only erase the current screen view, and thus the drawing can later be recalled for editing. Note that this command also erases information on layers that are turned off from the current screen view. It is also used to quickly erase all graphics to start the drawing over. DRAWING ERASE is most commonly used in this capacity by Generic CADD beginners.

TYPICAL OPERATION

In this exercise you create a drawing and then erase it from the screen.

1. Start Generic CADD. Type **CADD** and press **Return** at the DOS prompt. Press **Return** at the Generic CADD title page.

2. Start a new drawing called "DERASE."

```
ENTER A DRAWING FILE NAME> DERASE <CR>
IS THIS A NEW DRAWING (Y,N)> Y
```

3. Draw a rectangle

```
ENTER A COMMAND> RE
ENTER A CORNER OF RECTANGLE> 4,4 <CR>
ENTER NEXT CORNER OF RECTANGLE> 10,20 <CR>
```

4. Erase the entire drawing.

```
ENTER A COMMAND >  DX
!!!WARNING!!!
DO YOU REALLY WANT TO ERASE THE DRAWING (Y,N) >  Y
```

The drawing screen is now cleared.

5. Quit the program. No need to save the drawing, as there is nothing to save.

```
ENTER A COMMAND >  QU
SAVE CURRENT DRAWING (Y or N) >  N
"C" TO CONTINUE
"Q" TO QUIT >  Q
```

6. Turn to Module 24 to continue the learning sequence.

DESCRIPTION

DRAWING LOAD (DL) allows a previously saved drawing to be loaded onto the drawing screen for viewing or editing. Many small drawings may be loaded onto the same drawing to create a composite drawing.

APPLICATIONS

This command allows you to recall any number of previously saved drawings to the screen for viewing or editing during a single work period, without exiting Generic CADD each time. To clear the screen before issuing the DRAWING LOAD command, use the DRAWING ERASE command. DRAWING LOAD also allows loading of a drawing on top of another drawing currently on the screen to create a combined drawing. The origin alignment of the added drawing can be adjusted if needed. Refer to the DRAWING REORIGIN command in Module 21. In this manner, several smaller drawings can come together to create a complete drawing.

TYPICAL OPERATION

In this exercise you create two simple drawings, then you load one on top of the other with the origin points aligned.

1. Start Generic CADD. Type **CADD** and press **Return** at the DOS prompt. Press **Return** at the Generic CADD title page.

2. Start a new drawing called "LOAD."

```
ENTER A DRAWING FILE NAME>  LOAD  <CR>
IS THIS A NEW DRAWING (Y,N)>  Y
```

3. Draw a rectangle.

```
ENTER A COMMAND>  RE
ENTER A CORNER OF RECTANGLE>  2,2  <CR>
ENTER NEXT CORNER OF RECTANGLE>  18,12  <CR>
```

4. Save the drawing.

```
ENTER A COMMAND> DS
SAVE FILE: (LOAD.DWG)
```

5. Erase the drawing from the screen, since it is saved to the disk.

```
ENTER A COMMAND> DX
!!WARNING!!!
DO YOU REALLY WANT TO ERASE THE DRAWING (Y,N)> Y
```

The drawing screen is now cleared.

6. Draw a circle.

```
ENTER A COMMAND> C2
ENTER CENTER OF CIRCLE> 16,10  <CR>
ENTER A POINT ON THE CIRCLE> 18,18  <CR>
```

7. Save the drawing as "LOAD2."

```
ENTER A COMMAND> DS
SAVE FILE: (LOAD.DWG)> LOAD2  <CR>
```

8. Now load the LOAD drawing onto the screen on top of LOAD2, which is currently on the screen, and align the origins. Name the combination drawing LOAD3.

```
ENTER A COMMAND> DL
ENTER A DRAWING FILE NAME> LOAD  <CR>
RENAME WORKING DRAWING Y/N)> Y
WORKING FILENAME: (LOAD.DWG)> LOAD3  <CR>
ENTER AN INSERT ORIGIN>
PRESS RETURN FOR 0,0 ORIGIN>  <CR>
```

The LOAD drawing now appears on top of the current drawing LOAD2 on the screen, creating LOAD3.

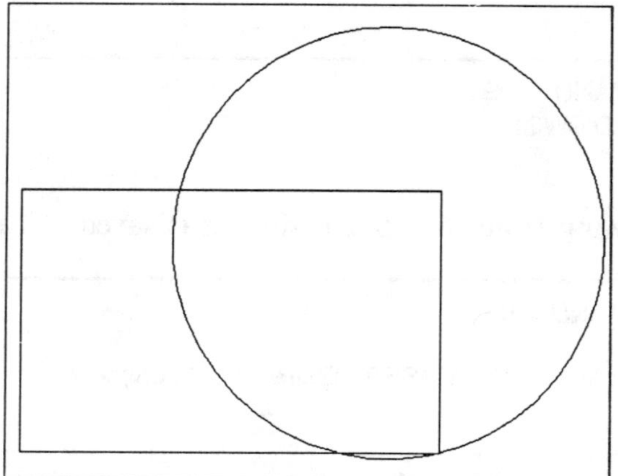

9. Quit the drawing without saving.

```
ENTER A COMMAND > QU
SAVE THE CURRENT DRAWING (Y or N) > N
"C" TO CONTINUE
"Q" TO QUIT > Q
```

10. Turn to Module 22 to continue the learning sequence.

Module 24
DRAWING PATH

DESCRIPTION

The DRAWING PATH (P1) command allows control over where Generic CADD saves or looks for drawings. Unless specified, the default drawing path is used. This path is automatically set to the same directory location as the Generic CADD software program.

APPLICATIONS

Often drawings of various types are stored in several hard drive subdirectories for easy reference. They may be divided according to drawing type or project, or according to the individual who created them. The floppy drive may also be used as a storage location if it is necessary to keep work off the hard drive. DRAWING PATH lets you direct where your work is saved and the location from which it is recalled. This path remains in effect until you change it or exit Generic CADD. Also note that you can change the drawing path for a specific DRAWING LOAD or DRAWING SAVE command if you enter the full path along with the drawing name.

TYPICAL OPERATION

In this activity you create a drawing, change the drawing path from the default to the A drive, and save the drawing to the A drive.

1. Start Generic CADD. Type **CADD** and press **Return** at the DOS prompt. Press **Return** at the Generic CADD title page.

2. Start a new drawing called "DWGPATH."

```
ENTER A DRAWING FILE NAME >  DWGPATH < CR >
IS THIS A NEW DRAWING (Y,N) > Y
```

3. Draw a circle.

```
ENTER A COMMAND > C2
ENTER CENTER OF CIRCLE > 15,15  <CR>
ENTER A POINT ON CIRCLE > 25,15  <CR>
```

4. Change the drawing path.

```
ENTER A COMMAND > P1
CHANGE DRAWING PATH FROM: CURRENT DRIVE & DIRECTORY TO: A:  <CR>
```

5. Save the drawing. Make sure you have a formatted floppy in the A drive.

```
ENTER A COMMAND > DS
SAVE FILE: (A:/DWGPATH.DWG) >  <CR>
```

Note that the full address of the drawing path is given.
6. Quit the drawing.

```
ENTER A COMMAND > QU
SAVE CURRENT DRAWING (Y or N) > N
```

No need to save the drawing as the most recent version has been saved.

```
"C" TO CONTINUE
"Q" TO QUIT > Q
```

7. Turn to Module 38 to continue the learning sequence.

Module 25
DRAWING PLOT

DESCRIPTION

The DRAWING PLOT (DP) command allows you to generate an actual drawing of your Generic CADD drawing file on paper using a pen plotter. The plotter you are using must be specified in the CONFIG program. See the Generic CADD manual for instructions on setup for your particular equipment. There are a number of options included in the DRAWING PLOT command. When you select the command, the following menu appears. The first five options control the way the drawing is to be plotted. The default selections appear in parentheses. To change any of the defaults, enter the number corresponding to the menu item and enter the new selection. Some of the menu options have additional menus. Your drawing screen may look different, depending upon your hardware configuration. Note that the plotter you are using is listed above the menu.

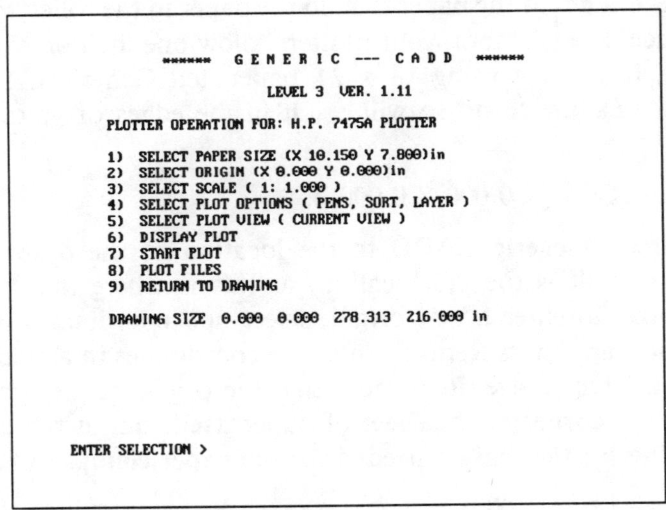

Each of the menu options is described below:

  1) SELECT PAPER SIZE (X 10.150 Y 7.800)in

Upon selection of option #1 the following submenu appears:

```
          ******  G E N E R I C  ---  C A D D   ******
                       LEVEL 3  VER. 1.11


          SELECT PLOT SIZE

                1) WIDTH 7.800          LENGTH 10.150in
                2) WIDTH 10.150          LENGTH 16.300in
                3) USER SELECTED SIZE








          ENTER SELECTION >
```

Select option 1 or 2 if this plot size is desired. The default option sizes that appear are based upon the configured plotter. Select 3 and you are prompted for the X plot length and the Y plot length. The plotter noted in this explanation has a maximum of 8-1/2"x 11"plot size. The paper size is the size of the total plotted area. Generic CADD plots within this entire area, while most plotters need a margin around the edges of the paper to hold the paper to the roller while plotting. The exact distance depends upon your plotter. Allow one inch on each side when in doubt. Thus, if you are using 18"x 24"paper, tell Generic CADD the plot area is 16"x 22". Failure to do so will result in the edges of your drawing not being plotted.

2) SELECT ORIGIN (X 0.000 Y 0.000)in

This options directs Generic CADD to the location of the drawing origin or basepoint. The default is the 0,0 location, as this is where the origin is most commonly located. To enter a new origin, select new coordinates in relation to the 0,0 coordinates and press Return. Enter the coordinates in actual size as they relate to the actual paper size. Remember that the origin of the drawing on the plotter is not at the corner of the sheet of paper itself, but at the corner of the plot area, allowing for the margin needed for the paper clamps or rollers.

3) SELECT SCALE (1:1.000)

This option sets the desired scale of the drawing. The default is 1 to 1, or actual size. To set another scale, enter the desired ratio and press Return. The first number in the ratio is assumed to be a value of one. A drawing one quarter the actual size is 1:4 scale. Twice the actual size is 1:1/2.

If you are using architectural or engineering scales, the conversion from feet to inches is necessary. For example, 1/8" = 1'0"scale is the same as 1/8" = 12" which is the same as 1" = 96. The scale ratio is thus 1:96. Using this example, 1/4"scale becomes 1:48; 1/2"scale becomes 1:24; and 3/4"scale becomes 1:16.

4) SELECT PLOT OPTIONS (PENS, SORT, LAYER)

Upon selection of option 4, the following submenu appears:

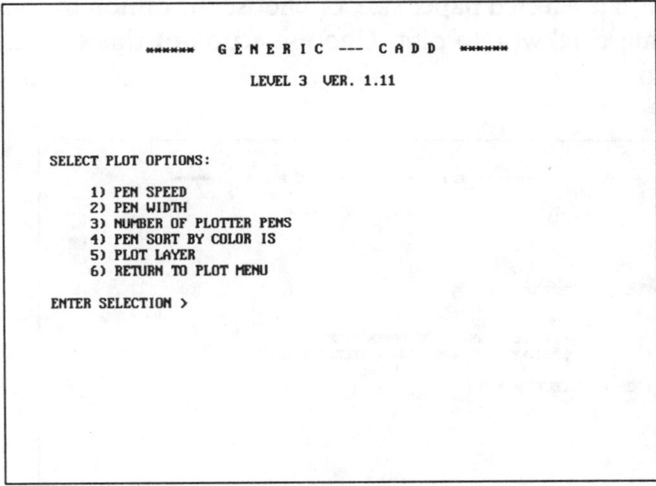

1) **PEN SPEED** sets the speed of the plotter pens if you are using a plotter with software programmable plotter speed. The default is 50. Refer to your plotter manual and change the value if needed.

2) **PEN WIDTH** sets a distance to enable the plotter to calculate how far to move the pen each time when filling a solid figure. This value is also used to plot lines with a width greater than 1.

3) **NUMBER OF PLOTTER PENS** sets the total number of different pens used in a plot to let the plotter know if pen changes are needed during the plot.

4) **PEN SORT BY COLOR IS ON** is a toggle, allowing you to plot the drawing, color by color. This option saves time when limited pen plotters are used, as pen changes happen only once per color. Select this option and the pen sort is toggled to the off position. The default is in the on position.

5) PLOT LAYER OFF is a toggle. If in the on position, you plot a single specified layer. After selecting this option, enter the layer number to plot.

6) RETURN TO PLOT MENU returns you to the main plot menu to continue setting parameters.

5) SELECT PLOT VIEW

This option allows you to let Generic CADD calculate a scale for the drawing plot by fitting it to a selected paper size, or choose the option to rotate the drawing 90 degrees counterclockwise to plot. Upon selection of this option, the following submenu appears:

```
****** GENERIC --- CADD ******
             LEVEL 3  VER. 1.11



SELECT PLOT VIEW :

        1) CURRENT VIEW
        2) FIT FULL DRAWING TO PAPER SIZE
        3) SPECIFY PLOT SCALE (USER SELECTED SCALE)

ENTER SELECTION >
```

1) CURRENT VIEW scales the current screen to fit the selected paper size, placing the corner of the view at the plot origin.

2) FIT FULL DRAWING TO PAPER SIZE scales the entire drawing file to fit the selected sheet size.

3) SPECIFY PLOT SCALE asks if you want to rotate the drawing 90 degrees counterclockwise to plot, using the plot scale specified in option 1 or 2. Enter Y or N at the prompt.

6) DISPLAY PLOT

This option allows you to see the drawing on the screen and set the scale to plot and the plot origin. If this option is selected, Generic CADD asks if you want fast redraw. If you select Y for yes, your drawing is shown as an X surrounded by a dotted box representing the drawing boundary. If you choose N for no, your drawing is shown normally. The FAST REDRAW can save time on larger, more complicated drawings. If you previously chose option 3 in the SELECT PLOT VIEW submenu, Generic CADD asks if the plot scale is correct. If the scale is wrong, enter N and enter the desired scale. The prompt appears again, asking for approval. Continue until you are satisfied the scale is correct and enter Y for yes. If the drawing was not rotated in the SELECT PLOT VIEW submenu, you are asked if you want to rotate the drawing 90 degrees. Enter Y or N at the prompt. Next, Generic CADD asks for confirmation on the location of the plot origin. If you respond with N for no, a box outlining your sheet boundaries appears, attached to your mouse. Drag it into the correct position. Enter Y in response to the origin location prompt only when you are satisfied with the placement.

7) START PLOT

This option sends the drawing plot to the plotter. Before plotting you are asked if you want to be prompted for pen changes. This option is important if you are using a single pen plotter and want to plot with more than one pen. The plotter will stop, giving you the opportunity to change pens. If you have a plotter with enough pens to complete your plot, select N at the prompt. The plot may be interrupted by pressing the Spacebar. This alerts Generic CADD to stop sending information to the plotter. It may take some time before the plot actually stops, however, as most plotters have a buffer that holds a certain amount of data as it comes from Generic CADD. Pressing the Spacebar or Esc resumes the plot.

The plotter pens selected correspond to the line and text colors used in the drawing. Color 1 is plotted with the pen in pen holder 1, color 2 maps to pen holder 2, etc. Color values greater than total number of pen holders in the plotter cycle around again. Thus a plotter with eight penholders maps color 9 to the pen in holder 1, and color 10 to the pen in holder 2, and so forth. It is entirely your responsibility to put the correct pen in each corresponding holder.

As the drawing is plotted, the drawing screen reveals the line number currently being plotted, along with the colors and line types being used.

8) PLOT FILES

This option allows you to save the plot file to a disk, which can be used to plot at a later date or another location. When this option is selected, the following menu appears:

```
******  G E N E R I C  ---  C A D D  ******
              LEVEL 3  VER. 1.11



SELECT PLOT OPTIONS:

        1)  SAVE PLOT TO DISK FILE IS
        2)  IMPORT PLOTTER COMMAND FILE
        3)  RETURN TO PLOT MENU

ENTER SELECTION >
```

1) **SAVE PLOT TO DISK FILE IS**   This option toggles between sending the plot information to the plotter or a specified disk. If toggled to on, specify the disk drive on which the plot is to be written. Give the complete path, including drive and directory and subdirectory, and the filename. The designated drive location must be ready to receive the information, so make sure you have a floppy disk in the **A** drive if this is the disk location you are using. The default setting for this option is the off position.

2) **IMPORT PLOTTER COMMAND FILE**   This option allows another plot file to be sent to the plotter before your drawing is plotted. When prompted, enter the name of the file, which must be located in the Generic CADD subdirectory. This feature is used to print a portion of a drawing, such as a title block on the same sheet as your drawing plot. The default is the off position.

3) **RETURN TO PLOT MENU**   This option returns you to the plot menu.

9) RETURN TO DRAWING

This option locates you back at the Generic CADD drawing menu.

APPLICATIONS

DRAWING PLOT is a critical part of any CAD program. You must be able to get your drawing files on paper for presentations, portability, and review with others. The Generic CADD plot options allow a variety of drawings on paper to be created from a single Generic CADD drawing file. Scales can be changed, depending upon the intended use of the hardcopy; pens and line weights are versatile to generate a quick check plot with a single line weight or a full presentation drawing with solid infill areas. Plots with multiple colors is a sure way to create an effective drawing when checking for accuracy of content. Layers can be turned on and off also, for when you plot, you get only what you see on the screen. Adjustable pen speed is used to create quality drawings, whether using liquid ink, felt tipped, or ball point pens.

DRAWING PLOT creates pen plots from a pen plotter, superior to printer plots in resolution, size, and color, but taking more time to produce.

TYPICAL OPERATION

In this exercise you plot the SAMPLE drawing created in the sample session module on 8-1/2"x 11"paper at 1/4"scale.

1. Start Generic CADD and load SAMPLE.DWG.

2. Prepare for the plot.

```
ENTER A COMMAND > DP
1) SELECT PAPER SIZE (X 10.150 Y 7.800)IN
2) SELECT ORIGIN (X 0.000 Y 0.000)IN
3) SELECT SCALE (1:1.000)
4) SELECT PLOT OPTIONS (PENS,SORT,LAYER)
5) SELECT PLOT VIEW (CURRENT VIEW)
6) DISPLAY PLOT
7) START PLOT
8) PLOT FILES
9) RETURN TO DRAWING

ENTER SELECTION >
```

3. Select paper size.

```
ENTER SELECTION > 1
SELECT PLOT SIZE
   1) WIDTH 7.800              LENGTH 10.150IN
   2) WIDTH 10.150             LENGTH 16.300IN
   3) USER SELECTED SIZE
ENTER SELECTION > 3
ENTER PLOT LENGTH (X) > 6.5  <CR>
```

NOTE

Generic CADD assumes the plot width (Y) to be equal to the plot length (X) until you change the entry by entering another dimension on top of the assumed value, thus overwriting the value.

```
ENTER PLOT WIDTH (Y) > 9.00  <CR>
```

4. Select the plot view.

```
ENTER SELECTION > 5
SELECT PLOT VIEW:
   1) CURRENT VIEW
   2) FIT FULL DRAWING TO PAPER SIZE
   3) SPECIFY PLOT SCALE (USER SELECTED SCALE)
ENTER SELECTION > 3
ROTATE 90 DEGREES? (Y/N) > N
```

5. Set the plot scale.

```
ENTER SELECTION > 3
ENTER PLOT SCALE 1:?? > 48
```

6. Display the plot.

```
ENTER SELECTION > 6
FAST REDRAW? (Y/N) > Y
CORRECT SCALE? (Y/N) > Y
ROTATE 90 DEGREES? (Y/N) > N
IS PLOT ORIGIN CORRECT? (Y/N) > N
ENTER NEW PLOT ORIGIN (Center the sheet border outline that is attached to your cursor
over the box representing the drawing contents and select the first button on your mouse.)
IS PLOT ORIGIN CORRECT? (Y/N) > Y
```

NOTE
Generic CADD sums up all the parameters you have chosen,
including calculating the exact origin points you chose visually
by selecting the drawing to be centered on the paper.

```
PLOT SIZE 9.000 BY 6.500 IN
SCALE 1:48.000 ORIGIN 69.015,44.458
 <RET> TO CONTINUE! <CR>
```

7. Begin the plot. Make sure your plotter is connected and ready to receive information.

```
ENTER SELECTION > 7
PROMPT FOR PEN CHANGE WITH COLOR VALUES GREATER THAN 6? (Y/N) > N
PLOTTING: SAMPLE
```

8. Quit the drawing when plotting is complete.

9. Turn to Module 20 to continue the learning sequence.

Module 26
DRAWING SAVE

DESCRIPTION

The DRAWING SAVE (DS) command allows the current version of a drawing on the screen to be saved onto a disk without leaving the Generic CADD program. Once saved, work can continue on the drawing.

APPLICATIONS

The DRAWING SAVE command creates a permanent copy of a drawing on a specified disk. This procedure protects your work from power fluctuations, computer failures, and operator mistakes that can destroy data. It is a good idea to save your drawing to disk often as you work to avoid drawing loss as a result of these problems. Avoid using a dollar sign as the first character in your drawing file name.

DRAWING SAVE is also used to save a number of different versions of your drawing. Name the current drawing as you save it, then continue to work and save it again with another name to represent a different version. The result is two versions of the same drawing.

DRAWING SAVE can also be used to save a drawing to a floppy disk drive for backup purposes should anything happen to the copy on the hard drive. A copy on a diskette should be created periodically to protect against loss.

TYPICAL OPERATION

In this session you load SAMPLE.DWG to the screen and save it to the default drive.

1. Start Generic CADD. Type **CADD** and press **Return** at the DOS prompt. Press **Return** at the Generic CADD title page.

2. Load SAMPLE.DWG.

```
ENTER A DRAWING FILE NAME >  SAMPLE
```

The drawing is loaded.

3. Save the drawing.

```
ENTER A COMMAND> DS
SAVE FILE: (SAMPLE.DWG)> <CR>
FILE EXISTS, OVERWRITE OR NAME OLD FILE TO *.BAK (O/R)> O
```

The drawing is now saved as SAMPLE.DWG. Generic CADD allows you to continue editing the drawing or quit the drawing.

4. Quit Generic CADD without saving the drawing again.

```
ENTER A COMMAND> QU
SAVE CURRENT DRAWING (Y OR N)> N
"C" TO CONTINUE
"Q" TO QUIT> Q
```

5. Turn to Module 23 to continue the learning sequence.

Module 27
ELLIPSE

DESCRIPTION

ELLIPSE (EP) creates a basic drawing element from which more complex figures are drawn. An ellipse is drawn by specifying the length and location of the major axis and the minor axis. An ellipse is either a true ellipse, acting as one object, or a construction ellipse, created of four arcs which can be modified.

APPLICATIONS

The ellipse is used as a basic drawing element. It may also be used to represent a circle in an isometric drawing.

TYPICAL OPERATION

In this exercise you draw two ellipses. One is a construction ellipse and the other is a true ellipse. The ellipses are then modified.

1. Start a new drawing called "ELLIPSE."

2. Draw the first ellipse.

```
ENTER A COMMAND > EP
ENTER START OF MAJOR AXIS > 10,5   <CR>
ENTER END OF MAJOR AXIS > 10,18   <CR>
ENTER START OF MINOR AXIS > 14,9   <CR>
ENTER END OF MINOR AXIS > 9,9   <CR>
TRUE OR CONSTRUCTION (T/C) > T
```

3. Draw the second ellipse.

```
ENTER A COMMAND > EP
ENTER START OF MAJOR AXIS > 20,6   <CR>
ENTER END OF MAJOR AXIS > 20,17   <CR>
ENTER START OF MINOR AXIS > 24,8   <CR>
ENTER END OF MINOR AXIS > 18,14   <CR>
TRUE OR CONSTRUCTION (T/C) > C
```

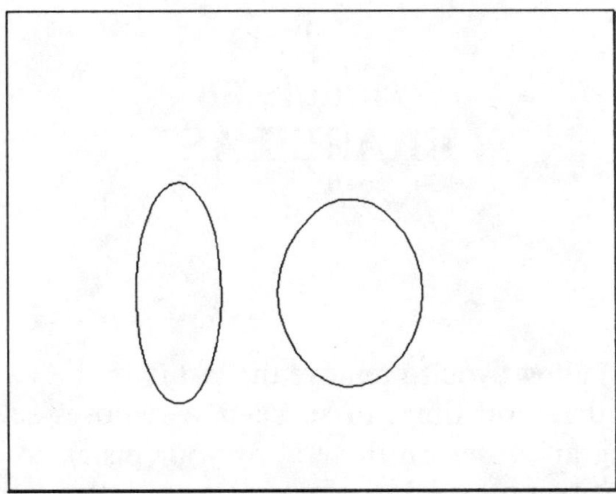

4. Observe how the second ellipse reacts to editing.

ENTER A COMMAND > **OE**
ENTER A POINT ON THE OBJECT TO ERASE > (Select a point on ellipse 2.) Notice that one of the four arcs of which the ellipse is created is deleted.

5. Observe how the first ellipse reacts to editing.

ENTER A COMMAND > **OE**
ENTER A POINT ON THE OBJECT TO ERASE > (Select a point on the first arc.) The entire ellipse is deleted, as it is a true ellipse.

6. Quit the drawing without saving.

7. Turn to Module 58 to continue the learning sequence.

Module 28
ERASE LAST

DESCRIPTION

ERASE LAST (EL) allows you to remove the last item drawn from your drawing. Using the command several times in succession removes several items. ERASE LAST is like having an eraser on the end of your pencil to catch errors as they occur. If by accident you press EL too many times, deleting more than you want, use UNERASE to restore the deleted items.

APPLICATIONS

ERASE LAST is used for corrections immediately after mistakes are made. This approach is a time saver during creation of your drawing and saves you from having to use another erase command and identify the object.

TYPICAL OPERATION

In this exercise you draw an object then partially erase it.

1. Start a new drawing called "LAST."

2. Draw a rectangle.

```
ENTER A COMMAND >  RE
ENTER A CORNER OF RECTANGLE >  6,6   <CR>
ENTER NEXT CORNER OF RECTANGLE >  20,20   <CR>
```

3. Erase two sides of the rectangle.

NOTE
Remember that even though you drew the rectangle as a single object, Generic CADD sees the rectangle as four separate lines. Thus, to remove the entire rectangle, you must press EL four times, one for each line.

```
ENTER A COMMAND >  EL   <CR>
ENTER A COMMAND >  EL   <CR>
```

Now two sides of the rectangle are deleted. Your drawing should look like this.

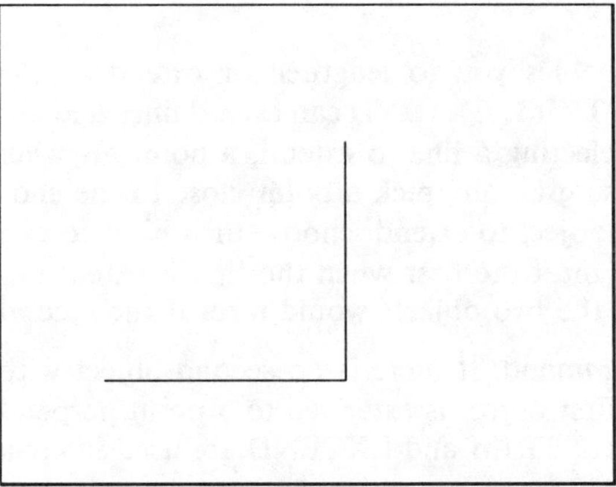

4. Quit the drawing without saving.

5. Turn to Module 60 to continue the learning sequence.

Module 29
EXTEND

DESCRIPTION

EXTEND (XT) enables you to lengthen or extend a selected object to meet another. Similar to TRIM, EXTEND can extend lines and arcs to other lines, arcs, or circles. When selecting a line to extend, a point anywhere on the object will suffice. When chosing an arc, pick a point close to the end you want to extend. After selecting the object to extend, choose the object to extend to. If the second object is unable to meet the first when the first is extended, the first is extended to the point where the two objects would meet if the second were larger.

Like the TRIM command, if there is no second object within the search radius of the cursor, the first object is extended to a point perpendicular to the second point selected. Often, TRIM and EXTEND are used interchangeably.

APPLICATIONS

EXTEND is a basic editing function, critical to clear, concise drawings.

TYPICAL OPERATION

In this activity you draw several lines and extend them.

1. Start a new drawing called "EXTEND."

2. Draw a series of lines.

```
ENTER A COMMAND > L1
ENTER START POINT > > 5,8  <CR>
ENTER NEXT POINT > 11,17  <CR>
ENTER NEXT POINT > PU
ENTER A COMMAND > L1
ENTER START POINT > > 16,2  <CR>
ENTER NEXT POINT > 11,9  <CR>
ENTER NEXT POINT > PU
```

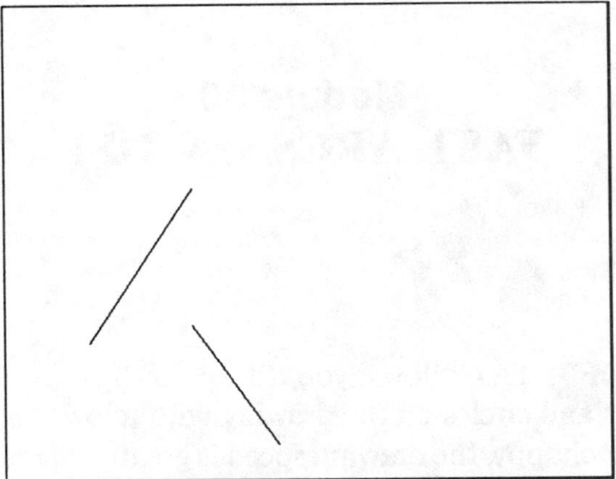

3. Extend the second line upward to meet the first line.

```
ENTER A COMMAND> XT
ENTER A POINT ON THE OBJECT TO EXTEND> 13,6 <CR>
SECOND OBJECT> 7,11
```

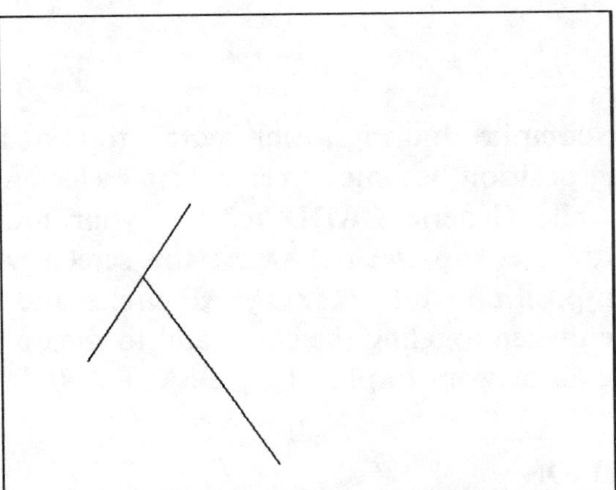

4. Quit the drawing without saving.

5. Turn to Module 7 to continue the learning sequence.

Module 30
FAST ARCS ON/OFF

DESCRIPTION

FAST ARC ON/OFF (FA) allows you to speed up the drawing display by representing all arcs and circles on the drawing with a lower resolution. While the circles and arcs look choppy, the drawing speed is greatly increased. This command is a toggle. The Generic CADD default is FAST ARCS to the off position. When toggled on, the resolution default is three segments to draw the circle or arc, on a scale of three to 12. Each number represents the number of segments used to draw the circles and arcs. Change the resolution value if necessary when you toggle the command to the on position. Each time the command is toggled on or off, a redraw of the screen is needed to see the changes. When plotting, if FAST ARC is toggled to the on position, circles and arcs are plotted as they appear on the screen.

APPLICATIONS

As you create more complex drawings, each redraw time of the screen when you change your viewing position becomes a critical time element. You soon become reluctant to wait while Generic CADD redraws your drawing. FAST ARCS ON/OFF is used to speed up the redraw of the screen. As a toggle, set the command to the on position while working. All circles and arcs are drawn with the value you entered when toggling the command to the on position. When you need to see more detail or want to plot, toggle FAST ARCS to the off position.

TYPICAL OPERATION

In this session you draw a circle and arc and toggle FAST ARCS to the on and off positions.

1. Start a new drawing called "FAST."

2. Draw a circle.

```
ENTER A COMMAND> C2
ENTER CENTER OF CIRCLE> 14,14  <CR>
ENTER A POINT ON CIRCLE> 14,23  <CR>
```

3. Draw an arc.

```
ENTER A COMMAND> A2
ENTER THE CENTER OF THE ARC> 10,4  <CR>
ENTER START OF ARC> 29,6  <CR>
ENTER THE END OF THE ARC> 1,21  <CR>
```

4. Zoom to fill the screen with the objects.

```
ENTER A COMMAND> ZA
```

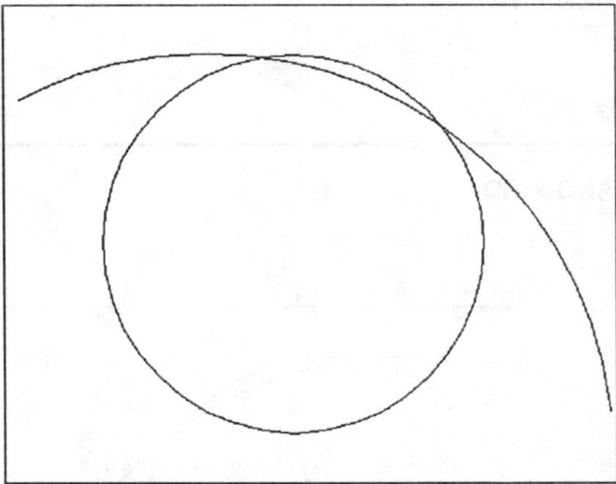

5. Toggle FAST ARCS to the on position.

```
ENTER A COMMAND> FA
CHANGE ARC SIDES (3) LIMITS: 3 TO 12> 4  <CR>
```

6. Redraw the screen.

```
ENTER A COMMAND> RD
```

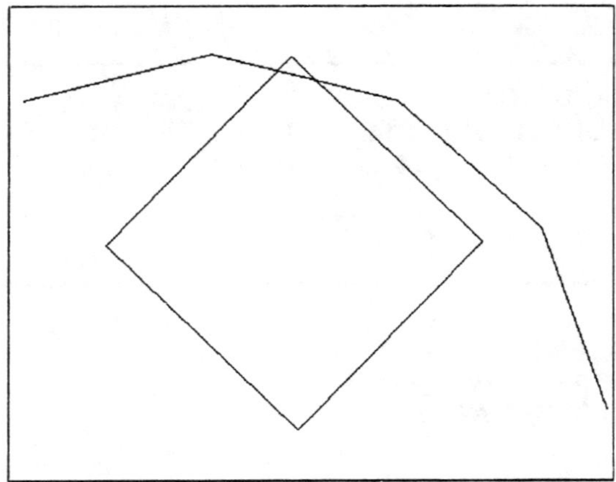

7. Toggle FAST ARCS to the off position.

```
ENTER A COMMAND> FA
FAST ARCS IS OFF
```

8. Redraw the screen.

```
ENTER A COMMAND> RD
```

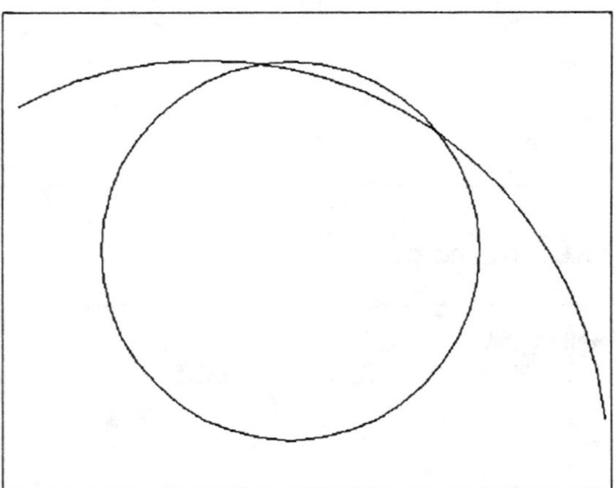

9. Toggle FAST ARCS on again and set a new resolution value.

```
ENTER A COMMAND > FA
CHANGE ARC SIDES (4) LIMITS: 3 TO 12 > 10  <CR>
```

10. Redraw the screen.

```
ENTER A COMMAND > RD
```

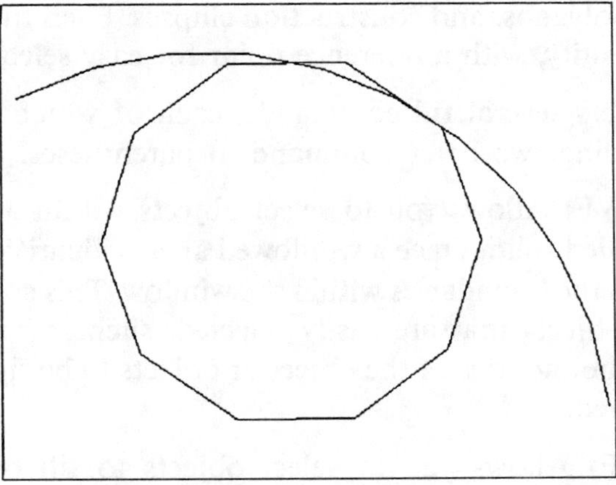

11. Quit the drawing without saving.

12. Turn to Module 51 to continue the learning sequence.

Module 31
FILL

DESCRIPTION

The fill commands allow you to fill selected area boundaries with a solid colored fill. The boundaries accepted are straight lines, arcs, and/or circles and include rectangles, regular polygons, and construction ellipses. Each fill is seen by Generic CADD as a single entity, with a reference point for easy selection.

Generic CADD offers several fill commands, each of which is described below with the corresponding two-letter command in parentheses.

WINDOW FILL (WF) Allows you to select objects within a windowed area to be filled solid. Once a windowed area is identified, Generic CADD finds the boundaries within the window. This command is designed for objects that are easily selected, such as rectangles or circles. The boundaries of the object or objects to be filled must be clearly defined.

OBJECT FILL (OF) Allows you to select objects to fill by identifying each boundary separately. Boundaries of objects not selected are disregarded. As with all the fill selection options, the boundaries must close properly and be clearly defined. At the prompt, select the boundaries you want, then enter PU to stop selection. Press Esc to begin again if you have selected an object by mistake.

FITTED FILL (FF) Allows you to fill areas defined by objects with poorly defined corners. Generic CADD establishes corners for the fill at the intersection or presumed intersection of the selected boundary lines. At the prompt, select the boundaries in order, proceeding clockwise or counterclockwise around the area to be hatched. Enter PU to halt selection.

FILL COLOR (FK) Allows you to specify the color of the area fill to be placed on the drawing. Previously placed fills are not affected. After you enter the command, enter a color number or select a color with the cursor bar from the color list in the screen menu area. Generic CADD accepts values between 0 and 255, but your entry depends upon your graphics card and monitor. This command also controls the color of fill used in the SOLID LINES command.

DISPLAY FILL (DF) Allows you to toggle on or off the visibility of placed area fills on your drawing. The Generic CADD default is area fill toggled to the on position. If the command is selected when the display is on, the display is turned off. If the command is selected when the display is off, the fill will be visible. In each case, redraw the screen or zoom or pan to see the change. DISPLAY FILL also controls the visibility of lines created in the SOLID LINES command.

APPLICATIONS

Area fills are used to make certain portions of a drawing stand out from the rest for emphasis. A common example is the use of area fills in double lines denoting walls. This technique is especially important for presentation drawings. FILL COLOR allows you to determine the color and therefore the corresponding line weight for plotting. DISPLAY FILL is important in drawings with a great quantity of fill, as the fill display slows the drawing redraw or zoom time. If not displayed, the time spent maneuvering around the drawing is much less.

TYPICAL OPERATION

In this activity you create several objects and fill the selected boundaries.

1. Start a new drawing called "FILL."

2. Draw a rectangle.

```
ENTER A COMMAND > RE
ENTER A CORNER OF RECTANGLE > 2,4  <CR>
ENTER NEXT CORNER OF RECTANGLE > 14,26  <CR>
```

3. Toggle reference points to on.

```
ENTER A COMMAND > PR
DISPLAY REFERENCE POINTS IS ON
```

4. Window the rectangle to fill.

```
ENTER A COMMAND > WF
PLACE WINDOW (Select two diagonal points to form a window around the rectangle.)
```

5. Draw two concentric circles.

```
ENTER A COMMAND >  C2
ENTER CENTER OF CIRCLE >  25,20 < CR >
ENTER A POINT ON CIRCLE >  30,20   < CR >
ENTER A COMMAND >  C2
ENTER CENTER OF CIRCLE >  25,20   < CR >
ENTER A POINT ON CIRCLE >  28,20   < CR >
```

6. Fill the larger circle.

```
ENTER A COMMAND >  OF
"PEN UP" WHEN DONE OR "ESC" TO CANCEL
ENTER A POINT ON BOUNDARY >  25,15   < CR >
ENTER A POINT ON BOUNDARY >  25,17 < CR >
ENTER A POINT ON BOUNDARY >  PU
```

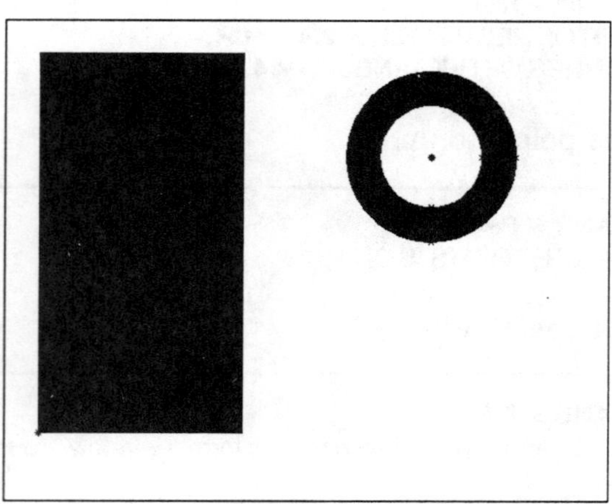

7. Draw a line series.

```
ENTER A COMMAND > L1
ENTER START POINT > > 20,4  <CR>
ENTER NEXT POINT > 19,12  <CR>
ENTER NEXT POINT > PU
ENTER A COMMAND > L1
ENTER START POINT > > 18,10  <CR>
ENTER NEXT POINT > 29,14  <CR>
ENTER NEXT POINT > PU
ENTER A COMMAND > L1
ENTER START POINT > > 19,5  <CR>
ENTER NEXT POINT > 31,2  <CR>
ENTER NEXT POINT > 28,12  <CR>
ENTER NEXT POINT > PU
```

8. Change the fill color.

```
ENTER A COMMAND > FK
CHANGE COLOR NUMBER (1) LIMITS: 0 TO 255 > 5  <CR>
```

9. Fill the area within the line series.

```
ENTER A COMMAND > FF
"PEN UP" WHEN DONE OR "ESC" TO CANCEL
ENTER A POINT ON BOUNDARY > (Select each line segment in the series in
succession, moving clockwise or counterclockwise around the shape. Select a total of four
points, one on each segment.)
ENTER A POINT ON BOUNDARY > PU
```

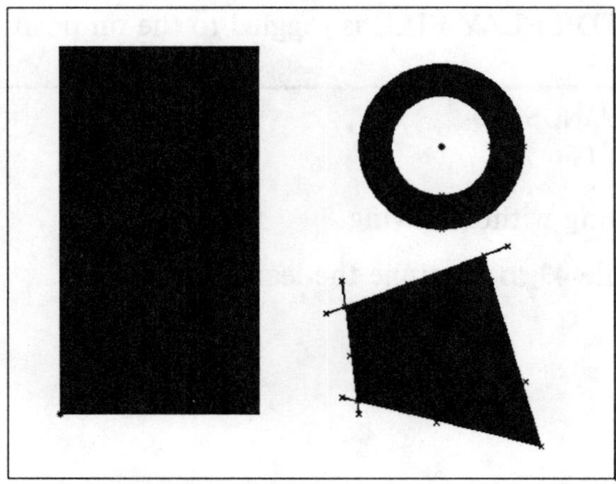

10. Toggle the fill display to the off position.

```
ENTER A COMMAND > DF
DISPLAY FILLS IS OFF
ENTER A COMMAND > RD
```

11. Toggle the fill display on again.

```
ENTER A COMMAND > DF
DISPLAY FILLS IS ON
```

NOTE

The redraw time of the drawing on the screen is considerably longer if DISPLAY FILL is toggled to the on position.

```
ENTER A COMMAND > RD
```

12. Quit the drawing without saving.

13. Turn to Module 43 to continue the learning sequence.

Module 32
FILLET/FILLET RADIUS

DESCRIPTION

The FILLET (FL) command creates an arc between two non-parallel lines or two arcs. The radius of the arc which defines the fillet is specified in the FILLET RADIUS (RF) command. At the prompt enter the actual distance or show Generic CADD the desired distance by typing D for distance and selecting the points on the screen as the prompts appear. After setting the FILLET RADIUS to the desired value, select two lines or arcs and the fillet is inserted. The default value for the fillet radius is .5. When a radius of 0 is used with two selected lines, the lines are extended to meet at a single point.

If you select two arcs to fillet, Generic CADD asks for a direction of trim. Select a point that is near the ends you want to trim and in between the two arcs. The color of the fillet is the same as the second arc or line identified. If the first arc or line chosen is of a different color, it is changed to match the second line or arc and the fillet.

APPLICATIONS

Fillets are used to represent curved edges of surfaces, from delicate machine parts to entire wall surfaces. Filleting with the radius set to zero is a useful cleanup technique for all lines that are hastily drawn and do not meet perfectly.

TYPICAL OPERATION

In this activity you draw fillets between lines.

1. Start a new drawing called "FILLET."

2. Set the radius of the fillet.

```
ENTER A COMMAND> RF
CHANGE FILLET RADIUS (0.500)in> 2  <CR>
```

3. Draw two lines.

```
ENTER A COMMAND> L1
ENTER START POINT>> 4,4 <CR>
ENTER NEXT POINT> 4,15  <CR>
ENTER NEXT POINT> PU
ENTER A COMMAND> L1
ENTER START POINT>> 3,16 <CR>
ENTER NEXT POINT> 16,16  <CR>
ENTER NEXT POINT> PU
```

4. Fillet the two lines.

```
ENTER A COMMAND> FL
```

NOTE

The points you select to identify the object to be filleted must be on the portion of the object that you want to retain after the fillet is complete.

```
ENTER A POINT ON THE OBJECT TO FILLET> 4,13  <CR>
SECOND OBJECT> 8,16  <CR>
```

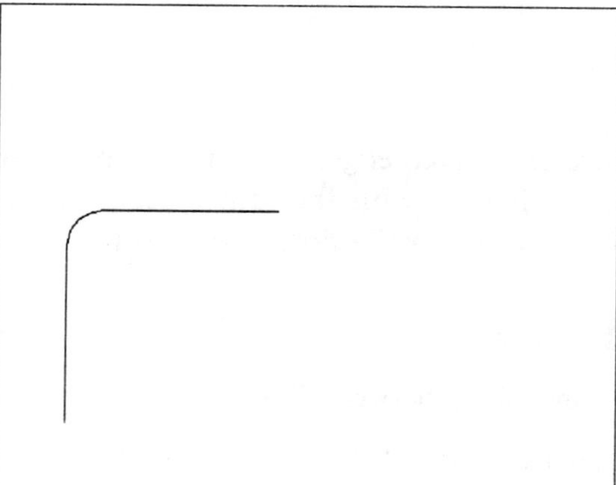

5. Draw another line.

```
ENTER A COMMAND> L1
ENTER START POINT>> 16,12  <CR>
ENTER NEXT POINT> 20,5  <CR>
ENTER NEXT POINT> PU
```

6. Set the fillet radius.

```
ENTER A COMMAND > RF
CHANGE FILLET RADIUS (2.000)in > O  <CR>
```

7. Create the zero radius fillet.

```
ENTER A COMMAND > FL
ENTER A POINT ON THE OBJECT TO FILLET > 16,12  <CR>
SECOND OBJECT > 12,16  <CR>
```

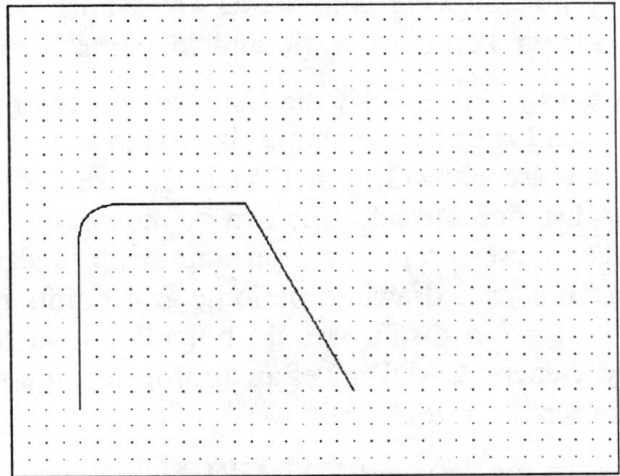

8. Quit the drawing without saving.

9. Turn to Module 4 to continue the learning sequence.

Module 33
GRIDS

DESCRIPTION

The grid commands allow you to specify an equal pattern of dots across the screen for easy reference. You specify the grid spacing, in addition to the color, display, and snap mode. The grid never plots, so you do not need to remember to turn it off before plotting. The following commands are available. Each command is followed by the two-letter keyboard command in parentheses.

GRID SIZE (GS) Allows you to specify the distance between grid points. The size of the grid is based on actual size to aid in input of your drawing. You can also show Generic CADD the size grid you want by typing D for distance and selecting two points on the screen. The distance between these two points determine the grid size. When you zoom back from your drawing, periodic grid points may not be shown, as too dense a display would not allow you to see the graphics easily. Generic CADD gives an appropriate message on the bottom of the screen in this case.

SNAP GRID (SG) When toggled on, SNAP GRID allows you to locate the cursor only on the grids points currently defined on the screen. Typing SG when SNAP GRID is off turns the command on; typing SG when SNAP GRID is on turns it off. As a toggle, GRID SNAP can be used while in the middle of a command without having to start the command over again. GRID SNAP functions regardless of whether the grid is displayed. When a large grid is selected and GRID SNAP is on, the screen cursor moves independently of the menu cursor, rather than moving together as is usually the case. The screen cursor moves in increments of the selected grid, while the menu cursor moves evenly up and down the menu.

GRID ON/OFF (GR) This command toggles on and off the display of the grid on the screen.

DISPLAY COLOR (DK) This command sets the color of the screen display text, including the prompt lines at the bottom of the screen, the side menu, the information at the top of the screen, and any grid that is displayed.

APPLICATIONS

Grids are the easy way to maintain accuracy in your drawing. Generic CADD allows points you select with the cursor to be snapped to the grid. The spacing of the grid can be modified as often as you need, depending upon the distances required. The grid can also be removed from the screen display, once your drawing gets too dense.

The grid does not affect the drawing; it is only a visual reference.

TYPICAL OPERATION

In this exercise you create several grids and coordinating lines.

1. Start Generic CADD. Type **CADD** and press **Return** at the DOS prompt. Press **Return** at the Generic CADD title page.

2. Start a new drawing called "GRIDS."

```
ENTER A DRAWING FILE NAME > GRIDS  <CR>
IS THIS A NEW DRAWING (Y,N) > Y
```

3. Change the 1" default grid to 6".

```
ENTER A COMMAND > GS
CHANGE GRID SIZE (1.000) in. > 6  <CR>
```

The grid is automatically displayed.

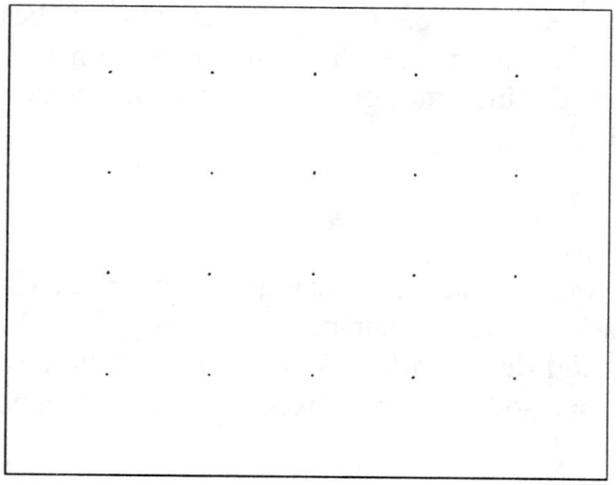

4. Draw a line snapping to the grid points.

```
ENTER A COMMAND> SG
SNAP TO GRID IS ON
ENTER A COMMAND> L1
ENTER START POINT> > (Select lower left grid point with the screen cursor.)
ESCAPE or PEN UP TO STOP
ENTER NEXT POINT (Move two grid points to the right and select the point with the
screen cursor.)
ENTER NEXT POINT> PU
```

You have drawn a 12"line.

5. Change the display.

```
ENTER A COMMAND> ZB
ENTER CENTER OF ZOOM> 24,24  <CR>
```

6. Change grid size to 2".

```
ENTER A COMMAND> GS
CHANGE GRID SIZE (6.000) in.)> 2  <CR>
```

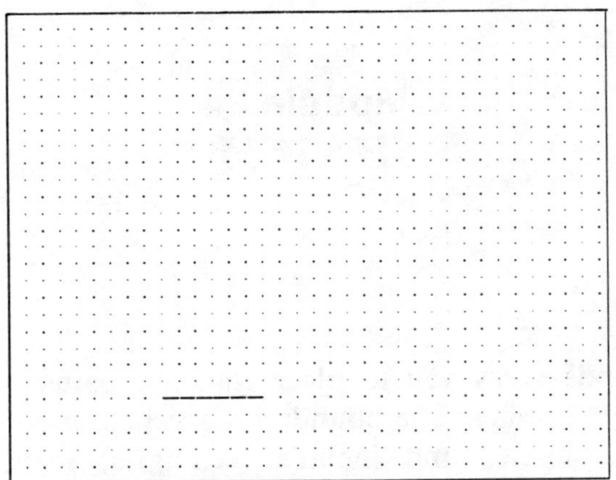

7. Draw a line.

```
ENTER A COMMAND > L1
ENTER START POINT > > (Draw a 6" horizontal line by selecting the grid points as a
visual guide.)
ENTER NEXT POINT > PU
```

8. Turn the grid display off.

```
ENTER A COMMAND > GR
DISPLAY GRID IS OFF
```

9. Toggle the display grid on again.

```
ENTER A COMMAND > GR
DISPLAY GRID IS ON
```

10. Quit the drawing without saving.

```
ENTER A COMMAND > QU
SAVE CURRENT DRAWING (Y or N) > N
"C" TO CONTINUE
"Q" TO QUIT > Q
```

11. Turn to Module 52 to continue the learning sequence.

Module 34
HATCH

DESCRIPTION

The hatch commands allow you to place standard patterns to infill specified boundaries on your drawing. The boundaries accepted are made up of straight lines, arcs, and/or circles and include rectangles, regular polygons, and construction ellipses. Each hatch placement is defined by selecting up to 150 total objects defining the boundary. The patterns can be scaled, rotated, and drawn in any selected color, so that a tremendous variety can be achieved. Each pattern placement is viewed by Generic CADD as a single object, with a reference point for easy selection.

Generic CADD offers several hatch options, each of which is described below with the appropriate two-letter command in parentheses.

HATCH NAME (HN) Allows you to enter the name of the hatch pattern you want to place. Patterns available with Generic CADD are shown in the Generic CADD Operator's Manual. Each hatch pattern is stored in the Generic CADD subdirectory with the .HCH filename extension. To select a hatch, enter the name without the extension at the prompt. Once a hatch is selected, it remains in effect until you change it or exit Generic CADD.

WINDOW HATCH (WH) Allows you to select objects within a windowed area to infill with a selected hatch pattern. Once a windowed area is identified, Generic CADD finds the boundaries within the window. This command is designed for objects that are easily selected, such as rectangles or circles. The boundaries of the object or objects to be hatched must be clealy defined. As the hatching proceeds, if Generic CADD locates a boundary which is not closed, it may complete the boundary and complete the hatch or it may completely ignore the boundary. Objects within objects are not hatched.

OBJECT HATCH (OH) Allows you to select objects to hatch by identifying each boundary separately. Boundaries of objects not selected are disregarded. As with all the hatch selection options, the boundaries must close properly and be clearly defined. At the prompt, select the boundaries you want, then enter PU to stop selection. Press ESC to begin again if you have selected an object by mistake.

FITTED HATCH (FH) Allows you to hatch areas defined by objects with poorly defined corners. Generic CADD establishes corners for the hatch at the intersection or presumed intersection of the selected boundary lines. At the prompt, select the boundaries in order, proceeding clockwise or counterclockwise around the area to be hatched. Enter PU to halt selection.

HATCH LIST Allows you to select hatch patterns to place by selecting the pattern name from a menu list. This command does not have a corresponding two-letter command and must be selected from the HATCH/FILL menu. Even though a hatch is listed, it must be in the Generic CADD subdirectory location to be able to be placed.

HATCH SCALE (HZ) Allows you to change the scale of hatch patterns to be placed on the drawing. Previously placed patterns are not affected. The default scale varies for each pattern, as the default scale is defined when the pattern is created. Enter the desired scale, in decimal format. An entry of 2 creates a pattern twice as large as the defalt size, while a .5 entry makes the hatch half the default size.

HATCH ROTATION (HR) Allows you to rotate hatch patterns to be placed on the drawing at a specified angle between −360 degrees and 360 degrees. All hatches placed after the hatch rotation is changed reflect the change. Existing hatch patterns are not affected. At the prompt, three options for entering the angle are available. You can enter the desired angle, if known; type A for angle to define the angle on the screen with a basepoint and a ray point; or type V for vertex to define the angle on the screen with a basepoint and two ray points. Generic CADD measures angles from the horizontal position in a counterclockwise rotation, beginning with the first ray selected and ending with the second ray selected. The resulting angle is displayed on the prompt line.

HATCH COLOR (HK) Allows you to specify the color of hatch patterns to be placed on the drawing. Previously placed patterns are not affected. After you enter the command, enter a color number or select a color with the cursor bar from the color list in the screen menu area. Generic CADD accepts values between 0 and 255, but your entry depends upon your graphics card and monitor.

DISPLAY HATCHING (DH) Allows you to toggle on or off the visibility of placed hatch patterns on your drawing. The Generic CADD default is hatch patterns to the on position. If the command is selected when the display is on, the display is turned off. If the command is selected when the display is off, the hatching will be visible. In each case, redraw the screen or zoom or pan to see the change.

APPLICATIONS

Hatch patterns are used to make certain drawing areas stand out and be more noticeable. They may also help to differentiate between different materials or textures. In addition, they may represent objects themselves, such as bricks, construction joints in concrete areas, or a 2' x 4' ceiling grid system. The rotation and scale options create variety with a small number of basic hatches. The HATCH COLOR allows you to determine the line weight with which the hatch is plotted, as Generic CADD plots according to color associated with plotter pens. DISPLAY HATCH is critical to drawings with many hatch patterns, as hatches slow the redraw or zoom time of the drawing. If not displayed, the movement about the drawing screen is faster.

TYPICAL OPERATION

In this activity you create several objects and hatch the selected boundaries.

1. Start a new drawing called "HATCH."

2. Draw a rectangle.

```
ENTER A COMMAND > RE
ENTER A CORNER OF RECTANGLE > 2,4  <CR>
ENTER NEXT CORNER OF RECTANGLE > 14,26  <CR>
```

3. Toggle reference points to the on position.

```
ENTER A COMMAND > PR
DISPLAY REFERENCE POINTS IS ON
```

4. Specify a hatch pattern.

```
ENTER A COMMAND>  HN
HATCH PATTERN [NET]>  ISO  <CR>
```

5. Window the rectangle to hatch.

```
ENTER A COMMAND>  WH
PLACE WINDOW (Select two diagonal points to form a window around the rectangle.)
```

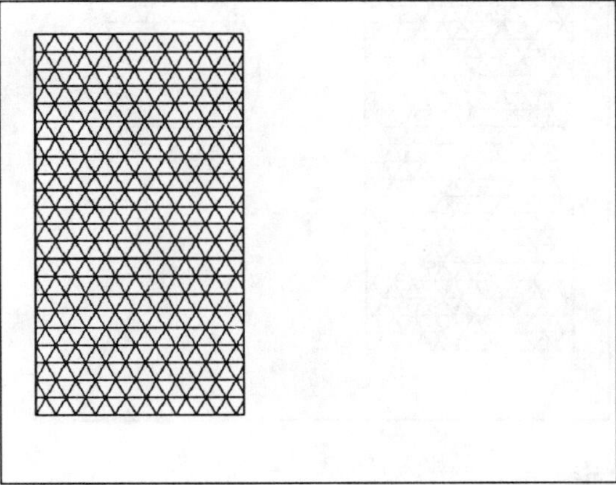

NOTE

The hatch is a single object. If you place a hatch and realize you made a mistake, the ERASE LAST removes the hatch from the drawing. Remember to redraw to restore the hatch boundaries that may temporarily disappear from view. To remove a hatch that was placed on your drawing before the most recent hatch placement, toggle REFERENCE POINTS to the on position and use the WINDOW ERASE command to window the hatch reference point. The entire hatch is deleted. Redraw the screen to restore a full graphic view.

6. Draw two concentric circles.

```
ENTER A COMMAND>  C2
ENTER CENTER OF CIRCLE>  25,20 <CR>
ENTER A POINT ON CIRCLE>  30,20  <CR>
ENTER A COMMAND>  C2
ENTER CENTER OF CIRCLE>  25,20  <CR>
ENTER A POINT ON CIRCLE>  28,20  <CR>
```

7. Hatch the larger circle.

```
ENTER A COMMAND >  OH
"PEN UP" WHEN DONE OR "ESC" TO CANCEL
ENTER A POINT ON BOUNDARY >  25,15   <CR>
ENTER A POINT ON BOUNDARY >  25,17   <CR>
ENTER A POINT ON BOUNDARY >  PU
```

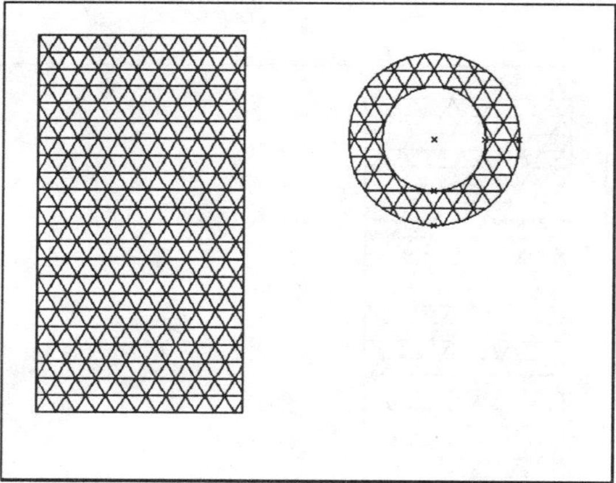

8. Draw a line series.

```
ENTER A COMMAND >  L1
ENTER START POINT > >  20,4   <CR>
ENTER NEXT POINT >  19,12   <CR>
ENTER NEXT POINT >  PU
ENTER A COMMAND >  L1
ENTER START POINT > >  18,10   <CR>
ENTER NEXT POINT >  29,14   <CR>
ENTER NEXT POINT >  PU
ENTER A COMMAND >  L1
ENTER START POINT > >  19,5   <CR>
ENTER NEXT POINT >  31,2   <CR>
ENTER NEXT POINT >  28,12   <CR>
ENTER NEXT POINT >  PU
```

9. Change the active hatch pattern.

```
ENTER A COMMAND >  HN
HATCH PATTERN [ISO] >  BRICKS   <CR>
```

10. Change the default rotation.

```
ENTER A COMMAND> HR
CHANGE HATCH ROTATION(0.000) LIMITS: -360.000 TO 360.000> 90   <CR>
```

11. Change the hatch scale.

```
ENTER A COMMAND> HZ
CHANGE HATCH SCALE (1.000) IN> .5  <CR>
```

12. Hatch the line series.

```
ENTER A COMMAND> FH
"PEN UP" WHEN DONE OR "ESC" TO CANCEL
ENTER A POINT ON BOUNDARY (Select each line segment of the series in succession,
moving clockwise or counterclockwise around the shape. Select a total of four points, one
for each segment.)
ENTER A POINT ON THE BOUNDARY PU
```

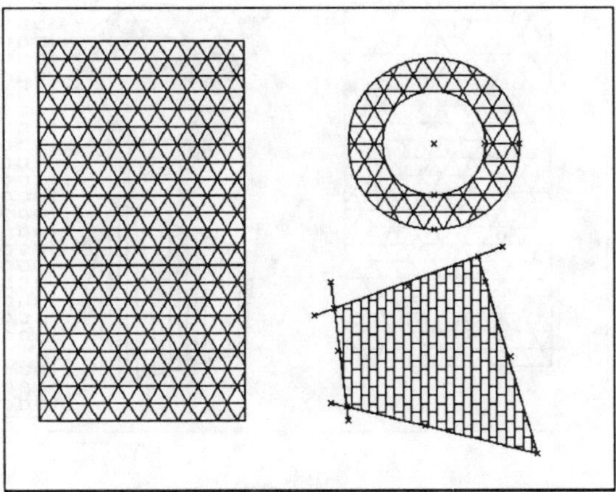

13. Draw another rectangle.

```
ENTER A COMMAND> RE
ENTER A CORNER OF RECTANGLE> 31,26  <CR>
ENTER NEXT CORNER OF RECTANGLE> 35,1  <CR>
```

14. Change the hatch color.

```
ENTER A COMMAND > HK
CHANGE COLOR NUMBER (1) LIMITS: 0 TO 255 > 5  <CR>
```

15. Change the active hatch pattern from the list.

```
ENTER A COMMAND > (Select the HATCH/FILL menu from the ROOT menu.)
ENTER A COMMAND > (Select HATCH LIST from the HATCH/FILL menu.)
ENTER A COMMAND > (Select SQUARES with the cursor bar.)
```

16. Hatch the rectangle.

```
ENTER A COMMAND > WH
PLACE WINDOW (Select two diagonal points to define a window completely containing
the rectangle.)
```

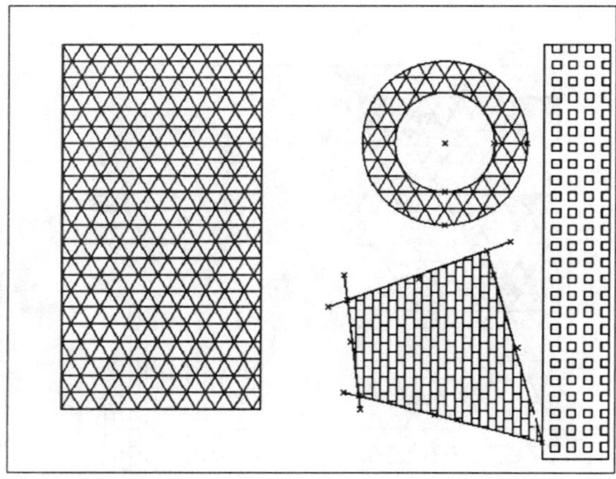

17. Toggle the hatch display to the off position.

```
ENTER A COMMAND > DH
DISPLAY HATCHES IS OFF
ENTER A COMMAND > RD
```

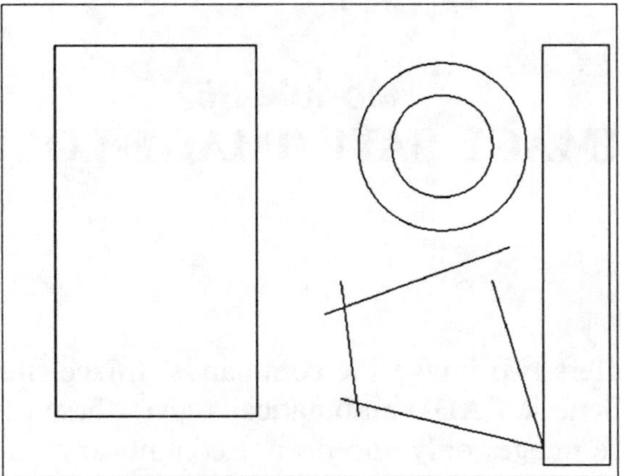

18. Toggle the hatch display on again.

```
ENTER A COMMAND >  DH
DISPLAY HATCHES IS ON
```

NOTE

The redraw time of the drawing on the screen is considerably longer if DISPLAY HATCH is toggled to the on position.

```
ENTER A COMMAND >  RD
```

19. Quit the drawing without saving.

20. Turn to Module 31 to continue the learning sequence.

Module 35
IMAGE SAVE/IMAGE LOAD

DESCRIPTION

Generic CADD offers two image file commands. Image files are picture copies of a screen view. Generic CADD automatically gives these files a .GX2 extension name. The files are images only and do not contain any information about the actual entities that make up the drawing itself. Not all monitor and graphics card combinations support image files. If this is the case with your configuration, Generic CADD displays the appropriate error message. Each of the image file commands is described below, with each corresponding two-letter command in parentheses.

IMAGE SAVE (IS) allows you to save a pixel image of the screen to a file with a .GX2 extension. At the prompt, enter the filename. Eight characters is the maximum allowable for a filename. Generic CADD adds the extension .GX2 automatically. Also include the drive and directory if you want the file to be saved to other than the default Generic CADD subdirectory. Then choose whether you want an image of the drawing only or the drawing plus the screen menu and prompts currently displayed. Generic CADD asks if you want an image of the entire screen. If you enter N for no, only the drawing within the rectangular drawing area is saved. If you answer Y for yes, the drawing plus the menu and prompt lines are saved.

IMAGE LOAD (IL) loads the saved pixel images of a .GX2 file into Generic CADD Level 3. Image files saved as an entire screen fill the current screen completely. Image files saved as only the drawing area are loaded into the drawing area only and the current menu and prompt lines remain the same. The image file loaded has no intelligence attached. It knows only the pixel representation of the image on the screen. Once an image file is loaded and you perform a ZOOM command or a REDRAW, the current drawing appears and the image file disappears. To load an image file, enter the name of the file you want to load at the prompt. Do not include the .GX2 extension, but add the drive and directory if applicable.

APPLICATIONS

Image files are used primarily with other Generic Software products, such as the Generic PRESENTATION package. A drawing is created in Generic CADD and transferred to the Presentation software as an image file for further visual modification. Image files can be used as a way to look at a drawing before actually loading the drawing file into your current drawing. Use it also to preview one of a series of drawings in a project for detailed information. Since the image file is only a static picture, it loads more quickly and does not add significantly to the current drawing size.

TYPICAL OPERATION

In this exercise, you create an image file and reload it into the current drawing for viewing.

1. Start a new drawing called "IMAGE."

2. Draw two rectangles.

```
ENTER A COMMAND> RE
ENTER A CORNER OF RECTANGLE> 2,2  <CR>
ENTER NEXT CORNER OF RECTANGLE> 7,25  <CR>
ENTER A COMMAND> RE
ENTER A CORNER OF RECTANGLE> 9,25 <CR>
ENTER NEXT CORNER OF RECTANGLE> 2'7, 1'10  <CR>
```

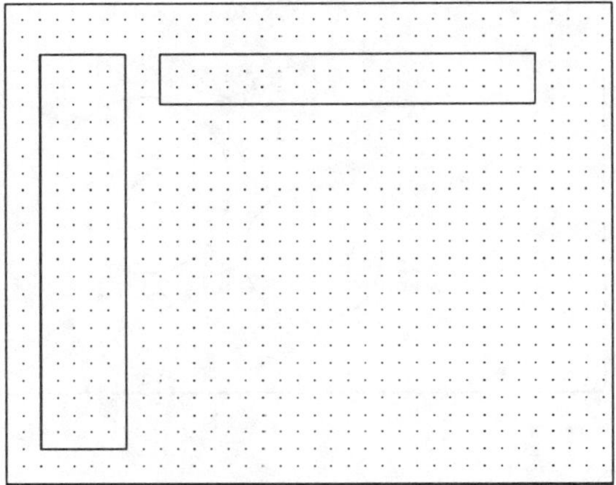

3. Save the current view as an image file.

```
ENTER A COMMAND> IS
ENTER IMAGE FILE NAME> TEST <CR>
SAVE FULL SCREEN IMAGE? (Y/N)> N
IMAGE SAVED
```

4. Clear current drawing from screen.

```
ENTER A COMMAND> DX
!!!WARNING!!!
DO YOU REALLY WANT TO ERASE THE DRAWING (Y,N)> Y
```

5. Draw additional figures.

```
ENTER A COMMAND> C2
ENTER CENTER OF CIRCLE> 1'5, 8   <CR>
ENTER A POINT ON CIRCLE> 1'5, 12   <CR>
ENTER A COMMAND> C2
ENTER CENTER OF CIRCLE> 2'3, 12 <CR>
ENTER A POINT ON CIRCLE> 1'10, 13   <CR>
```

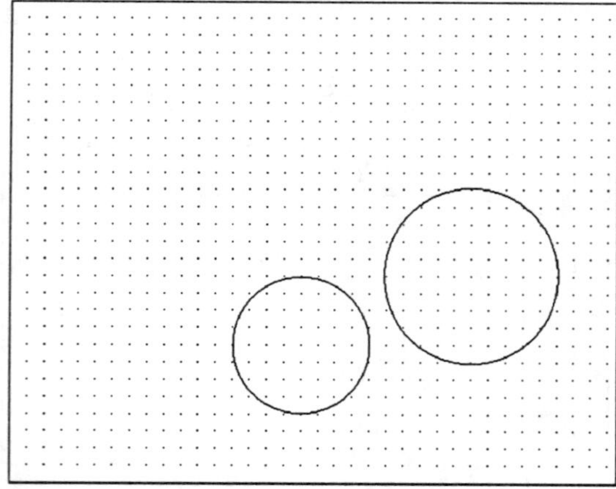

6. View the previously saved image file.

```
ENTER A COMMAND >  IL
```

NOTE

When an image file is loaded, it sweeps onto the screen from top to bottom, rather than redrawing all the entities as a drawing files does when loaded.

```
ENTER IMAGE FILE NAME >  TEST
IMAGE LOADED
```

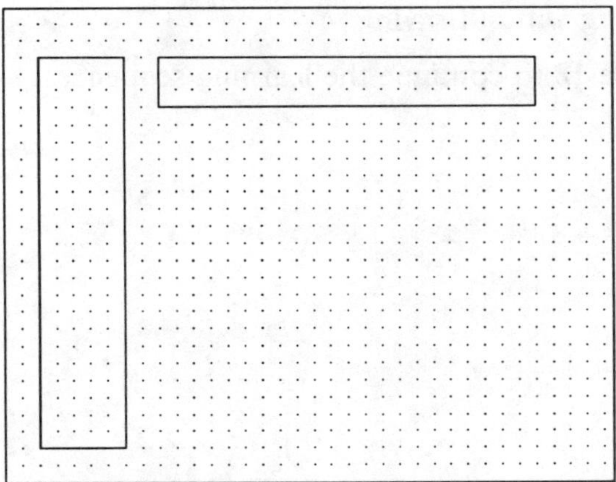

7. Zoom back from the current screen view.

```
ENTER A COMMAND >  ZB
ENTER CENTER OF ZOOM >  12,12  <CR>
```

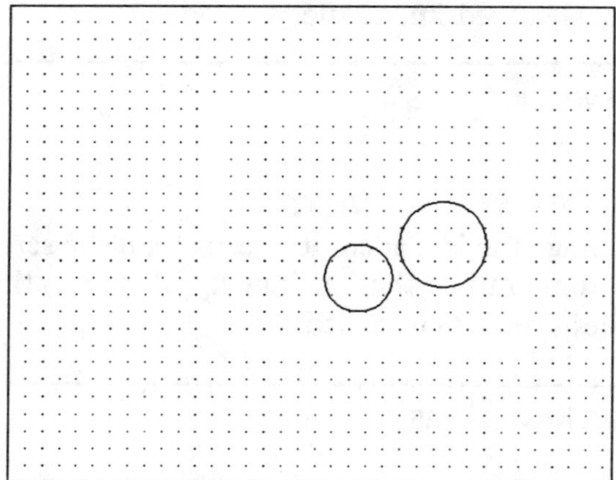

8. Quit the drawing without saving.

9. Turn to Module 18 to continue the learning sequence.

Module 36
LAYERS

DESCRIPTION

The layer series of commands control various special editing functions pertaining only to layers. Layers can be envisioned as transparent sheets of paper which stack together to create a drawing. Different portions of the drawing contents are on each sheet. The sheets can be viewed or turned off, depending upon which information you want to see.

Generic CADD offers a total of 256 layers per drawing file, numbered from 0 to 255. The various layer commands are described with each corresponding two-letter command in parentheses.

LAYER CURRENT (YC) Sets the current drawing layer. Each object drawn must be on a layer. The Generic CADD default is layer 0. The current setting for the current layer remains in effect until you change it.

LAYER DISPLAY (YD) Sets the layers which are viewed on the screen. When plotting, only the displayed layers are plotted. All the layers in the drawing file, even though they may not currently be displayed, are saved when the drawing file itself is saved. To see all the available drawing layers, type 256 at the prompt in the LAYER DISPLAY command. You cannot draw on a layer which is not displayed. When choosing a layer to be displayed that is currently turned off from view, notice that Generic CADD redraws the screen to display the added layer.

LAYER HIDE (YH) Allows you to turn off from view or hide a selected layer. If a layer is not visible, you cannot edit the graphics on the layer. The command DRAWING ERASE erases all layers, visible or not. After entering the layer number at the command prompt, enter a REDRAW to see the layers removed from view on your screen. To see only the current layer, enter 256 at the command prompt. This value turns off all layers, except the current layer.

LAYER ERASE (YX) Erases all information on a selected layer. Enter the layer to be erased at the command prompt. The UNERASE command brings the data back again if you make a mistake.

LAYER CHANGE (YG) Allows you to modify certain characteristics of all objects on a selected layer. The characteristics are line type, line color, and layer. Enter the new line type or color at the command prompt. For a layer change, enter the new layer, and all information on the selected layer is changed to the new layer.

LAYER ROTATE (YR) Rotates all objects on a selected layer. At the command prompt, enter the layer to be rotated and select an axis point about which all objects on the selected layer rotate. At the angle prompt, three options for entering the angle are available. You can enter the desired angle, if known; type A for angle to define the angle on the screen with a basepoint and a ray point; or type V for vertex to define the angle on the screen with a basepoint and two ray points. Generic CADD measures angles from the horizontal position in a counterclockwise rotation, beginning with the first ray selected and ending with the second ray selected. The resulting angle is displayed on the prompt line. Generic CADD rotates only a single layer at a time.

LAYER RESCALE (YZ) Allows you to rescale all objects on a selected layer. Sizes and proportions are changed, similar to the WINDOW RESCALE command. After entering the X and Y scale factor at the command prompt, enter a reference point. This is the single point which remains in the same location while the roation occurs. Generic CADD rescales only one layer at a time.

LAYER LOAD (YL) Allows you to load a previously saved drawing onto a single selected layer, regardless of the layer or layers on which the saved drawing was originally created. At the command prompt, enter the desired target layer, then the dawing filename, complete with drive and path designation, if necessary. The origins of the current drawing and the drawing being loaded are aligned.

LAYER SAVE (YS) Saves all information on a selected layer to a separate drawing file. Enter the layer you want to save and the name of the file to be saved. You are limited to a total of eight characters in the name. Specify the drive and path location if needed. Components placed on the selected layer are saved with the drawing file, even if created on other layers.

ALL LAYERS EDIT (AL) Allows you to determine whether the Generic CADD editing commands affect all the visible drawing layers or only the current layer. This command is a toggle between editing all layers and editing only the current layer. The default in ALL LAYERS EDIT off.

APPLICATIONS

Various layer combinations can be created for on-screen viewing or for plotting. For an architectural plan, for example, separate layers are created for walls, doors, room names, titles, reflected ceiling grid, light fixtures, mechanical diffusers, smoke detectors, electrical outlets, and so forth. If all this information is viewed at once, the drawing contents are difficult to read. Yet, all the information needs the architectural walls and doors, so these layers are viewed in all combinations. The mechanical diffusers probably never appear in the same plan as the light fixtures, yet on screen they can be viewed together to check for interferences.

LAYER HIDE is used to turn off from view a layer whose information you do not need at that time. LAYER ERASE permits quick and easy editing of a number of objects at once, while LAYER ROTATE and LAYER RESCALE allow you to change the shape and orientation of a number of objects at once.

TYPICAL OPERATION

In this exercise you create objects in several different layers, then edit by layer.

1. Start a new drawing called "LAYER."

2. Draw a rectangle in the default layer 0.

```
ENTER A COMMAND > RE
ENTER A CORNER OF RECTANGLE > 4,4  <CR>
ENTER NEXT CORNER OF RECTANGLE > 8,26  <CR>
```

3. Change the current layer.

```
ENTER A COMMAND > YC
CHANGE CURRENT LAYER (0) LIMITS: 0 TO 255 > 3  <CR>
```

4. Draw two squares in the current layer.

NOTE

The prompt line at the bottom of the screen displays the current drawing layer.

```
ENTER A COMMAND>  RE
ENTER A CORNER OF RECTANGLE>  20,20 <CR>
ENTER NEXT CORNER OF RECTANGLE>  24,24  <CR>
ENTER A COMMAND RE
ENTER A CORNER OF RECTANGLE>  26,19  <CR>
ENTER NEXT CORNER OF RECTANGLE>  30,23  <CR>
```

5. Change the current layer again.

```
ENTER A COMMAND>  YC
CHANGE CURRENT LAYER (3) LIMITS: 0 TO 255>  135  <CR>
```

6. Draw two circles.

```
ENTER A COMMAND>  C2
ENTER CENTER OF CIRCLE>  14,12 <CR>
ENTER A POINT ON CIRCLE>  18,12 <CR>
ENTER A COMMAND>  C2
ENTER CENTER OF CIRCLE>  20,9  <CR>
ENTER A POINT ON CIRCLE>  22,9  <CR>
```

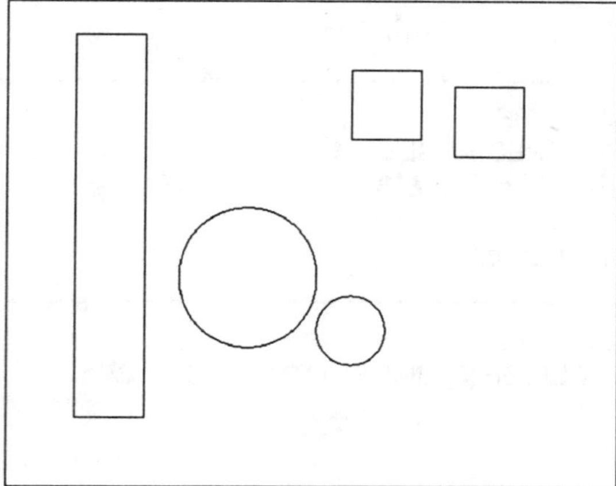

7. Turn off layer 0.

```
ENTER A COMMAND> YH
HIDE LAYER [0-255] OR HIDE ALL = 256> 0  <CR>
```

8. Redraw the screen to remove the rectangle from view.

```
ENTER A COMMAND> RD
```

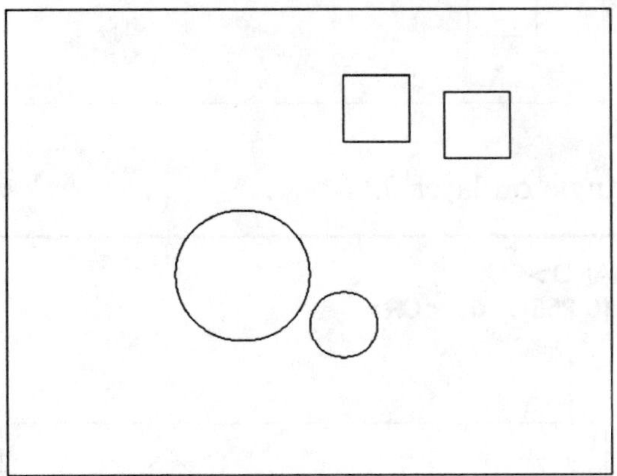

9. Display layer 0.

```
ENTER A COMMAND> YD
DISPLAY LAYER [0-255] OR DISPLAY ALL = 256> 0  <CR>
```

10. Redraw the screen to view the layer.

```
ENTER A COMMAND> RD
```

11. Rotate the squares drawn in layer 3.

```
ENTER A COMMAND> YR
SELECT LAYER [0-255] 3
ENTER AN AXIS POINT> 24,20  <CR>
ENTER ANGLE OF ROTATION ABOUT THE AXIS> 45 <CR>
```

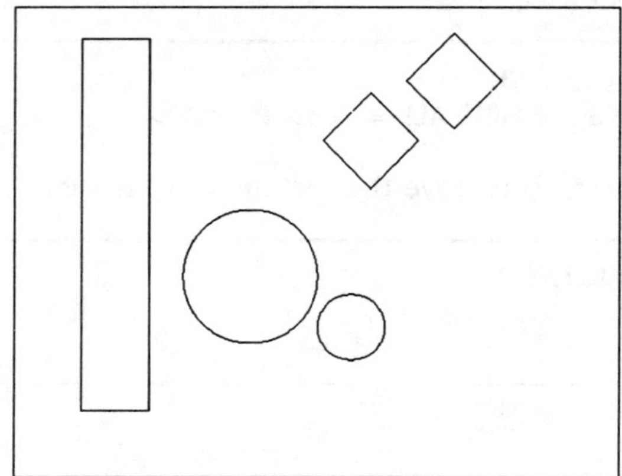

12. Erase the rectangle on layer 0.

```
ENTER A COMMAND> YX
SELECT LAYER [0-255]> 0   <CR>
```

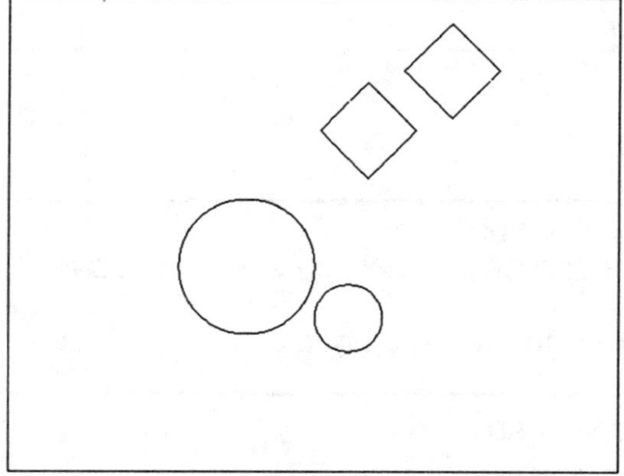

13. Delete the squares on layer 3 and the circles on layer 135.

```
ENTER A COMMAND > AL
EDIT ALL VISIBLE LAYERS IS ON
ENTER A COMMAND > WE
PLACE WINDOW (Select two diagonal points to define a window around the squares and
the circles.)
```

14. Quit the drawing without saving.

15. Turn to Module 46 to continue the learning sequence.

LEADER/SHOULDER LENGTH

DESCRIPTION

The LEADER (LE) command allows you to draw a leader line complete with a selected arrowhead type from one point to another. At the command prompt, select the point to be on the opposite end from the arrowhead, choose a direction for the horizontal shoulder line, then select an end point for the automatic location of the selected arrowhead. The size of the selected arrowhead is controlled by the dimensional LETTER SIZE command. Text notes are added with the TEXT PLACE command. The SHOULDER LENGTH (LL) command controls the length of the horizontal portion of the leader line. The Generic CADD default is one unit. At the shoulder prompt, enter the desired length. Once a new size is chosen, all new leaders placed reflect the change. Existing leader lines are not affected. The arrowhead type and its closed or open mode are controlled by the current settings of the ARROW TYPE and ARROW MODE commands.

APPLICATIONS

LEADER is most commonly used to locate text notes on a drawing. The leader line may connect an object to a text note or tie together two objects to denote alignment. The arrowhead type is capable of change, depending upon whether you measure the surface or the interior of an object shown.

TYPICAL OPERATION

In this session you draw a leader line to connect an object to a text note.

1. Start a new drawing called "LEADER."

2. Set the LETTER SIZE to determine the length of the arrowhead lines.

```
ENTER A COMMAND> LH
CHANGE LETTER HEIGHT (1.000) IN> .5  <CR>
```

3. Draw a rectangle.

```
ENTER A COMMAND> RE
ENTER A CORNER OF RECTANGLE> 5,8 <CR>
ENTER NEXT CORNER OF RECTANGLE> 11,11 <CR>
```

4. Set the SHOULDER LENGTH of the leader line.

```
ENTER A COMMAND> LL
CHANGE LEADER SHOULDER SIZE (1.000)> 2 <CR>
```

5. Draw a leader to the rectangle.

```
ENTER A COMMAND> LE
ENTER LEADER STARTING POINT> 18,14 <CR>
ENTER A POINT INDICATING SHOULDER DIRECTION (LEFT OR RIGHT)> 14,14 <CR>
ENTER LEADER TERMINAL POINT> 11,11 <CR>
```

6. Place the text note.

```
ENTER A COMMAND> TP
SELECTED FONT IS: MAIN
ENTER TEXT STARTING POINT> 19,13 <CR>
PLACE TEXT—ESC TO QUIT!
ENTER A CHARACTER> (Type TEXT NOTE and <ESC>)
```

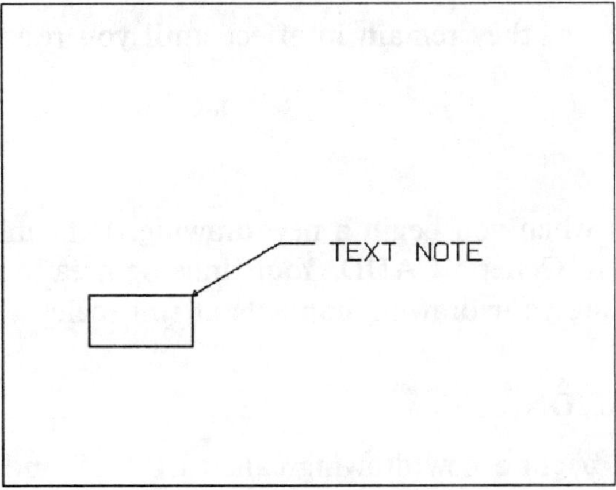

7. Quit the drawing without saving.

8. Turn to Module 19 to continue the learning sequence.

Module 38
LIMITS

DESCRIPTION

The LIMITS (LS) command establishes the boundaries of your drawing sheet. Actually, the LIMITS command sets the upper right corner limit of your drawing. The lower left corner is the drawing origin and can be reset using the DRAWING REORIGIN command (DO).

To set the limits with the LS command, enter the X and Y coordinates of the limits you desire. You may also show Generic CADD the limits you want by typing D for distance and selecting two points on the screen to define the limits. Generic CADD uses these points to calculate the size of the limits.

The limits which are preset when you begin a new drawing are 24"in height and 36"in length. These settings are the default limits.

The ZOOM LIMITS (ZL) command brings the defined limits of your drawing onto the screen. You can draw beyond the limits, however. If you do so, ZL does not bring your entire drawing into view. Then you should use the ZOOM ALL (ZA) command to bring all of the drawing into view.

Once the limits are set, they remain in effect until you resize them or you quit Generic CADD.

APPLICATIONS

You must set limits when you begin a new drawing. Remember that you always draw in actual size in Generic CADD. Your drawing area must be appropriately sized to accommodate your drawing contents at full scale.

TYPICAL OPERATION

In this activity you begin a new drawing called LIMITS and change the default limits of 24 and 36 to 48 and 72.

1. Start Generic CADD. Type **CADD** and press **Return** at the DOS prompt. Press **Return** at the Generic CADD title page.

2. Begin a new drawing called "LIMITS."

```
ENTER A DRAWING FILE NAME > LIMITS  <CR>
IS THIS A NEW DRAWING (Y,N) > Y
```

3. Use the LIMITS command to change the height and width.

```
ENTER A COMMAND > LS
CHANGE HEIGHT LIMIT (24.000) > 8  <CR>
CHANGE WIDTH LIMIT (36.000) > 72  <CR>
```

4. Draw a rectangle.

```
ENTER A COMMAND > RE
ENTER A CORNER OF RECTANGLE > 3,3  <CR>
ENTER NEXT CORNER OF RECTANGLE > 24,24 <CR>
```

5. Zoom to the extent of the limits to bring the rectangle and the overall limits into view.

NOTE

When you establish the limits of your drawing, Generic CAD automatically holds to the Y coordinate or vertical dimension as entered and adjusts the X dimension proportionally to show correctly on the drawing screen.

```
ENTER A COMMAND > ZL
```

6. Quit the drawing without saving.

```
ENTER A COMMAND >  QU
SAVE CURRENT DRAWING (Y or N) >  N
"C" TO CONTINUE
"Q" TO QUIT >  Q
```

7. Turn to Module 70 to continue the learning sequence.

Module 39
LINES

DESCRIPTION

The lines group of commands control the settings of four default attributes of lines. Any changes made affect only those entities created after the changes are made. Characteristics of lines already on the drawing are not modified in this way. To change items once they are on your drawing, use OBJECT CHANGE, WINDOW CHANGE, LAYER CHANGE, or DRAWING CHANGE.

Generic CADD offers four lines commands. Each two-letter command is in parentheses.

LINE COLOR (LK) Allows an onscreen color to be associated with lines or objects. Once selected, each item placed takes on the chosen color. Objects already drawn are not changed. Components are not affected, using the line color in effect when they were originally created. Text color is controlled through the TEXT COLOR command. The graphics card you use determines the actual color on the monitor. Colors named 0 through 255 are allowed. The line color default is 0. The line color of each object determines which pen is used to plot the object.

LINE WIDTH (LW) Allows selection of eleven different widths, each represented by a number 0 through 10. Each number refers to the number of pixels (dots on the screen) used to represent the line. Your monitor and printer resolutions determine the real-world width. Once a width is selected, each line or object drawn assumes that width. Objects already drawn are not affected. Text and components are not affected.

LINE TYPE (LT) Allows selection of a line type, designated with a number from 0 to 255. The Generic CADD default is 0. Once a type is selected, each line or object drawn takes on the chosen line type. Objects already drawn are not changed. Neither components nor text is affected. When you select the LINETYPE command, a representative sample appears on the screen.

The first ten line types are automatically scaled to always appear the same on your monitor, regardless of the zoomed position. Line types 10 through 19 are scaled to have one repeat (dash plus space) to equal one unit as set by the line scale.

LINE SCALE (LZ) Allows setting of the interval at which the pattern of a line repeats. All line types, with the exception of the solid line, are created of repeating patterns. Changing the line scale affects all line types number 10 and above, which are automatically scaled to appear exactly as they are in the menu, regardless of how far in or out you are zoomed.

APPLICATIONS

LINE COLOR is available to provide easier viewing of your drawing on the screen, thus enabling you to differentiate between the drawing parts. You are also able to associate a line color with a particular pen in your plotter, enabling multi-pen plots.

LINE WIDTH also insures a legible drawing on the screen, by adding a variety of widths to add "punch" to your drawing.

LINE TYPE contributes to your drawing's legibility by allowing use of a variety of linetypes to denote hidden items, items above or behind the drawing plane, or items supplied by another source.

LINE SCALE works with the LINE TYPE command to provide infinite variety to the available line types.

TYPICAL OPERATION

In this activity, you draw lines and objects using the various lines commands.

1. Start a new drawing called "LINES."

2. Draw a line. Note the status line defaults for line type and line color.

```
ENTER A COMMAND > L1
ENTER START POINT > > 4,4  <CR>
ESC OR PEN UP TO STOP
ENTER NEXT POINT > 10,5  <CR>
EXC OR PEN UP TO STOP
ENTER NEXT POINT > PU
```

3. Change the line color from default of color 1 to color 5.

```
ENTER A COMMAND > LK
```

NOTE
Your monitor and graphics card must be EGA or better to support the color options of Generic CADD. CGA and monochrome combinations do not support the colors.

NOTE
Fifteen colors are available. Choose the color by entering a number between 0 and 255 or by selecting with the mouse or keyboard from the color bar to the right of the screen. Note that the 15 colors available rotate evenly through all 255.

```
CHANGE COLOR NUMBER (1) LIMITS: 0 TO 255 > 5   <CR>
```

Note the change on the status line.

4. Draw another line in the new line color.

```
ENTER A COMMAND > L1
ENTER START POINT > > 10,8   <CR>
ESC OR PENUP TO STOP
ENTER NEXT POINT > 12,10   <CR>
ESC OR PENUP TO STOP
ENTER NEXT POINT > PU
```

5. Change the line type from the default of 0 to 7.

```
ENTER A COMMAND > LT
CHANGE LINE TYPE (0) LIMITS: 0 TO 255 > 7   <CR>
```

Note the 10 sample line types to the right of the drawing screen.

6. Draw a line with the new line type.

```
ENTER A COMMAND > L1
ENTER START POINT > > 15,15   <CR>
ESC OR PEN UP TO STOP
ENTER NEXT POINT > 25,15   <CR>
ESC OR PEN UP TO STOP
ENTER NEXT POINT > PU
```

7. Change the line width from the default of 0 to 5.

```
ENTER A COMMAND> LW
CHANGE LINE WIDTH (0) LIMITS: 0 TO 10> 5  <CR>
```

8. Draw a line with the new line width.

```
ENTER A COMMAND> L1
ENTER START POINT> > 15,10  <CR>
ESC OR PEN UP TO STOP
ENTER NEXT POINT> 28,10  <CR>
ESC OR PEN UP TO STOP
ENTER NEXT POINT> PU
```

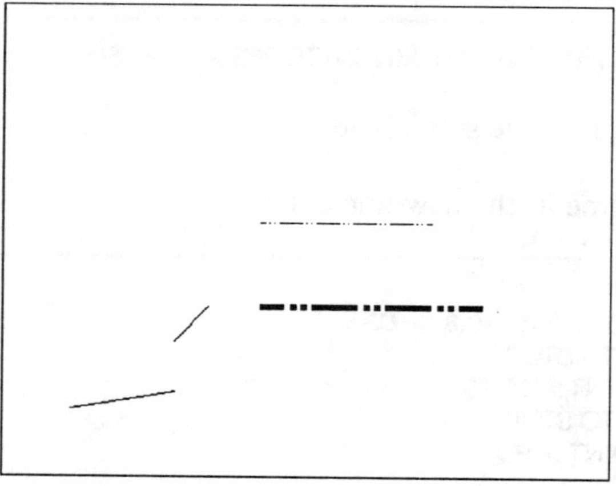

9. Quit the drawing without saving.

10. Turn to Module 8 to continue the learning sequence.

Module 40
LOAD BATCH FILE/SAVE BATCH FILE

DESCRIPTION

Batch files allow you to enter multiple commands automatically. Batch files can be made from a drawing file using the SAVE BATCH FILE command, or you can write your own batch files using a text editor. A drawing can be saved as a batch file with a .TXT extension and printed in a text format. As a batch file, the drawing file can be examined with a text editor program. Each command and point location is recorded in the program. Generic CADD provides two commands for use in saving and loading batch commands. Each option is described below, with the corresponding two-letter command in parentheses.

SAVE BATCH FILE (SB) allows you to save a drawing file as a batch file. The .TXT extension is automatically given to the designated filename. All parts of the drawing file are saved except components. Components must be saved to disk with the COMPONENT DUMP command or the COMPONENT SAVE command. After selecting the command, Generic CADD asks for a filename. The program assumes you want to name it the same as the drawing file name, except that it will have a .TXT extension rather than the .DWG extension of a drawing file. Enter another name if you want, complete with drive and directory designations if needed, or press Return to accept the designated name.

LOAD BATCH FILE (LB) allows you to load a .TXT file into Generic CADD and automatically execute the commands as the loading occurs. After entering the command, enter the name of the file you want to load, together with the drive and directory if needed. You do not need to add the .TXT extension. The drawing is then recreated.

APPLICATIONS

Batch files are used to gather information from a drawing or to create simple commands to create a series of repetitious steps. For example, batch files enable you to start a drawing, set layers and line weights, and draw the sheet border for a new drawing.

TYPICAL OPERATION

In this activity you load a drawing, create a batch file, and then load the batch file.

1. Begin Generic CADD by loading the SAMPLE.DWG drawing created in Module 2.

2. Save the drawing as a batch file.

```
ENTER A COMMAND > SB
SAVE TEXT FILE: (SAMPLE.TXT) > CR
SAVE IS COMPLETED
```

3. Clear the drawing screen.

```
ENTER A COMMAND > DX
!!!WARNING!!!
DO YOU REALLY WANT TO ERASE THE DRAWING (Y,N) > Y
```

4. Load the batch file.

```
ENTER A COMMAND > LB
ENTER THE BATCH FILE NAME > SAMPLE
```

The drawing is recreated on the screen.

5. Zoom to bring all the drawing into view.

```
ENTER A COMMAND > ZA
```

6. Quit the drawing without saving.

7. Turn to Module 35 to continue the learning sequence.

Module 41
MANUAL ENTRY OFFSET ORIGIN

DESCRIPTION

MANUAL ENTRY OFFSET ORIGIN (MO) allows you to enter the X and Y coordinates of a point offset from the drawing origin point. This mode is the Generic CADD default until set to another manual entry mode, either basepoint (MB) or relative (MR). Choose MO only when you are in another entry mode and want to return to offset your point entry from the origin of the drawing.

APPLICATIONS

MANUAL ENTRY OFFSET ORIGIN is used when you want all points entered to be in direct relation to the drawing origin, rather than to each other or to a selected basepoint.

TYPICAL OPERATION

In this activity you draw lines using the default manual entry setting. After changing the manual entry mode, you again return to MANUAL ENTRY OFFSET ORIGIN to enter additional lines.

1. Start a new drawing called "MEORIGIN."

2. Display the default grid for easy reference.

```
ENTER A COMMAND >  GR
DISPLAY GRID IS ON
```

3. Draw a line.

NOTE

The default entry mode is MANUAL ENTRY OFFSET ORIGIN. Note that the coordinates given for the line are in reference to the drawing origin.

```
ENTER A COMMAND >  L1
ENTER START POINT > >  4,4  <CR>
ENTER NEXT POINT >  4,8  <CR>
ENTER NEXT POINT >  PU
```

4. Change the manual entry to offset relative.

```
ENTER A COMMAND >  MR
MANUAL ENTRY/LAST POINT
```

5. Draw a line.

```
ENTER A COMMAND >  L1
ENTER START POINT > >  4,4  <CR
ENTER NEXT POINT >  4,8  <CR>
ENTER NEXT POINT >  PU
```

6. Return the manual entry to offset origin.

```
ENTER A COMMAND >  MO
MANUAL ENTRY/ORIGIN
```

7. Draw a line.

```
ENTER A COMMAND >  L1
ENTER START POINT > >  8,8  <CR>
ENTER NEXT POINT >  10,10  <CR>
ENTER NEXT POINT >  PU
```

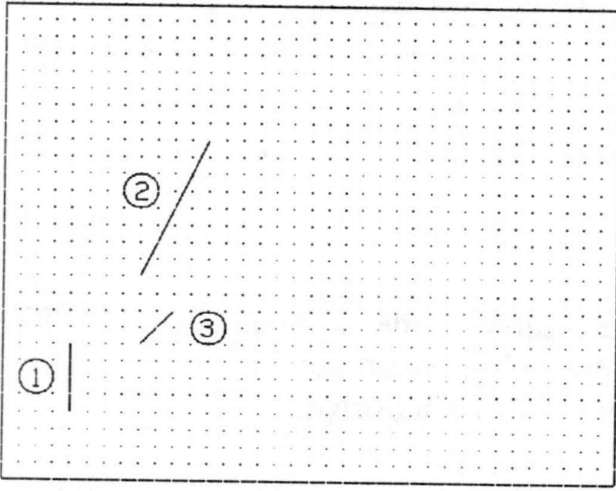

8. Quit the drawing without saving.

9. Turn to Module 5 to continue the learning sequence.

Module 42
MANUAL ENTRY OFFSET RELATIVE

DESCRIPTION

MANUAL ENTRY OFFSET RELATIVE (MR) allows entry of a point to be a specified distance from the last point entered. The coordinates have no bearing on the origin or basepoint of the drawing, but only to the previous point.

APPLICATIONS

Most often when drawing, lines are drawn with a specific length, relative only to each other. MR selection means that lengths are entered as they exist on the real object, not as they are in relation to an origin on a Generic CADD drawing. For example, when drawing a horizontal wall 12' in length, you want to enter 12' for the X coordinate. MR mode lets you do this. Otherwise, you spend time calculating the X coordinate in relation to the origin of the drawing.

Once this mode is selected, it remains in effect until you quit the drawing. The command can be activated at any time, even in the middle of another command.

TYPICAL OPERATION

In this exercise you create a line drawing using MANUAL ENTRY OFFSET RELATIVE.

1. Begin a new drawing called "MR."

2. Begin the series of lines.

```
ENTER A COMMAND> L1
ENTER START POINT>> 4,5  <CR>
```

3. Select the MANUAL ENTRY OFFSET RELATIVE mode.

```
ESC or PEN UP TO STOP
ENTER NEXT POINT> MR
MANUAL ENTRY/LAST POINT
```

4. Continue the line series.

```
ESC or PEN UP TO STOP
ENTER NEXT POINT > 6,0  <CR>
ESC or PENUP TO STOP
ENTER NEXT POINT > 0,6  <CR>
ESC or PEN UP TO STOP
ENTER NEXT POINT > 6,0  <CR>
ESC or PEN UP TO STOP
ENTER NEXT POINT > PU
```

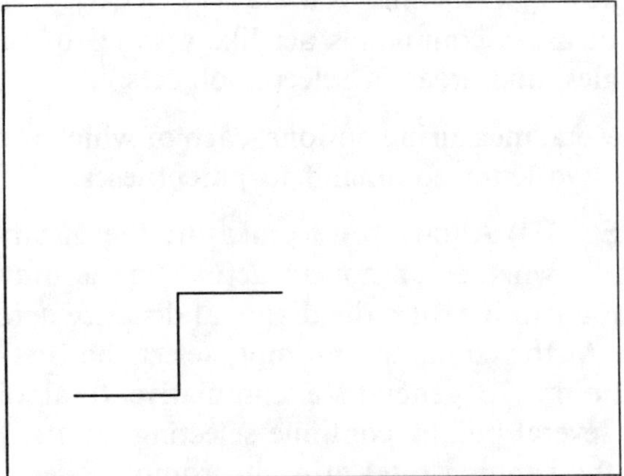

Three lines, each 6" in length, are on the drawing.

5. Quit the drawing without saving.

6. Turn to Module 63 to continue the learning sequence.

Module 43
MEASURE

DESCRIPTION

The measure commands allow you to obtain specific dimensional information about objects on your drawing. The lines you draw in Generic CADD are created in actual size, and the measure commands act like a series of tape measures to give exact distances, angles, and areas of selected objects.

Generic CADD offers several measuring options, each of which is described below with the corresponding two-letter command in parentheses.

MEASURE DISTANCE (MD) Allows you to measure the distance between any two points, whether or not an actual line is drawn between the points. You can measure the diagonal distance across a square for example. At the command prompt, select the first point, then the second point. To generate a cumulative total distance passing through several points, continue selecting points. Generic CADD adds to the running total at each prompt. Select pen up to stop selecting points. For accurate measurements, it is important to use the Generic CADD snap modes to snap exactly to a desired point.

MEASURE ANGLE (MA) Allows you to measure the angle between any two selected points. Horizontal is considered a zero degree angle, with all angles originating from the horizontal and increasing in value in the counterclockwise direction.

MEASURE AREA (MV) Allows you to calculate the area of a chosen figure by selecting the corner points in a continuous manner until the figure is closed. You can close the figure by selecting the start point as the final point, or Generic CADD closes it automatically with a pen up command, drawing a straight line between the last point selected and the starting point. Any number of points are allowed in defining the area to be calculated. All areas are displayed in the units that have been defined for the drawing.

APPLICATIONS

The measure commands are important to create an accurate drawing. Most commonly they are used to generate quantities of materials needed for a job. Measure an angle to accurately duplicate it elsewhere on the drawing. Use MEASURE AREA to measure an area to generate a square footage calculation for use by a commercial office tenant. Measure a room's perimeter with MEASURE DISTANCE to determine the linear footage of base or wall covering needed.

TYPICAL OPERATION

In this activity you create several objects and take measurements.

1. Start a new drawing called "MEASURE."

2. Draw a line series.

```
ENTER A COMMAND >  L1
ENTER START POINT > >  4,14   <CR>
ENTER NEXT POINT >  11,14   <CR>
ENTER NEXT POINT >  15,20   <CR>
ENTER NEXT POINT >  27,4   <CR>
ENTER NEXT POINT >  14,7   <CR>
ENTER NEXT POINT >  6,5   <CR>
ENTER NEXT POINT >  4,14   <CR>
ENTER NEXT POINT >  PU
```

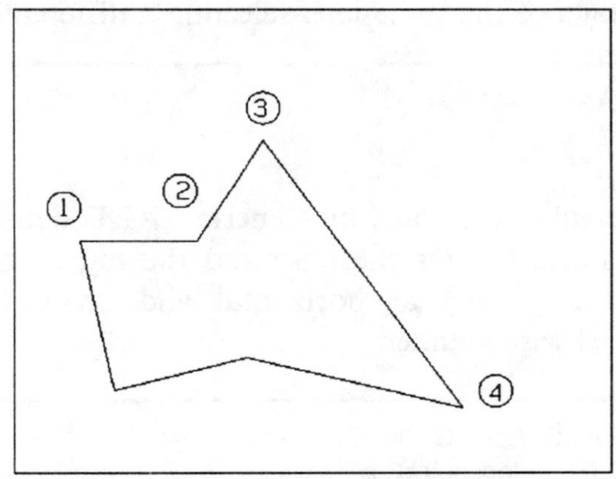

3. Measure the total distance between points 1 and 3.

```
ENTER A COMMAND > MD
```

NOTE
The NEAREST POINT (NP) snap command is also used to accurately select the corner points.

```
ENTER STARTING POINT > > SC
CLOSEST POINT TO > (Select point 1 with screen cursor.)
ENTER NEXT POINT > (ESC OR PENUP TO QUIT) > SC
CLOSEST POINT TO > (Select point 2 with screen cursor.)
DISTANCE = 0' 7.00"
ENTER NEXT POINT(ESC OR PENUP TO QUIT) > SC
CLOSEST POINT TO > (Select point 3.)
DISTANCE = 1' 2.211"
ENTER NEXT POINT(ESC OR PENUP TO QUIT) > PU
DISTANCE = 1' 2.211"
```

4. Measure the angle of the longest line in the series.

```
ENTER A COMMAND > MA
ENTER BASE OF ANGLE > SC
CLOSEST POINT TO (Select point 4.)
ENTER A POINT ON THE RAY > SC
CLOSEST POINT TO (Select point 3.)
THE ANGLE IS > 126.870   DEGREES.
```

5. Measure the angle of the same line, selecting a different base point.

```
ENTER A COMMAND > MA
```

NOTE
The angle value generated by Generic CADD depends upon the points selected for the base and the ray, as angles are calculated beginning at horizontal and proceeding in a counterclockwise manner.

```
ENTER BASE OF ANGLE > SC
CLOSEST POINT TO (Select point 3.)
ENTER A POINT ON THE RAY > SC
CLOSEST POINT TO (Select point 4.)
THE ANGLE IS > 306.870 degrees.
```

6. Measure the area defined by the line series.

```
ENTER A COMMAND > MV
ENTER FIRST POINT > SC
CLOSEST POINT TO > (Select point 1.)
ENTER ESC OR PENUP TO SHOW AREA!
ENTER NEXT POINT > SC
CLOSEST POINT TO > (Select point 2.)
ENTER NEXT POINT > (Select each successive point in the series, using CLOSEST
POINT each time. End the sequence at the beginning point.)
ENTER NEXT POINT >   <ESC>
AREA: 1' 27.500" square
```

7. Quit the drawing without saving.

8. Turn to Module 25 to continue the learning sequence.

Module 44
MOVE POINT

DESCRIPTION

MOVE POINT (MP) allows you to move any point on an object. A point is any defining point used to initially create the object. For lines, the endpoints may be moved. A rectangle may have a segment endpoint moved, while a circle moves at the center. The point that moves may be different on each object type, depending upon how the object is created.

APPLICATIONS

MOVE POINT is used to edit objects after they have been placed on the drawing. A line may need to be relocated at one endpoint, or a circle or curve resized.

TYPICAL OPERATION

In this activity, you draw several objects and modify them with the MOVE POINT command.

1. Start a new drawing called "MOVEPT."

2. Draw a rectangle.

```
ENTER A COMMAND> RE
ENTER A CORNER OF RECTANGLE> 2,2  <CR>
ENTER NEXT CORNER OF RECTANGLE> 8,10  <CR>
```

3. Draw a standard point.

```
ENTER A COMMAND> PO
ENTER THE POINT> 12,10  <CR>
```

4. Draw a regular polygon.

```
ENTER A COMMAND > RP
ENTER THE CENTER OF POLYGON > 20,15  <CR>
ENTER A POINT ON POLYGON > 20,10  <CR>
ENTER THE NUMBER OF SIDES > 6 <CR>
```

5. Draw a circle.

```
ENTER A COMMAND > C2
ENTER CENTER OF CIRCLE > 25,5  <CR>
ENTER A POINT ON CIRCLE > 25,1  <CR>
```

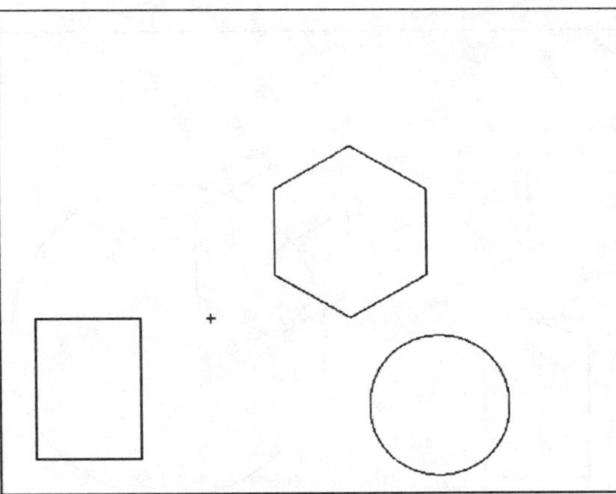

6. Modify the rectangle.

```
ENTER A COMMAND > MP
ENTER A POINT ON THE OBJECT TO MOVE POINT > 6,10  <CR>
ENTER POINT TO BE MOVED > 8,10  <CR>
ENTER NEW LOCATION > 8,12  <CR>
```

7. Move the standard point.

```
ENTER A COMMAND > MP
ENTER A POINT ON THE OBJECT TO MOVE POINT > 12,10  <CR>
ENTER POINT TO BE MOVED > 12,10  <CR>
ENTER NEW LOCATION > 12,20  <CR>
```

8. Modify the polygon.

```
ENTER A COMMAND>  MP
ENTER A POINT ON THE OBJECT TO MOVE POINT>  17,18  <CR>
ENTER POINT TO BE MOVED>  20,20  <CR>
ENTER NEW LOCATION>  20,15  <CR>
```

9. Modify the circle.

```
ENTER A COMMAND>  MP
ENTER A POINT ON THE OBJECT TO MOVE POINT>  25,1  <CR>
ENTER POINT TO BE MOVED>  25,5  <CR>
ENTER NEW LOCATION>  26,10  <CR>
```

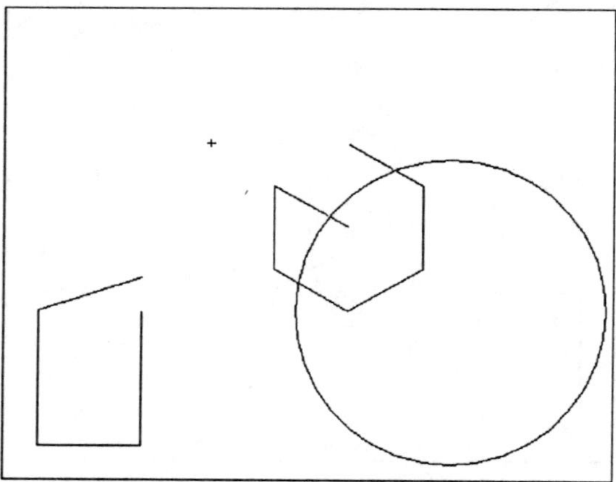

10. Quit the drawing without saving.

11. Turn to Module 45 to continue the learning sequence.

Module 45
OBJECT BREAK

DESCRIPTION

OBJECT BREAK (OB) removes a section of an existing object between any two selected points. Affected objects are straight lines, arcs, circles, and curves. After an object is broken, the two remaining portions of the object become separate objects.

APPLICATIONS

OBJECT BREAK is used to modify an existing object. When breaking a straight line, the broken area may be replaced with a dashed line to denote a hidden portion. Often, portions of objects are broken to accommodate other basic drawing elements in an adjacent position. The number of variations of basic drawing elements is expanded with the ability to break out portions of the object.

TYPICAL OPERATION

In this activity you draw several objects and break out portions of each.

1. Start a new drawing called "BREAK."

2. Draw a rectangle.

```
ENTER A COMMAND> RE
ENTER A CORNER OF RECTANGLE> 15,15  <CR>
ENTER NEXT CORNER OF RECTANGLE> 25,25  <CR>
```

3. Draw a circle.

```
ENTER A COMMAND> C3
ENTER FIRST POINT ON CIRCLE> 15,5  <CR>
ENTER SECOND POINT ON CIRCLE> 25,5  <CR>
ENTER THIRD POINT ON CIRCLE> 20,0  <CR>
```

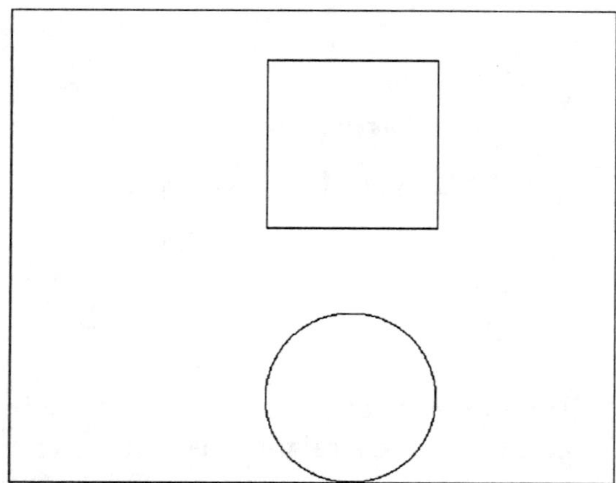

4. Break the circle.

```
ENTER A COMMAND> OB
ENTER A POINT ON THE OBJECT TO BREAK> 20,0  <CR>
ENTER BREAK POINT> 15,5  <CR>
ENTER SECOND BREAK POINT> 25,5  <CR>
```

5. Break the rectangle.

```
ENTER A COMMAND> OB
ENTER A POINT ON THE OBJECT TO BREAK> 20,25  <CR>
ENTER BREAK POINT> 17,25  <CR>
ENTER SECOND BREAK POINT> 23,25  <CR>
```

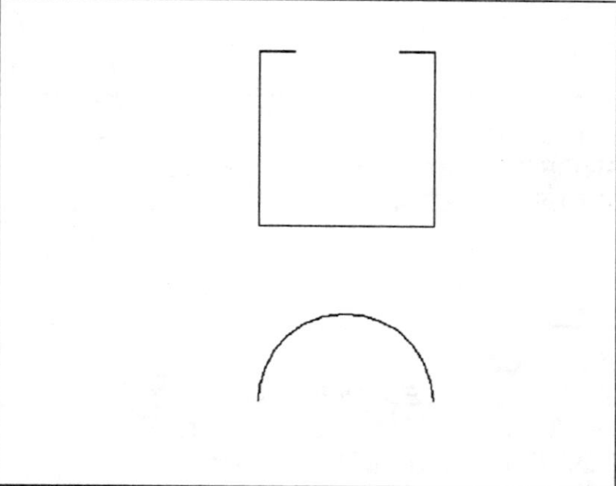

6. Quit the drawing without saving.

7. Turn to Module 48 to continue the learning sequence.

OBJECT CHANGE/WINDOW CHANGE

DESCRIPTION

The change commands allow you to change certain parameters about an object that has been drawn on the screen. The line type, line width, line color, and layer of an object or group of objects can be changed. Generic CADD offers two ways to change objects, depending upon whether you want to change a single object or window a group of objects to change. The available options are described below, with the corresponding two-letter command in parentheses.

OBJECT CHANGE (OG) Allows you to change the line type, line width, line color, and layer of a single object already placed on the screen.

WINDOW CHANGE (WG) Allows you to change the line type, line width, line color, and layer of a group of items on your drawing within a selected window.

APPLICATIONS

OBJECT CHANGE and WINDOW CHANGE allow easy editing of objects previously placed on your drawing. Often during the development of a drawing, mistakes are made or design changes occur that necessitate changing the drawing. These commands allow those changes to occur easily, without erasing and redrawing the objects.

TYPICAL OPERATION

In this session you draw a variety of objects and change them.

1. Start a new drawing called "CHANGE."

2. Draw a rectangle and a circle with the default values.

```
ENTER A COMMAND> RE
ENTER A CORNER OF RECTANGLE> 5,11 <CR>
ENTER NEXT CORNER OF RECTANGLE> 20,19 <CR>
ENTER A COMMAND> C2 <CR>
ENTER CENTER OF CIRCLE> 28,21  <CR>
ENTER A POINT ON CIRCLE> 32,20 <CR>
```

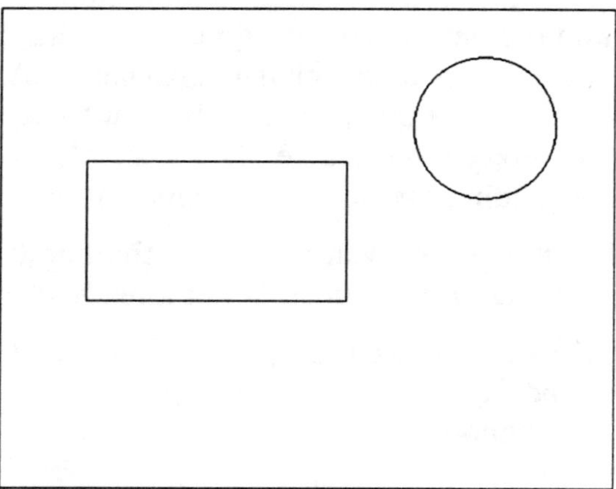

3. Change the paramenters of the circle.

```
ENTER A COMMAND> OG  <CR>
ENTER A POINT ON THE OBJECT TO CHANGE> 32,20  <CR>
```

4. Notice the available linetypes graphically shown in the menu area of the screen.

```
CHANGE LINE TYPE (0) LIMITS:0 TO 255> 1  <CR>
```

5. Notice the available line widths graphically shown in the menu area of the screen.

```
CHANGE LINE WIDTH (0) LIMITS:0 TO 10> 6 <CR>
```

6. Notice the available colors shown in the menu area of the screen.

```
CHANGE COLOR NUMBER (1) LIMITS:0 TO 255 > 13   <CR>
When you do not want to change a parameter, press < Return >.
CHANGE LINE LAYER (0) LIMITS: 0 TO 255 >  <CR>
```

7. Window the rectangle to change the parameters.

NOTE

To change the entire rectangle, select WINDOW CHANGE. Using OBJECT CHANGE results in only the selected rectangle segment being changed, as a rectangle is actually four lines, not a single object.

```
ENTER A COMMAND >  WG
PLACE WINDOW (Select two diagonal points to define a window around the entire
rectangle. >
(1)POINT (2)LINE (3)CIRCLE (4)ARC (5)ELLIPS (6)CURV (7)TXT (8)CMP
ENTER TYPE OF OBJECT FROM ABOVE (RETURN FOR ALL) > 2   <CR>
ENTER PARAMETERS TO CHANGE
LINE TYPE (0-255) RETURN FOR ALL >  <CR>
LINE WIDTH (0-255) RETURN FOR ALL >  <CR>
COLOR (0-255) RETURN FOR ALL >  <CR>
LAYER (0-255) RETURN FOR ALL >  <CR>
CHANGE THEM TO >
LINE TYPE (0-255) RETURN FOR NO CHANGE > 4   <CR>
LINE WIDTH (2-255) RETURN FOR NO CHANGE > 6   <CR>
COLOR (0-255) RETURN FOR NO CHANGE > 14   <CR>
LAYER (0-255) RETURN FOR NO CHANGE >  <CR>
CHANGE LINES, ALL LINETYPES, ALL WIDTHS, ALL COLORS, ALL LAYERS
TO NEW LINETYPE:4 NEW WIDTH:6 NEW COLOR:14 SAME LAYERS (Y,N) > Y
```

8. Quit the drawing without saving.

9. Turn to Module 10 to continue the learning sequence.

Module 47
OBJECT COPY/WINDOW COPY

DESCRIPTION

The copy commands allow you to repeat graphic objects on your drawing quickly and easily. The object to be copied is selected, a reference point chosen, a new reference point located, and the number of copies needed is entered. The copies are placed the same distance from each other as the first copy is from the original. The copy distance is the distance between the chosen reference point and the new reference point location. The original object remains in its original position. Generic CADD offers several copy methods, two of which are described below. Each two-letter command is included in parentheses.

OBJECT COPY (OC) Allows you to create up to 100 copies of a single object at a specified location.

WINDOW COPY (WC) Allows you to create up to 99 copies of a windowed group of objects at a specified location.

APPLICATIONS

Using the copy commands insures that you never have to draw the same object more than once. One of the great benefits of CAD, copying enables tremendous drawing creation speed. Items from stair treads and toilet fixtures to titles and column reference bubbles are ideal for copying.

TYPICAL OPERATION

In this session you create several objects and make numerous copies.

1. Start a new drawing called "COPY."

2. Draw a rectangle.

```
ENTER A COMMAND> RE
ENTER A CORNER OF RECTANGLE> 10,10  <CR>
ENTER NEXT CORNER OF RECTANGLE> 15,15 <CR>
```

3. Draw a circle.

```
ENTER A COMMAND >  C2  <CR>
ENTER CENTER OF CIRCLE > 12,6  <CR>
ENTER A POINT ON CIRCLE > 14,6  <CR>
```

4. Copy the circle.

```
ENTER A COMMAND >  OC
ENTER A POINT ON THE OBJECT TO COPY > (Select a point on the perimeter of the
circle with the screen cursor.)
ENTER A REFERENCE POINT >  SC
CLOSEST POINT TO > (Select the circle center with the screen cursor.)
ENTER NEW REFERENCE POINT OR OFFSET > 18,9  <CR>
ENTER NUMBER OF COPIES (1-100) > 4  <CR>
```

The circle is copied.

5. Copy the rectangle and the original circle.

```
ENTER A COMMAND >  WC
PLACE WINDOW (Select two points on the screen to form a single window around the
rectangle and the original circle.)
ENTER REFERENCE POINT >  10,10 <CR>
ENTER NEW REFERENCE POINT OR OFFSET >  1,10  <CR>
ENTER NUMBER OF COPIES (1-99) > 1  <CR>
```

The objects are copied directly to the left of the original objects.

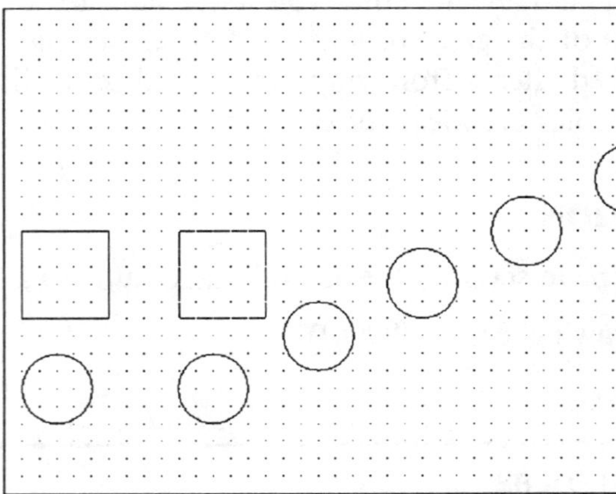

6. Quit the drawing without saving.

7. Turn to Module 54 to continue the learning sequence.

Module 48
OBJECT ERASE/WINDOW ERASE

DESCRIPTION

The erase commands allow objects to be removed from your drawing. Generic CADD offers two types, depending upon whether you want to erase a single item or several items. Each is described below, with the two-letter command in parentheses.

OBJECT ERASE (OE) Allows erasing of any single object each time the command is entered.

WINDOW ERASE (WE) Allows erasing of all objects completely within a windowed area that you define.

APPLICATIONS

The erase commands allow easy editing of objects already placed on your drawing. A single item is easily deleted with the OBJECT ERASE command, while a number of items can be quickly deleted all at once with WINDOW ERASE.

TYPICAL OPERATION

In this session you create several objects, then erase them.

1. Start a new drawing called "OWERASE."

2. Draw three rectngles.

```
ENTER A COMMAND > RE
ENTER A CORNER OF RECTANGLE > 4,4   <CR>
ENTER NEXT CORNER OF RECTANGLE > 12,12  <CR>
ENTER A COMMAND > RE
ENTER A CORNER OF RECTANGLE > 5,6   <CR>
ENTER NEXT CORNER OF RECTANGLE > 15,14  <CR>
ENTER A COMMAND > RE
ENTER A CORNER OF RECTANGLE > 10,10  <CR>
ENTER NEXT CORNER OF RECTANGLE > 16,25 <CR>
```

3. Draw a circle.

```
ENTER A COMMAND>  C2
ENTER CENTER OF CIRCLE>  25,20  <CR>
ENTER A POINT ON CIRCLE>  25,15 <CR>
```

4. Draw a series of straight lines.

```
ENTER A COMMAND>  L1
ENTER START POINT> >  5,5  <CR>
ENTER NEXT POINT>  10,8  <CR>
ENTER NEXT POINT>  7,15  <CR>
ENTER NEXT POINT>  15,20  <CR>
ENTER NEXT POINT>  20,10  <CR>
ENTER NEXT POINT>  PU
```

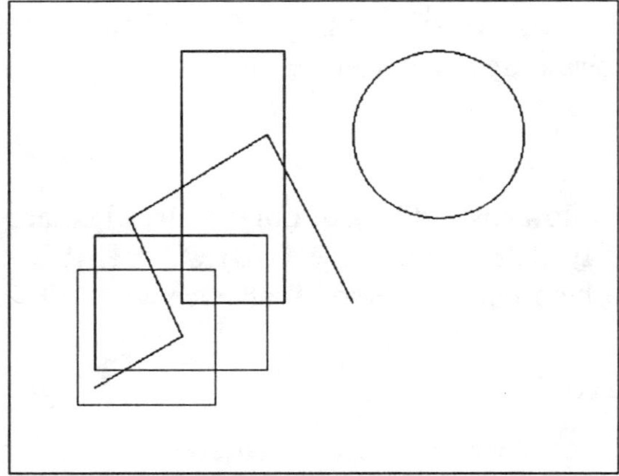

5. Erase a rectangle segment.

NOTE

A rectangle is actually four line segments. When OBJECT
ERASE is used, only one segment is deleted.

```
ENTER A COMMAND>  OE
ENTER A POINT ON THE OBJECT TO ERASE>  4,5  <CR>
```

6. Erase a group of objects.

> ENTER A COMMAND > **WE**

NOTE

Only those objects completely and totally within the window are erased.

> PLACE WINDOW (Select two diagonal points on the screen to encompass several of the objects drawn.)

Your drawing should look similar to this.

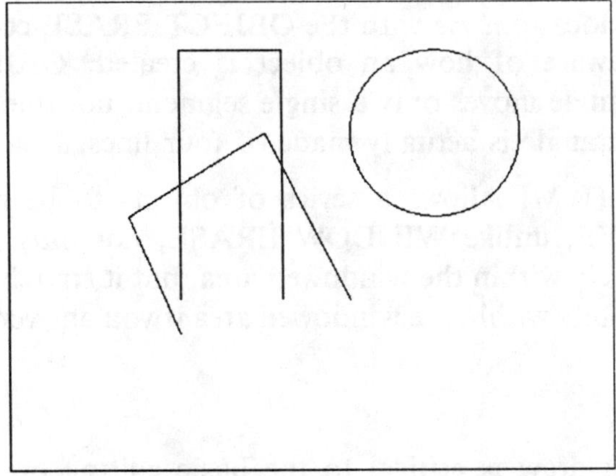

7. Quit the drawing without saving.

8. Turn to Module 69 to continue the learning sequence.

Module 49
OBJECT MOVE/WINDOW MOVE

DESCRIPTION

The move commands allow you to move a single object or a series of objects on
the screen. You must identify what you want to move and where you want the
new position to be. The two available options for moving are described below,
with the corresponding two-letter command in parentheses.

OBJECT MOVE (OM) Allows a single object to be identified and moved to a
new location. As with the OBJECT ERASE command, you must
be aware of how an object is created. OBJECT MOVE to a
rectangle moves only a single segment, not the entire rectangle, as
a rectangle is actually made of four lines.

WINDOW MOVE (WM) Allows a series of objects to be moved. WINDOW
MOVE, unlike WINDOW ERASE, not only moves the objects
entirely within the windowed area, but it stretches all lines that are
partially within the windowed area if you answer yes at the prompt.

APPLICATIONS

Moving objects you draw is critical to the basic editing process of creating a
drawing. Generic CADD allows movement of a single object as well as a group
of objects. The stretch capability in the WINDOW MOVE option gives even
greater flexibility by allowing easy change of the size of an object.

TYPICAL OPERATION

In this activity you draw several objects, then move and stretch them.

1. Start a new drawing called "MOVE."

2. Draw a rectangle.

```
ENTER A COMMAND> RE
ENTER A CORNER OF RECTANGLE> 5,6  <CR>
ENTER NEXT CORNER OF RECTANGLE> 15,10  <CR>
```

3. Draw a circle.

```
ENTER A COMMAND >  C2  <CR>
ENTER CENTER OF CIRCLE >  20,15 <CR>
ENTER A POINT ON CIRCLE >  25,15  <CR>
```

4. Draw a line series.

```
ENTER A COMMAND >  L1
ENTER START POINT > >  25,5  <CR>
ENTER NEXT POINT >  25,8  <CR>
ENTER NEXT POINT >  30,8  <CR>
ENTER NEXT POINT >  30,5  <CR>
ENTER NEXT POINT >  35,5  <CR>
ENTER NEXT POINT >  35,1  <CR>
ENTER NEXT POINT >  20,1  <CR>
ENTER NEXT POINT >  20,5  <CR>
ENTER NEXT POINT >  25,5  <CR>
ENTER NEXT POINT >  PU
```

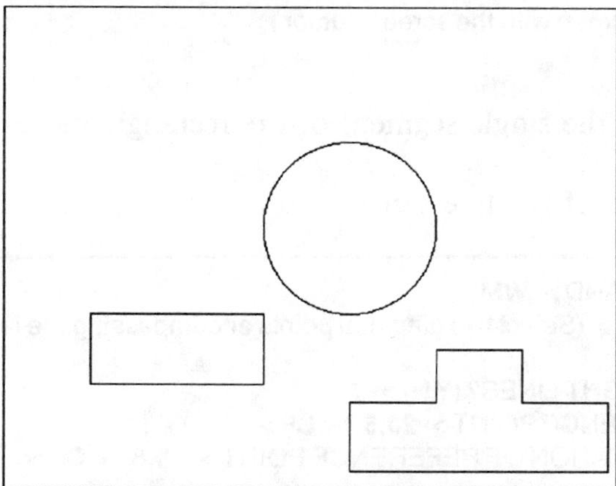

5. Move the circle.

```
ENTER A COMMAND >  OM
ENTER POINT ON THE OBJECT TO MOVE > 25,15  <CR>
ENTER A REFERENCE POINT >  20,15  <CR>
ENTER NEW REFERENCE POINT OR OFFSET >  10,15  <CR>
```

6. Move the rectangle.

ENTER A COMMAND > **WM**
PLACE WINDOW > (Select two diagonal points to encompass the rectangle with a window.)
STRETCH STRAIGHT LINES?(Y,N) > **N**
ENTER A REFERENCE POINT > **15,10** **<CR>**
ENTER NEW LOCATION OF REFERENCE POINT > (Pull screen cursor to upper right corner of drawing screen.)

Note the rubber banding line following your cursor.

7. Move a segment of the rectangle.

ENTER A COMMAND > **OM**
ENTER A POINT ON THE OBJECT TO MOVE > (Select the top segment of the rectangle with the screen cursor.)
ENTER A REFERENCE POINT > **SC** (Now select the upper left corner of the rectangle and the cursor will snap to the corner.)
ENTER NEW REFERENCE POINT OR OFFSET > (Select a point in the upper left corner of your drawing screen with the screen cursor.)

Note that only the single segment of the rectangle moves.

8. Move a portion of the line series.

ENTER A COMMAND > **WM**
PLACE WINDOW > (Select two diagonal points encompassing the left end of the line series.)
STRETCH STRAIGHT LINES? (Y,N) > **Y**
ENTER A REFERENCE POINT > **20,5** **<CR>**
ENTER NEW LOCATION OF REFERENCE POINT > **15,8** **<CR>**

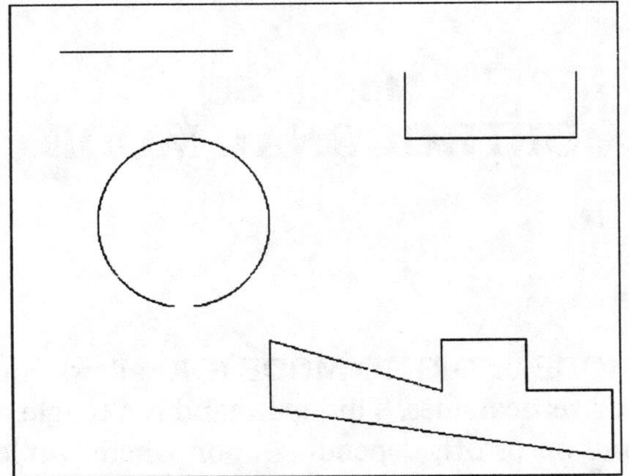

9. Quit the drawing without saving.

10. Turn to Module 47 to continue the learning sequence.

Module 50
ORTHOGONAL MODE

DESCRIPTION

ORTHOGONAL MODE or ORTHO MODE (OR) allows you to draw perfectly straight horizontal or vertical lines. This command is a toggle, with each selection turning the command on or off, depending upon where you left it last.

APPLICATIONS

With the resolution of your screen, it is impossible to tell whether you are drawing straight horizontal or vertical lines. What may look straight on the screen may actually be at a slight angle if ORTHO MODE is not selected. This command allows you fast entry of your linework, yet assures straight horizontal or vertical lines.

When a straight line is drawn, the line may not go to the point selected with the screen cursor. Instead, the point selected will align horizontally or vertically with the point you are drawing from. Thus, the lines are not only straight horizontally or vertically, but all corners are 90 degrees. Since ORTHO is a toggle, it can be used while in the midst of a command without disturbing the command itself.

TYPICAL OPERATION

In this exercise you draw a series of lines with the ORTHO MODE on and off.

1. Start Generic CADD. Type **CADD** and press **Return** at the DOS prompt. Press **Return** again at the Generic CADD title page.

2. Start a new drawing called "ORTHO."

```
ENTER A DRAWING FILE NAME >  ORTHO   <CR>
IS THIS A NEW DRAWING (Y,N) >  Y
```

3. Draw the line series to approximate those in the drawing.

```
ENTER A COMMAND >  L1
```

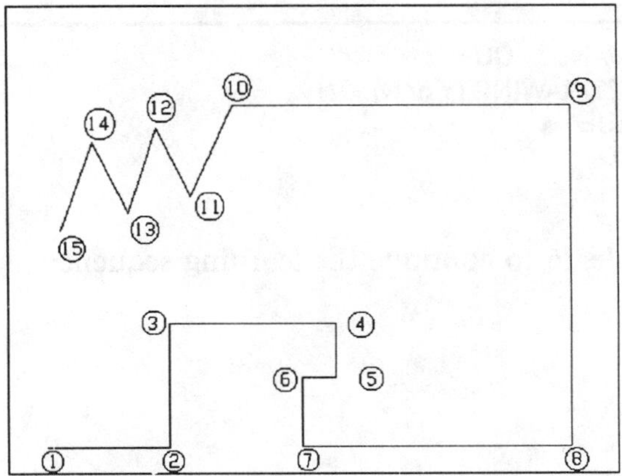

4. Toggle the **ORTHO MODE** on.

> ENTER START POINT > > **OR**
> ORTHO MODE IS ON

5. Now draw the lines.

> ENTER A COMMAND > (Select a point to begin in the lower left corner of the screen.)
> ENTER NEXT POINT > (Select each of the numbered points 2 through 11 on the screen
> to approximate the drawing.)

6. Toggle **ORTHO MODE** off to draw the angled lines and complete the
drawing.

> ENTER NEXT POINT > **OR**
> ORTHO MODE IS OFF

7. As the cursor moves on the screen, note that it is still connected to the lines
series at point 11.

> ENTER A COMMAND > (Select points 12 through 15 on the screen.)
> ENTER NEXT POINT > **PU**

8. Quit the drawing without saving.

```
ENTER A COMMAND > QU
SAVE CURRENT DRAWING (Y or N) > N
"C" TO CONTINUE
"Q" TO QUIT > Q
```

9. Turn to Module 76 to continue the learning sequence.

Module 51
PACK DATA

DESCRIPTION

PACK DATA (PD) removes erased objects from memory. As objects are erased from your drawing, Generic CADD removes them from the drawing itself, but not from the memory of your computer. This approach saves time when erasing and also means you can use the UNERASE command to bring back selected objects to the screen as needed. When the memory is packed, the resulting space is then available for new data you add to your drawing, and UNERASE does not bring back previously erased objects to the screen. Generic CADD also runs faster after packing. To use, select PD. The memory is then packed and you can continue with your drawing. The commands DRAWING LOAD, DRAWING SAVE, and FONT SELECT automatically pack the memory.

APPLICATIONS

PACK DATA is used primarily for large, complex drawings to increase the speed of Generic CADD, clearing the memory for additional new data.

TYPICAL OPERATION

As this command is self explanatory, no practice activity is included.

Turn to Module 41 to continue the learning sequence.

Module 52
PEN UP

DESCRIPTION

The PEN UP (PU) command allows you to stop drawing single or double lines, thus freeing Generic CADD to accept another command entry.

APPLICATIONS

Similar to picking up the pen when drawing lines, PEN UP stops the drawing line and allows entry of another command. If you are drawing single lines and issue a PEN UP command, the line will be stopped. No rubber band will follow your cursor. You are free to draw more lines or issue a different command. The PEN UP command may also be invoked by pressing Esc.

TYPICAL OPERATION

In this exercise you draw several sets of lines, using PEN UP between each series.

1. Start Generic CADD. Type **CADD** and press **Return** at the DOS prompt. Press **Return** at the Generic CADD title page.

2. Start a new drawing called "PENUP."

```
ENTER A DRAWING FILE NAME> PENUP <CR>
IS THIS A NEW DRAWING (Y,N)> Y
```

3. Draw the first group of lines.

```
ENTER A COMMAND> L1
ENTER START POINT>> 2,2  <CR>
ENTER NEXT POINT> 8,20  <CR>
ENTER NEXT POINT>15,5  <CR>
ENTER NEXT POINT> PU
```

4. Draw another series of lines.

```
ENTER A COMMAND> L1
ENTER START POINT>> 22,10  <CR>
ENTER NEXT POINT> 30,10  <CR>
ENTER NEXT POINT> 30,25  <CR>
ENTER NEXT POINT> PU
```

Now two distinct groups of lines are on the screen.

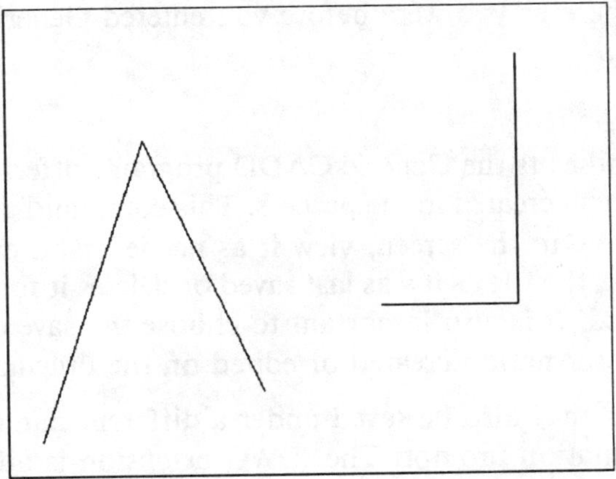

5. Quit Generic CADD without saving the drawing.

```
ENTER A COMMAND> QU
SAVE CURRENT DRAWING (Y or N)> N
"C" TO CONTINUE
"Q" TO QUIT> Q
```

6. Turn to Module 64 to continue the learning sequence.

Module 53
QUIT

DESCRIPTION

The QUIT (QU) command leaves the Generic CADD program and returns to the DOS prompt or wherever you were before you entered Generic CADD.

APPLICATIONS

The QUIT command exits the Generic CADD program, offering the opportunity to save the drawing you created in the process. This command gives you the option to bring up a drawing to the screen, view it as needed, and exit without saving. This action preserves the file as it was last saved or deletes it forever if the drawing had never been saved. It is also important to choose the save option if you want the latest graphic information created or edited on the drawing to be saved.

The current drawing may also be saved under a different name. Type the desired name at the confirmation prompt. The .DWG extension is added automatically by Generic CADD.

Unless directed otherwise, Generic CADD saves the drawing to the current path for drawing files. To chose another location, add the drive and the desired directory in addition to the file name.

TYPICAL OPERATION

In this operation you save the SAMPLE drawing, then you use the QUIT command to exit Generic CADD. Begin with SAMPLE.DWG on your screen from Module 2.

1. Respond to the following prompts to save the drawing and quit Generic CADD.

```
ENTER A COMMAND >  QU
SAVE CURRENT DRAWING (Y or N) >  Y
SAVE FILE: (SAMPLE.DWG) >  <CR>
FILE EXISTS, OVERWRITE OR RENAME OLD FILE TO *.BAK (O,R) > O   <CR>
"C" TO CONTINUE
"Q" TO QUIT >  Q
```

You are now at the same location from which you entered Generic CADD.

2. Turn to Module 26 to continue the learning sequence.

Module 54
RADIAL COPY

DESCRIPTION

RADIAL COPY (RC) allows you to copy a windowed object into a circular pattern. An axis or reference point is specified, together with the degree span and the number of copies desired. At the prompt, three options for entering the angle are available. You can enter the desired angle if known; type A for angle to define the angle on the screen with a basepoint and a ray point; or type V for vertex to define the angle on the screen with a basepoint and two ray points. Angles are measured from the horizontal position in a counterclockwise rotation, beginning with the first ray selected and ending with the second ray selected. The copies can be duplicated on only a portion of the circle if desired. As the windowed item is copied radially, the item rotates around the selected axis.

APPLICATIONS

Copies in a circular pattern are used in a variety of ways, from copying chairs around a table, to locating gear teeth around a wheel and placing seats in a curving theater plan.

TYPICAL OPERATION

In this activity you draw a table and place the chairs around the perimeter.

1. Start a new drawing called "RCOPY."

2. Draw a circle.

```
ENTER A COMMAND >  C2
ENTER CENTER OF CIRCLE >  18,12   <CR>
ENTER A POINT ON CIRCLE >  18,16   <CR>
```

3. Draw a chair.

```
ENTER A COMMAND> RE
ENTER A CORNER OF RECTANGLE> 17,17  <CR>
ENTER NEXT CORNER OF RECTANGLE> 19,19  <CR>
```

4. Copy the chair around the table by selecting the center of the table as the axis.

```
ENTER A COMMAND> RC
PLACE WINDOW> (Use the screen cursor to place a window around the chair.)
ENTER AN AXIS POINT> 18,12  <CR>
ENTER TOTAL DEGREES TO SPAN> 360  <CR>
```

NOTE

The number of items in the span includes the original item that you select to copy.

```
ENTER NUMBER OF ITEMS IN SPAN> 6  <CR>
```

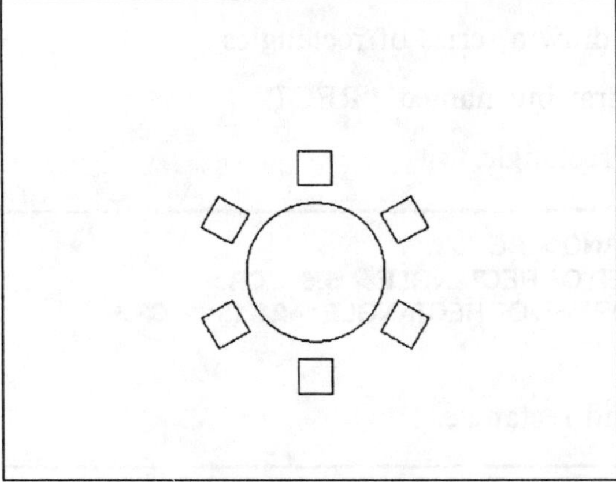

5. Quit the drawing without saving.

6. Turn to Module 72 to continue the learning sequence.

Module 55
RECTANGLE

DESCRIPTION

RECTANGLE (RE) allows a rectangle to be drawn by specification of two diagonal points. Faster than drawing four separate lines, RECTANGLE assures that opposite sides are parallel and all corners are 90 degrees.

APPLICATIONS

Created as a basic drawing element, RECTANGLE draws simple items such as furniture or room number references, as well as more complex objects, such as entire rooms and various schedules. Note that each rectangle is actually four STRAIGHT LINES, and editing takes place accordingly.

TYPICAL OPERATION

In this exercise you draw a series of rectangles.

1. Begin a new drawing named "RECT."

2. Draw the first rectangle.

```
ENTER A COMMAND> RE
ENTER A CORNER OF RECTANGLE> 5,6 <CR>
ENTER NEXT CORNER OF RECTANGLE> 21,15  <CR>
```

3. Draw the second rectangle.

```
ENTER A RECTANGLE> RE
ENTER A CORNER OF RECTANGLE> 15,15  <CR>
ENTER NEXT CORNER OF RECTANGLE> 28,20  <CR>
```

The drawing should look like this.

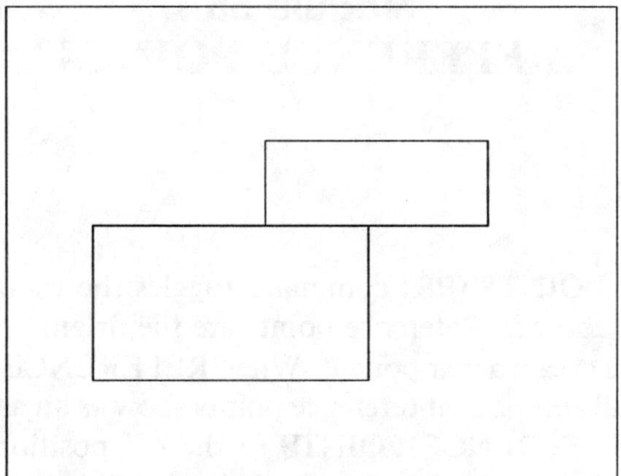

4. Quit the drawing without saving.

5. Turn to Module 57 to continue the learning sequence.

Module 56
REFERENCE POINTS

DESCRIPTION

The REFERENCE POINTS (PR) command toggles the visibility of component reference points on and off. Reference points are the origin or handle points that you define when you create a component. When REFERENCE POINTS is toggled to the on position, all component reference points show as an asterisk. The Generic CADD default is REFERENCE POINTS to the off position. Reference points never plot, so you do not need to toggle their visibility to off before plotting. After toggling the command to on or off, redraw the screen to see the up-to-date status of the reference points' visibility. An asterisk always appears at the drawing origin if REFERENCE POINTS is toggled to the on position.

APPLICATIONS

When creating a drawing using a number of components, viewing the reference points is helpful for aligning other components or objects and to refresh your memory of how a component was originally created. The visibility of a reference point also reveals whether an object is a component or a series of objects, perhaps an image. Yet, if the asterisks are bothersome or tend to mask parts of your drawing, they can be visually suppressed.

TYPICAL OPERATION

In this exercise you load a drawing with components and toggle REFERENCE POINTS on and off.

1. Load the "COMP.DWG" drawing you created in Module 10.

2. Toggle the reference points to the on position.

```
ENTER A COMMAND > PR
DISPLAY REFERENCE POINTS IS ON
```

NOTE

The screen may also be refreshed using any of the zoom or pan commands.

```
ENTER A COMMAND > RD
```

The reference points are visible only on true components.

3. Toggle the reference points to the off position.

```
ENTER A COMMAND > PR
DISPLAY REFERENCE POINTS IS OFF
ENTER A COMMAND > RD
```

4. Quit the drawing without saving.

5. Turn to Module 34 to continue the learning sequence.

Module 57
REGULAR POLYGON

DESCRIPTION

REGULAR POLYGON (RP) creates an equal sided and equal angled geometric figure. Specification of the center, a vertex point, and the total number of sides is all that is required.

The minimum number of sides specified is three and the maximum number of sides is 255. This constraint never presents a problem, since a polygon approaching 255 sides looks like a circle!

APPLICATIONS

Polygons are used in parts design, as well as for various reference symbols in the architectural discipline. As with the RECTANGLE command, Generic CADD offers an easy way to create a polygon without drawing each separate line segment individually.

TYPICAL OPERATION

In this activity you draw two polygons of six sides, each with a different rotation.

1. Start a new drawing called "POLY."

2. Draw the first polygon.

```
ENTER A COMMAND>  RP
ENTER THE CENTER OF POLYGON>  20,15  <CR>
ENTER A POINT ON POLYGON>  25,15  <CR>
```

The second point selected is a vertex of the polygon. Note also that this vertex point determines the rotation angle of the polygon.

```
ENTER THE NUMBER OF SIDES>  6  <CR>
```

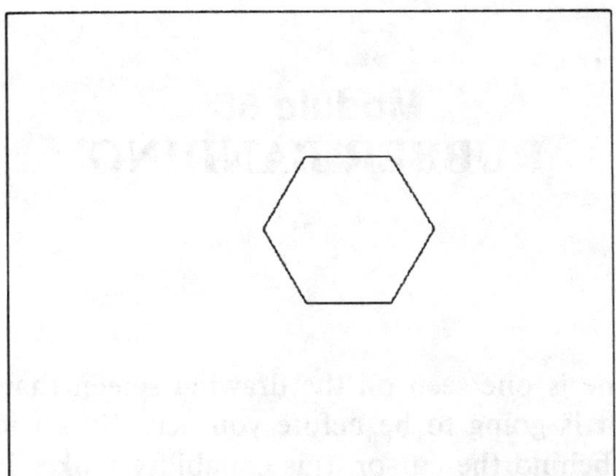

3. Draw an additional polygon at a different rotation.

```
ENTER A COMMAND > RP
ENTER THE CENTER OF POLYGON > 8,8   <CR>
ENTER A POINT ON POLYGON > 12,6   <CR>
ENTER THE NUMBER OF SIDES > 6   <CR>
```

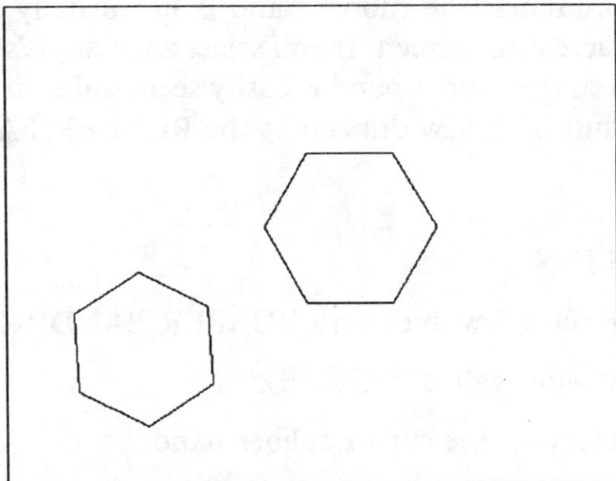

4. Quit the drawing without saving.

5. Turn to Module 3 to continue the learning sequence.

Module 58
RUBBER BANDING

DESCRIPTION

A rubber banded line is one seen on the drawing screen that allows you to see where your endpoint is going to be before you actually set it down. Similar to dragging a shadow behind the cursor, this capability makes it easier to visually select any point correctly the first time.

APPLICATIONS

A rubber banded line makes the transition to computer drafting easier. Whether or not you work with the rubber band feature is entirely up to you. This command is a toggle, with each RB turning the rubber band feature on or off. If RUBBER BAND is off, the commands using the feature all work exactly the same, except there is no rubber band attached to the screen cursor. When you enter a rectangle, for example, by coordinates, the rubber band is not usually seen, as the screen cursor is not moved across the screen. If you select a rectangle's two points visually on the screen, however, the rubber band is easily seen, unless it is toggled off. The Generic CADD default on a new drawing is the RUBBER BAND toggled to the on position.

TYPICAL OPERATION

In this activity you draw a few lines with RUBBER BANDING both on and off.

1. Start a new drawing called "RBAND."

2. Draw a line, observing the cursor rubber band.

```
ENTER A COMMAND> L1
ENTER START POINT> > 2.2 <CR>
ENTER NEXT POINT> (Move the cursor away form the previously selected point and
observe the rubber banding line attached to the cursor.) 8,8  <CR>
ENTER NEXT POINT> PU
```

3. Toggle off the RUBBER BAND feature and draw another line.

```
ENTER A COMMAND > RB
RUBBER BANDING IS OFF
ENTER A COMMAND > L1
ENTER START POINT > > 8,4  <CR>
ENTER NEXT POINT > (Move the cursor away form the previously selected point and
observe that the rubber banding line is not shown.) 12,8  <CR>
ENTER NEXT POINT > PU
```

NOTE

Even with the rubber banding option off, the line is drawn
correctly.

4. Quit the drawing without saving.

5. Turn to Module 28 to continue the learning sequence.

Module 59
SCREEN FLIP

DESCRIPTION

SCREEN FLIP (SF) allows you to temporarily replace the drawing screen with a text screen, which provides additional information about the status of the drawing. Generic CADD contains a number of information screens which need a full screen to display. You can send any information screen to your printer by selecting the Shift and Print Screen keys on your keyboard. Upon selection of SCREEN FLIP a menu appears. Each option and corresponding selection number is described below:

1) DISPLAY DRAWING STATUS displays a greater variety of information about the current drawing than is available on the drawing screen prompt line. The information includes the drawing name; current zoom value; the number of points, line, text characters, and components; available memory; distance between the basepoint and the origin; and current settings for the line type, text color, display color, and cursor color. Also displayed is the tolerance setting; current layer; trace mode, ortho mode, and batch mode toggle settings; current grid size, grid display, and grid snap mode; and the current path settings for drawings, fonts, and components. Select Return to return to the SCREEN FLIP menu.

2) DISPLAY DIRECTORY FILES displays a list of all the drawing files in the default drawing path. If you need to see a list of files in another location, enter the complete path location, including the drive, directory, subdirectory, file name, and extension. Note that if the filename is designated by the DOS wildcard, the asterisk (*), all files with the designated extension are listed. If the directory is larger than it takes to display on a single screen, you must select <CR> to see each additional page. Select <Esc> to return to the SCREEN FLIP menu.

3) LIST OBJECTS IN CURRENT VIEW displays a list of all the objects currently in the screen view, along with each object's linetype, width, color, and layer. If the list is longer than a single screen view, select

<CR> to view each additional page. Select <Esc> to return to the SCREEN FLIP menu.

4) SHOW LAYER STATUS shows all layers with data, then displays a list of the currently viewed layers. After selecting SHOW LAYER STATUS and reviewing the layers with data, select <CR> to view the layers currently displayed or select <Esc> to return to the SCREEN FLIP menu.

5) LIST NAMED VIEWS displays a list of the views that have been saved with the NAME VIEW (NV) command. If the list is longer than a single screen view, select <CR> to view each additional page. Select <Esc> to return to the SCREEN FLIP menu.

6) RETURN TO DRAWING removes the text screen menu from view and takes you back to the drawing on the drawing screen.

APPLICATIONS

SCREEN FLIP allows you to check the status of your drawing quickly and easily from a single source. You can run a check of drawings in a specified location without exiting Generic CADD to run a directory using DOS. A listing of all named views is helpful if you are working on a drawing that someone else created. The drawing status list is important for refreshing your memory of a a drawing that you have not worked on for sometime. The layer status is useful on large drawings with many layers.

TYPICAL OPERATION

In this activity, you load the SAMPLE.DWG and use the SCREEN FLIP command to display more information about the drawing.

1. Load the SAMPLE.DWG drawing you created in Module 2.

2. Select the SCREEN FLIP command.

```
ENTER A COMMAND> SF
```

```
******  G E N E R I C  ---  C A D D  ******

              LEVEL 3  VER. 1.11




     1)  DISPLAY DRAWING STATUS
     2)  DISPLAY DIRECTORY FILES
     3)  LIST OBJECTS IN CURRENT VIEW
     4)  SHOW LAYER STATUS
     5)  LIST NAMED VIEWS
     6)  RETURN TO DRAWING



         ENTER SELECTION >
```

3. Display information about the drawing status.

```
ENTER A SELECTION > 1
```

```
******  G E N E R I C  ---  C A D D  ******

          D R A W I N G   S T A T U S


DRAWING NAME IS:  SAMPLE  ,  AT ZOOM:   34.903521
POINTS:    928 , LINES:   259 , CHARACTERS:   22 , COMPONENTS:     0
MEMORY AVAILABLE:   135230 MEMORY USED:     9280 MEMORY REMAINING:  125950
BASE POINT IS:     0.000000       0.000000 in FROM DRAWING ORIGIN.

LINE COLOR IS: 1, LINE TYPE IS: 0, TEXT COLOR IS: 1
DISPLAY COLOR IS: 11, CURSOR COLOR IS:

TOLERANCE IS:  0.2500      CURRENT LAYER IS:    0
TRACE MODE IS: OFF,  ORTHO MODE IS: OFF,  BATCH MODE IS: OFF
GRID SIZE IS:  1.0000 , GRID DISPLAY IS: OFF, GRID SNAP IS: OFF

PATH FOR DRAWING FILES:    CURRENT DRIVE & DIRECTORY
PATH FOR FONT FILES:    CURRENT DRIVE & DIRECTORY
PATH FOR COMPONENT FILES: CURRENT DRIVE & DIRECTORY

HIT RETURN TO EXIT >
```

4. Return to the SCREEN FLIP menu.

```
HIT RETURN TO EXIT >  < CR  >
```

5. Display a list of all the files in the current default directory. Your particular list will vary from the listing below.

```
ENTER SELECTION> 2
Please enter the (drive:/directory/*.EXT ) of the files to be listed [*.dwg] <CR>
```

```
******  G E N E R I C  ---  C A D D  ******

              LEVEL 3  VER. 1.11

CIRCLE.DWG    ZOOM5.DWG    CHANGE2.DWG    MOVEPT.DWG
RECT.DWG      ZOOM6.DWG    ELLIPSE.DWG    MOVEPT1.DWG
POLY.DWG      ZOOM7.DWG    CHANGE.DWG     BREAK.DWG
SAMPLE.DWG    LAYER1.DWG   COMP1.DWG      BREAK1.DWG
TEXT.DWG      LOAD2.DWG    COMP2.DWG      OWERASE.DWG
ARC.DWG       PENUP.DWG    SNAPS.DWG      OWERASE1.DWG
ZOOM.DWG      L1.DWG       LINES.DWG      UNERASE.DWG
LOAD.DWG      MR.DWG       CONPT.DWG      UNERASE1.DWG
ZOOM2.DWG     UNITS.DWG    POINT.DWG      OWMOVE1.DWG
ZOOM1.DWG     GRIDS.DWG    LAST.DWG       OWMOVE.DWG
ORTHO.DWG     DWGPATH.DWG  STDPT.DWG      COPY.DWG
LAYER.DWG     LAYER2.DWG   CURVES.DWG     RCOPY.DWG
ZOOM3.DWG     LAYER3.DWG   BEZIER.DWG     MIRROR.DWG
ZOOM4.DWG     LAYER4.DWG   BEZIER1.DWG    ROTATE.DWG

HIT RETURN TO CONTINUE OR [ESC] TO EXIT >
```

6. Return to the SCREEN FLIP menu.

```
HIT RETURN TO CONTINUE OR [ESC] TO EXIT >  <ESC>
```

7. View the objects in the current drawing view.

```
ENTER SELECTION> 3
```

```
******  G E N E R I C  ---  C A D D  ******

           LIST OBJECTS IN CURRENT VIEW

STRAIGHT LINE,  TYPE:  0, WIDTH:  0, COLOR:  1, LAYER:  0
STRAIGHT LINE,  TYPE:  0, WIDTH:  0, COLOR:  1, LAYER:  0
STRAIGHT LINE,  TYPE:  0, WIDTH:  0, COLOR:  1, LAYER:  0
STRAIGHT LINE,  TYPE:  0, WIDTH:  0, COLOR:  1, LAYER:  0
STRAIGHT LINE,  TYPE:  0, WIDTH:  0, COLOR:  1, LAYER:  0
STRAIGHT LINE,  TYPE:  0, WIDTH:  0, COLOR:  1, LAYER:  0
STRAIGHT LINE,  TYPE:  0, WIDTH:  0, COLOR:  1, LAYER:  0
STRAIGHT LINE,  TYPE:  0, WIDTH:  0, COLOR:  1, LAYER:  0
STRAIGHT LINE,  TYPE:  0, WIDTH:  0, COLOR:  1, LAYER:  0
STRAIGHT LINE,  TYPE:  0, WIDTH:  0, COLOR:  1, LAYER:  0
STRAIGHT LINE,  TYPE:  0, WIDTH:  0, COLOR:  1, LAYER:  0
STRAIGHT LINE,  TYPE:  0, WIDTH:  0, COLOR:  1, LAYER:  0
STRAIGHT LINE,  TYPE:  0, WIDTH:  0, COLOR:  1, LAYER:  0
STRAIGHT LINE,  TYPE:  0, WIDTH:  0, COLOR:  1, LAYER:  0

HIT RETURN TO CONTINUE OR [ESC] TO EXIT >
```

8. Press Return to continue through the several page listing.

```
HIT RETURN TO CONTINUE OR [ESC] TO EXIT >  <CR>
HIT RETURN TO CONTINUE OR [ESC] TO EXIT >  <CR>
HIT RETURN TO CONTINUE OR [ESC] TO EXIT >  <CR>
HIT RETURN TO CONTINUE OR [ESC] TO EXIT >  <CR>
HIT RETURN TO CONTINUE OR [ESC] TO EXIT >  <CR>
HIT RETURN TO CONTINUE OR [ESC] TO EXIT >  <CR>
HIT RETURN TO CONTINUE OR [ESC] TO EXIT >  <CR>
HIT RETURN TO CONTINUE OR [ESC] TO EXIT >  <CR>
HIT RETURN TO CONTINUE OR [ESC] TO EXIT >  <CR>
HIT RETURN TO CONTINUE OR [ESC] TO EXIT >  <CR>
HIT RETURN TO CONTINUE OR [ESC] TO EXIT >  <CR>
HIT RETURN TO CONTINUE OR [ESC] TO EXIT >  <CR>
```

9. Show the layer status.

```
ENTER SELECTION >  4
```

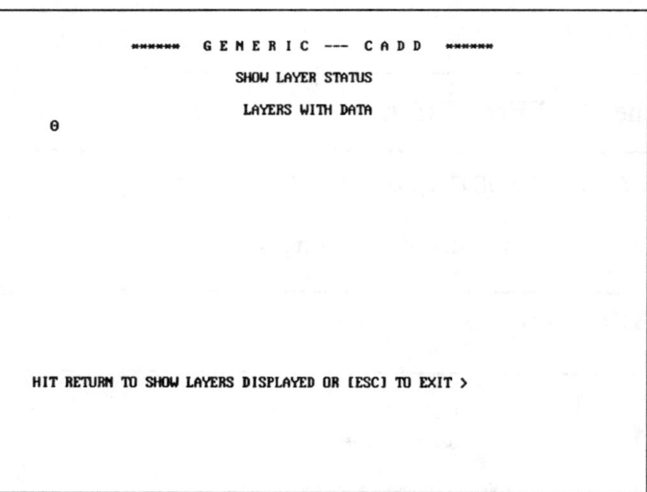

10. Continue to the page of displayed layers.

```
HIT RETURN TO SHOW LAYERS DISPLAYED OR [ESC] TO EXIT >  <CR>
```

```
****** G E N E R I C  ---  C A D D  ******

               SHOW LAYER STATUS

                 LAYERS DISPLAYED
 0  15  30  45  60  75  90 105 120 135 150 165 180 195 210 225 240 255
 1  16  31  46  61  76  91 106 121 136 151 166 181 196 211 226 241
 2  17  32  47  62  77  92 107 122 137 152 167 182 197 212 227 242
 3  18  33  48  63  78  93 108 123 138 153 168 183 198 213 228 243
 4  19  34  49  64  79  94 109 124 139 154 169 184 199 214 229 244
 5  20  35  50  65  80  95 110 125 140 155 170 185 200 215 230 245
 6  21  36  51  66  81  96 111 126 141 156 171 186 201 216 231 246
 7  22  37  52  67  82  97 112 127 142 157 172 187 202 217 232 247
 8  23  38  53  68  83  98 113 128 143 158 173 188 203 218 233 248
 9  24  39  54  69  84  99 114 129 144 159 174 189 204 219 234 249
10  25  40  55  70  85 100 115 130 145 160 175 190 205 220 235 250
11  26  41  56  71  86 101 116 131 146 161 176 191 206 221 236 251
12  27  42  57  72  87 102 117 132 147 162 177 192 207 222 237 252
13  28  43  58  73  88 103 118 133 148 163 178 193 208 223 238 253
14  29  44  59  74  89 104 119 134 149 164 179 194 209 224 239 254

HIT RETURN OR [ESC] TO EXIT > LAYED OR [ESC] TO EXIT >
```

11. Return to the SCREEN FLIP menu.

```
HIT RETURN OR [ESC] TO EXIT >  <ESC>
```

12. List the named views.

```
ENTER SELECTION > 5
```

```
****** G E N E R I C  ---  C A D D  ******
              LIST NAMED VIEWS   1.11




















        HIT RETURN TO CONTINUE OR [ESC] TO EXIT >
```

There are no views named at this time.

13. Return to the SCREEN FLIP menu.

HIT RETURN TO CONTINUE OR [ESC] TO EXIT > <**ESC**>

14. Return to the drawing screen.

ENTER SELECTION > **6**

15. Quit the drawing without saving.

16. This is the last module in the learning sequence.

Module 60
SNAPS

DESCRIPTION

Snaps are a series of commands which allow you to be extremely accurate in the placement of points on your drawing. With snaps, your input is extremely fast and Generic CADD makes sure your lines are going exactly where you want them. The following list exlains the available snap options. Each two-letter command is in parentheses.

CLOSEST POINT (SC) Allows selection of a new point by locating it in the same place as an existing point. Used while drawing or editing, SNAP CLOSEST POINT overrides any other snap mode currently activated. The layer of the point you snap to must be turned on.

NEAREST LINE (NL) Allows selection of a point on a line. NEAREST LINE SNAP insures that you are actually touching the object you want. Similar to CLOSEST POINT, this command selects any point on a line. NEAREST LINE can be used when Generic CADD asks for a point.

INTERSECTION (SI) Allows selection of the common crossing point of any two entities, such as lines, circles, or arcs. This common point is an intersection. INTERSECTION SNAP can be used when Generic CADD asks for a point.

MIDPOINT (SM) Allows selection of the exact midpoint of an existing line. This command can be used when Generic CADD asks for a point.

PARALLEL (SA) Allows you to draw lines parallel to existing lines. Used when Generic CADD asks for the endpoint of a straight line, this command can also be used when beginning to draw a 3-point arc or a 2-point circle.

PERPENDICULAR (SP) Allows you to draw a line perpendicular to an existing line. This command can be used when Generic CADD asks for the endpoint of a straight line.

ARC CENTER (SN) Allows selection of the center of an existing circle or arc. This command can be used when Generic CADD asks for a point to be selected on the drawing screen.

ARC TANGENT (SX) Allows selection of a point tangent to an existing arc or circle. This command can be used when Generic CADD asks for the endpoint of a straight line.

NEAREST POINT (NP) Allows selection of a point by snapping to an existing point. This command is similar to CLOSEST POINT except that selection of the closest point is automatic rather than waiting for you to select the point. NEAREST POINT overrides any other currently activated snap command. This command can also be activated by pressing the third mouse button if you are using a three-button mouse.

COMPONENT SNAPS (GC) Allows you to use the snap commands on the points which are within a component. Refer to Module 10 (COMPONENTS) for more detail.

APPLICATIONS

Your ability to edit your drawing visually, relying only upon what you can see on the screen, is limited by the resolution of the monitor. Generic CADD can see in much more detail than you can on your monitor. Using the snap modes enables you to take advantage of the detailed capability of Generic CADD.

Use SNAP CLOSEST POINT to insure that all your polygons are closed. Use NEAREST POINT to create accurate plots by enabling one desk to be aligned with an adjacent desk. SNAP MIDPOINT usage means that a conference room can be easily divided into two smaller equal sized conference rooms. SNAP PERPENDICULAR insures that a ninety degree angle forms between the new line and an existing one. Use ARC CENTER to draw a series of concentric circles. In short, if the snap commands are implemented, your drawing will be precise, yet easily created.

TYPICAL OPERATION

In this activity you draw a series of objects using the snap commands.

1. Start a new drawing called "SNAPS."

2. Draw a rectangle.

```
ENTER A COMMAND> RE
ENTER A CORNER OF RECTANGLE> 2,2  <CR>
ENTER NEXT CORNER OF RECTANGLE> 14,18  <CR>
```

3. Draw a line to divide the rectangle into two equal parts.

```
ENTER A COMMAND> L1
```

NOTE

While selecting a point in a snap mode, it is not necessary to select the point exactly. Just get close, and Generic CADD and the snap insure that your cursor jumps to the correct point.

```
ENTER START POINT>> SM
MIDPOINT OF> (Select the lower edge of the rectangle.)
ENTER NEXT POINT> OR
ORTHO MODE IS ON
ENTER A COMMAND> NL
NEAREST LINE TO> (Select the top edge of the rectangle.)
ENTER A COMMAND> PU
```

Your drawing should now look like this.

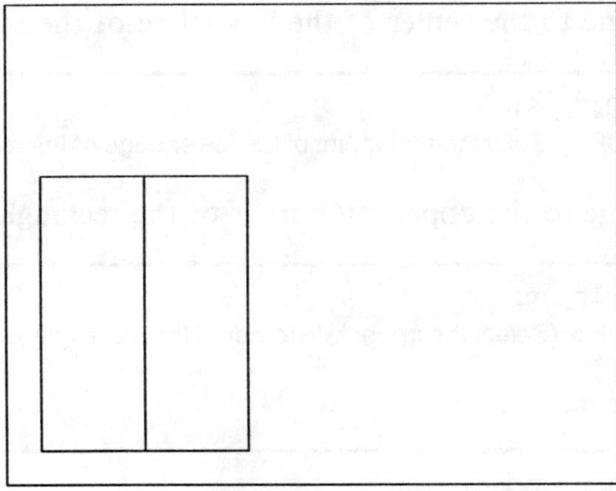

4. Draw a circle.

```
ENTER A COMMAND > C2
ENTER CENTER OF CIRCLE > 26,10  <CR>
ENTER A POINT ON CIRCLE > 30,10  <CR>
```

5. Draw another circle.

```
ENTER A COMMAND > C2
ENTER CENTER OF CIRCLE > 26,20 <CR>
ENTER A POINT ON CIRCLE > 20,20 <CR>
```

6. Draw a line from the center of the first circle tangent to the second circle.

```
ENTER A COMMAND > L1
ENTER START POINT > > SN
CENTER OF > (Select the center of the lower circle.)
ESC OR PEN UP TO STOP
ENTER NEXT POINT > OR
ORTHO MODE IS OFF
ENTER A COMMAND > SX
TANGENT TO > (Select the right edge of the larger circle.)
```

7. Continue the line to attach to a rectangle corner.

```
ENTER NEXT POINT > SC
CLOSEST POINT TO (Select upper right corner of rectangle.)
```

8. Continue the line to the center of the lower line of the rectangle.

```
ENTER NEXT POINT > SI
INTERSECTION OF > (Select the midpoint of the lower edge of the rectangle.)
```

9. Continue the line to the upper left corner of the rectangle.

```
ENTER NEXT POINT > SI
INTERSECTION OF > (Select the upper left corner of the rectangle.)
```

10. Discontinue the line.

```
ENTER NEXT POINT > PU
```

11. Erase the line segment you just drew.

```
ENTER A COMMAND >  EL
```

12. Restart the line at the midpoint of the rectangle's lower edge.

```
ENTER A COMMAND >  L1
ENTER START POINT > >  SC
CLOSEST POINT TO > (Select the midpoint of the recrangle's lower edge.)
```

13. Draw the line to the center of the smaller circle.

```
SC OR PEN UP TO STOP
ENTER NEXT POINT >  SC
CLOSEST POINT TO > (Select the center of the smaller circle.)
ESC OR PEN UP TO STOP
ENTER NEXT POINT >  PU
```

Your drawing should look like this.

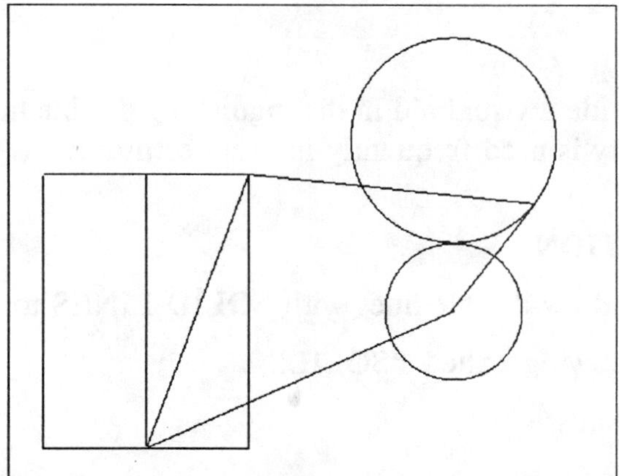

14. Quit the drawing without saving.

15. Turn to Module 66 to continue the learning sequence.

Module 61
SOLID LINES

DESCRIPTION

SOLID LINES (SO) creates solid infill in double lines, both on the screen and on the plotted drawing. The SOLID LINES command is an on/off toggle. When toggled on, all lines created with the DOUBLE LINE command are filled. When toggled off, lines created with the DOUBLE LINE command are drawn with no fill. The size of the solid fill is controlled by the DOUBLE WIDTH command. The color of the fill is controlled by the FILL COLOR command. The display of the fill is controlled by the DISPLAY FILL command. When SOLID LINES is toggled on as DOUBLE LINES are placed on your drawing, SOLID LINES adds additional lines onto the ends of parallel lines to further define the area to be filled.

APPLICATIONS

SOLID LINES provide a visual aid in distinguishing double lines from other line types. This capability is used frequently in architectural plans to highlight walls.

TYPICAL OPERATION

In this exercise you draw double lines with SOLID LINES toggled on and off.

1. Start a new drawing called "SOLID."

2. Draw several walls.

NOTE

When you begin a new drawing, the solid lines default is set
to off.

```
ENTER A COMMAND > L2
ENTER START POINT > > 4,4  <CR>
ENTER NEXT POINT > 10,8  <CR>
ENTER NEXT POINT > 12,4  <CR>
ENTER NEXT POINT > 18,4  <CR>
ENTER NEXT POINT > PU
```

3. Toggle SOLID LINE on.

```
ENTER A COMMAND >  SO
SOLID DOUBLE LINE IS ON
```

4. Draw double lines.

```
ENTER A COMMAND >  L2
ENTER START POINT >  26,4   <CR>
```

NOTE

SOLID LINE does not fill the double lines drawn until there are at least two line segments on the screen or until the PU command is given.

```
ENTER NEXT POINT >  8,15   <CR>
ENTER NEXT POINT >  8,18   <CR>
ENTER NEXT POINT >  22,21   <CR>
ENTER NEXT POINT >  PU
```

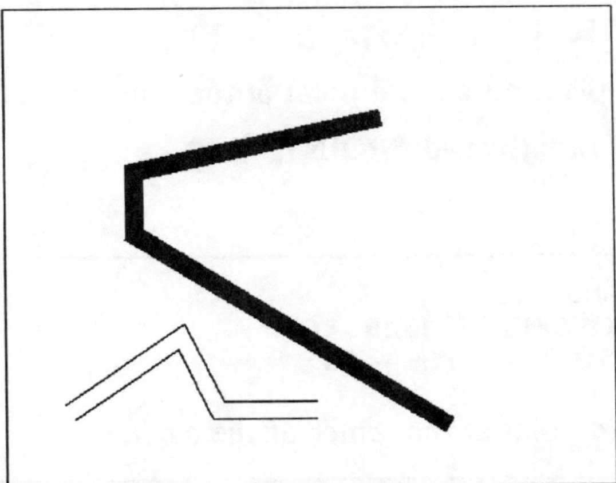

5. Quit the drawing without saving.

6. Turn to Module 32 to continue the learning sequence.

Module 62
STANDARD POINTS

DESCRIPTION

A STANDARD POINT (PO) is a small cross placed on your drawing as your own reference point. These points may be toggled on and off with the PS command. The Generic CADD default is standard points on. As with construction points, the screen must be refreshed to see a change after the toggling on or off. This toggle is useful, as you may not want the standard points to plot. The standard points plot if toggled on while plotting.

APPLICATIONS

Standard points are most often used to mark the center of a circle or a point where an object is to align with another at a future date.

TYPICAL OPERATION

In this activity, you place a standard point at the center of a circle.

1. Start a new drawing called "POINT."

2. Draw a circle.

```
ENTER A COMMAND > C2
ENTER CENTER OF CIRCLE > 10,10   <CR>
ENTER POINT ON CIRCLE > 14,8   <CR>
```

3. Place a standard point at the center of the circle.

```
ENTER A COMMAND > PO
ENTER THE POINT > SN
CENTER OF >   (Select a point on the circle perimeter.)
```

The standard point is placed.

4. Place additional standard points on your drawing.

```
ENTER A COMMAND> PO
```

NOTE

To place points in succcession, remember that it is easiest to use the Spacebar to repeat the command.

```
ENTER THE POINT> 15,10  <CR>
ENTER A COMMAND>   <SPACEBAR>
ENTER THE POINT> 20,15  <CR>
```

5. Toggle the standard points off.

```
ENTER A COMMAND> PS
DISPLAY STANDARD POINTS IS OFF
ENTER A COMMAND> RD
```

6. Toggle the standard points on again.

```
ENTER A COMMAND> PS
DISPLAY STANDARD POINTS IS ON
ENTER A COMMAND> RD
```

Your drawing should look like this.

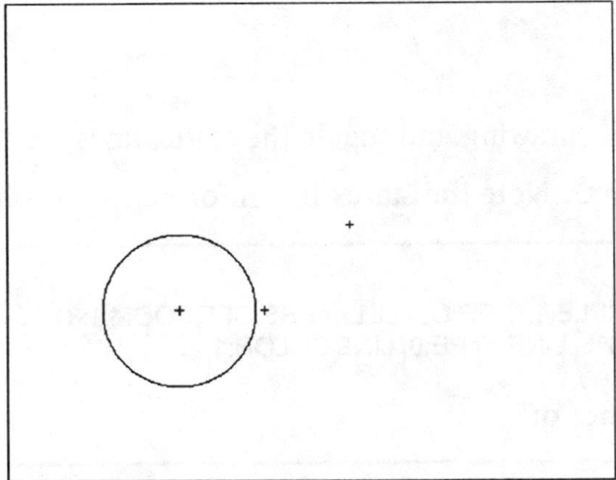

7. Quit the drawing without saving.

8. Turn to Module 13 to continue the learning sequence.

Module 63
STATUS LINE

DESCPIPTION

The status line is the information at the bottom of the drawing screen. The information revealed is the drawing name, the current layer, All Layers Edit On/Off, the zoom factor, the amount of memory used by the drawing, the current line type, and the current line color.

The STATUS LINE (SL) command allows you to turn this information on or off from view. Typing SL when STATUS LINE is on removes the STATUS LINE from view. Typing SL when STATUS LINE is off redisplays the STATUS LINE information. The Generic CADD default is to view the status line. If the STATUS LINE is turned off, the lines previously occupied by the status line are available to be used by the drawing graphics.

APPLICATIONS

The STATUS LINE is toggled off to gain more screen room to display the drawing graphics. With increased experience on Generic CADD, an operator may not need to refer to the STATUS LINE as often.

TYPICAL OPERATION

In this session you load a drawing and toggle the status lines on and off.

1. Load SAMPLE.DWG. Note the status line information displayed.

```
ENTER A COMMAND>
DRAWING NAME:SAMPLE, LAYER:O, ALL LAYERS:OFF, ZOOM 1:31.23
MEMORY USED:6.606%, LINE TYPE:0, LINE COLOR:1
```

2. Toggle the status lines off.

```
ENTER A COMMAND> SL
DISPLAY STATUS LINES IS OFF
```

Note that the status line information is not visible.

3. Redisplay the status line information.

```
ENTER A COMMAND > SL
DISPLAY STATUS LINES IS ON
```

4. Press **Esc** to view the status lines.

   Now the status lines are visible.

5. Quit the drawing without saving.

6. Turn to Module 39 to continue the learning sequence.

Module 64
STRAIGHT LINE

DESCRIPTION

The STRAIGHT LINE (L1) command, located in the DRAW command, is used to draw a single straight line. Single lines may connect to form a series of straight lines. Each line is defined by one of the three following methods:

1. Selecting the two endpoints with the screen cursor.

2. Typing the X and Y coordinates for the endpoints.

3. Typing the angle and distance along the line from the last point.

APPLICATIONS

The straight line is a basic drawing element used to create complex objects. Generic CADD sees a line as its two endpoints and treats each line segment as a separate entity.

TYPICAL OPERATION

In this activity you draw a figure using a series of straight lines.

1. Start Generic CADD. Type **CADD** and press **Return** at the DOS prompt. Press **Return** at the Generic CADD title page.

2. Start a new drawing called "LINE."

```
ENTER A DRAWING FILE NAME >  LINE   <CR>
IS THIS A NEW DRAWING (Y,N) >  Y
```

3. Set the coordinate entry to relative mode.

```
ENTER A COMMAND >  MR
MANUAL ENTRY/LAST POINT
```

4. Begin the line.

```
ENTER A COMMAND > L1
ENTER START POINT > > (Select a point near the center of the upper edge of the
screen to begin the line.)
```

5. Continue the line, entering the X and Y coordinates.

```
ENTER NEXT POINT > 12,0   <CR>
ENTER NEXT POINT > 0,-15   <CR>
ENTER NEXT POINT > -6,0   <CR>
```

NOTE

As each coordinate is entered, the text is visible on the prompt
line at the bottom of the screen. If you make a mistake, erase
the text with the Backspace key on the keyboard and try again.
Always check for the correct entry on the prompt line before
pressing < CR > .

6. Enter coordinates using an angle and line distance.

```
ENTER NEXT POINT > 10,<135 <CR>
ENTER NEXT POINT >  6, <225 <CR>
```

7. Enter coordinates using the X and Y endpoint coordinates.

```
ENTER A COMMAND >  0,-10   <CR>
```

8. Pick up your "pen" with the PEN UP command.

```
ENTER A COMMAND > PU
```

Your drawing should look like the following illustration.

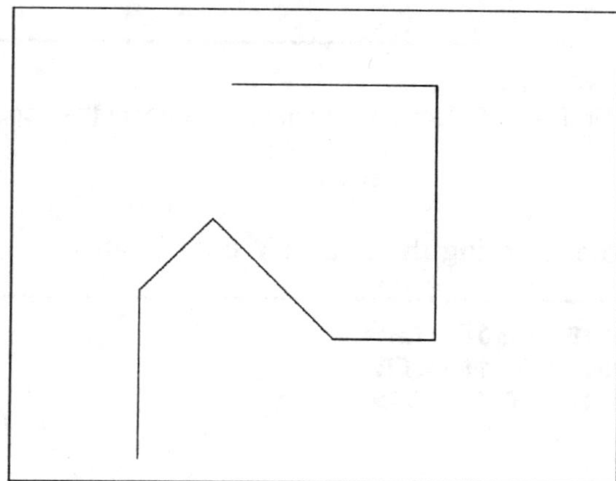

9. Quit the drawing without saving.

```
ENTER A COMMAND> QU
SAVE CURRENT DRAWING (Y or N)> N
"C" TO CONTINUE
"Q" TO QUIT> Q
```

10. Turn to Module 50 to continue the recommended learning sequence.

Module 65
TEXT

DESCRIPTION

The text commands allow you to place letters and numbers on your drawing. The font or lettering style must be selected before adding text to your drawing. After selecting a font, choose the color, size, rotation, angle, aspect, ratio, and slant of the text. Once these parameters are defined, all text you place on the drawing has these characteristics. When these parameters are changed, you place new text on the drawing according to these new parameters. Text already on the drawing remains the same as it was when originally placed.

Generic CADD offers a large variety of text commands. Each is described below with the corresponding two-letter command in parentheses.

FONT SELECT (FS) Selects the lettering style for the text characters placed on the screen. Generic CADD offers seven styles, and you can create your own. The default text style is Main. After pressing FS to select a font, enter the font name and the drive and directory if the font is not in the default directory. If you ask for a font that Generic CADD cannot find, you are asked if you want to create a new font. If you do not, press N for no and try again. Once a font is chosen, it remains active until you change it or exit Generic CADD.

TEXT COLOR (TK) Allows you to select the onscreen color of text placed on the drawing. The default color is one. When changing text color, all text placed after the change is drawn with the new color. All text placed prior to the change remains the same as it was when originally placed. As the colors available depend upon the graphics card you are using, refer to your graphic card instruction documentation. Generic CADD accepts any number between 0 and 255 for color. For example, if your graphics card offers 16 colors, and you enter 18 for a color number, Generic CADD understands that as 2, since it cycles the colors over and over. Color numbers can be entered by number or chosen from the color bars in the menu area. Generic CADD plots according to color, so it is usually advantageous to use a variety of colors to achieve a variety of line weights on the plotted drawing. Once a text color is set, it remains in effect until you change it or exit Generic CADD.

TEXT SIZE (TZ) Allows you to select the height of the lettering you place on the drawing. The default is 1" height. When prompted for the text height, enter the height desired or type D for distance to select two points on the screen to represent the height of the text. Generic CADD displays the resulting height on the prompt line. Your Generic CADD drawings are created in actual size and not scaled until you plot. If you plan to plot at other than actual size, you must overscale your text appropriately to be the correct size when plotted. Once a text size is set, it remains in effect until you change it or exit Generic CADD.

TEXT ROTATION (TR) Allows you to place text on the drawing already rotated to a selected angle, specified in degrees. The default is zero degrees, enabling you to read the text horizontally. At the prompt, three options for entering the angle are available. You can enter the desired angle if known; type A for angle to define the angle on the screen with a basepoint and a ray point; or type V for vertex to define the angle on the screen with a basepoint and two ray points. Generic CADD measures angles from the horizontal position in a counterclockwise rotation, beginning with the first ray selected and ending with the second ray selected. The resulting angle is displayed on the prompt line. Once a rotation is set, it remains in effect until you change it or exit Generic CADD.

TEXT ASPECT (TA) Allows you to stretch or compress text by adjusting the width of each character. The height remains the same, unless changed with TEXT SIZE. The default aspect is 1, which is the width with which each character in the font was originally defined. A new aspect is in relation to the original width. For example, a .5 creates thin letters (half as wide as originally defined), while a 2 value creates wide letters (twice as wide as originally created). The allowable range is .1 to 10. Once an aspect is set, it remains in effect until you change it or exit Generic CADD.

TEXT SLANT (TS) Controls the slant of each character in a text string. The default slant of zero results in vertical characters read horizontally. At the prompt, three options for entering the angle are available. You can enter the desired angle if known; type A for angle to define the angle on the screen with a basepoint and a ray point; or type V for vertex to define the angle on the screen with a basepoint and two ray points. Generic CADD measures angles from the horizontal position in a counterclockwise rotation, beginning with the first ray selected and ending with the second ray selected. The resulting angle is displayed on the prompt line. A positive number slants the character to the right, while a negative number slants the character to the left. The allowed limit is 45 degrees in either direction. Once a slant is set, it remains in effect until you change it or exit Generic CADD.

TEXT PLACE (TP) Places text on your drawing at a specified location. Upper and lower case can be used. Prior to placement, a font must be selected. With the cursor, locate the point to begin the lower left corner of the text string. Begin typing, and you see the letters appear on the screen. If you make mistakes, use the Delete or Backspace keys to correct yourself. When the string is complete, press Return and continue to the next line. If you are finished placing text, press Esc.

TEXT INSERT (TI) Allows you to insert new characters into an existing string of text. Generic CADD automatically adjusts the existing string to make room for the added text. Select the insertion point, making sure to use the CLOSEST POINT snap mode to align the new text with the existing, and type the text to be added. All the defining parameters used in the existing text are carried through to the inserted text, even though these values may not be the current values.

TEXT DELETE (TD) Allows you to delete characters in an existing string of text. The opposite of TEXT INSERT, TEXT DELETE adjusts the existing string to the left to compensate for the deleted characters. Select the character to be deleted using the CLOSEST POINT snap mode and locate the screen cursor near the lower left corner of the character.

TEXT REPLACE (TX) Allows you to replace existing characters in a text string. Select the text starting point at the lower left corner of the text you want to replace using the CLOSEST POINT snap mode. As you type each character, it replaces an existing character. Pressing Esc completes the process. All the defining parameters used in the existing text are carried through to the new text, even though these values may not be the current values.

TEXT CREATE/EDIT (TC) Allows you to define characters to create an individual font style. To begin, select a font with the FS command and enter the name of the font you will define. Enter yes when asked if this is a new font. Choose the letter on the keyboard you want the upcoming definition to reference. Be aware of upper and lower case letters. A reference box 1" x 1" appears to fill the screen. Draw the character as you want it to look, using the box as reference. You cannot use other text characters to define the new font. You can draw outside the box. All Generic CADD drawing commands can be used. When finished, select TEXT CREATE to end and begin another character. Newly defined fonts are stored in the location specified in the FONT PATH. You can also use FONT CREATE/EDIT to bring up characters of a previously defined font for editing. Any graphic object can be drawn and referenced to a keyboard character, not just text.

WINDOW TEXT (WT) Allows you to create new font characters from objects already on the screen. New characters cannot be created from existing font characters. First place a window around the object to be defined, select a reference point, then the character on the keyboard with which it will be associated. The reference point does not have to be on the selected object. The window you place around the object is assumed to be one inch in height, to create a reference dimension. After the character is defined with WINDOW TEXT, all occurrences on the drawing are changed to the new definition.

FAST TEXT (TF) Allows you to temporarily turn off all text on your drawing from view. Each text character is represented by a standard point, so you are aware of the location. This command is a toggle. The default is FAST TEXT off. When TF is selected, FAST TEXT becomes active, and each character appears as a standard point. After toggling TF on or off, the visual effect does not become apparent until the next redraw of the screen. If STANDARD POINTS DISPLAY is off, nothing appears to represent the text if FAST TEXT is toggled on.

FAST TEXT VIEW (TV) Allows you to be selective and see certain selected text even though FAST TEXT is toggled on. FAST TEXT must be toggled on if FAST TEXT VIEW is to function. With FAST TEXT toggled on and STANDARD POINTS on, place a window around the points representing the text you want to see, and the text appears.

FONT PATH (P3) Allows you to specify the drive and directory where Generic CADD looks for and saves fonts. The default path is the same directory location as the Generic CADD operating software. When changing the path, be sure to end the path location with a backslash (\) to separate the directory from the font filename which Generic CADD adds.

APPLICATIONS

Text is used to label the contents of your drawing and provide general information in note form as well as in dimensions. A number of the text commands are particularly useful in special ways.

TEXT COLOR allows you to associate different on-screen colors with different types of text, therefore providing an easy way to plot in varying line thicknesses to highlight text as needed.

TEXT SIZE, ROTATION, ASPECT, and SLANT allow you to adjust the text exactly to fit the situation. Slanted text creates visual interest in a note to be emphasized, while rotation lets the text follow the lines of the object being noted, as well as allowing text in a vertically oriented title block on a drawing sheet. ASPECT allows text to fit in tight spaces on a dense drawing.

TEXT INSERT and TEXT DELETE and REPLACE allow easy correction of mistakes and changing information.

TEXT CREATE/EDIT gives the option to create special fonts for visual interest, presentation drawings, or a need to meet preset standards set by others.

FAST TEXT capability gives the opportunuty to turn off memory-consuming text, creating a faster drawing display, while FAST TEXT VIEW allows you to read the text in the immediate vicinity of your editing area.

TYPICAL OPERATION

In this exercise you create a variety of text strings and manipulate them as in the editing process.

1. Start a new drawing called "TEXT."

2. Place a text string with the defaults active.

```
ENTER A COMMAND> TP
SELECTED FONT IS: MAIN
ENTER TEXT STARTING POINT> (Select a point at the top left of your screen.)
```

NOTE

A line appears on the screen when you select a text starting point. This line approximates the width of the text selected.

NOTE

If you make a typographical error entering a text string, use the Backspace key to back up and enter again.

```
ENTER A CHARACTER> THIS IS A TEST.  <Esc>
```

3. Change the text slant.

```
ENTER A COMMAND> TS
CHANGE TEXT SLANT (0.000) LIMITS: -45.000 TO 45.000> 30   <CR>
```

4. Place the text.

```
ENTER A COMMAND> TP
SELECTED FONT IS: MAIN
ENTER TEXT STARTING POINT> (Select a point under the first text string.)
ENTER A CHARACTER> LET US TRY   <CR>
ENTER A CHARACTER> TWO LINES THIS TIME.  <Esc>
```

5. Change the text rotation and on-screen color.

```
ENTER A COMMAND> TR
CHANGE TEXT ROTATION (0.000) LIMITS:-360.000 TO 360.000> 90   <CR>
```

NOTE

Your monitor and graphics card must be EGA or better to support the color options of Generic CADD. CGA and monochrome combinations do not support the colors. Omit the following step if needed.

```
ENTER A COMMAND> TK
CHANGE COLOR NUMBER (1) LIMITS: 0 TO 255> 10   <CR>
```

6. Place the text.

```
ENTER A COMMAND > TP
SELECTED FONT IS: MAIN
ENTER TEXT STARTING POINT > 3,3  <CR>
ENTER A CHARACTER > THIS TEXT IS TALL. <CR>
```

7. Reset the rotation angle.

```
ENTER A COMMAND > TR
CHANGE TEXT ROTATION (90.000) LIMITS:-360.000 TO 360.000 > 0  <CR>
```

8. Change the text aspect.

```
ENTER A COMMAND > TA
CHANGE TEXT ASPECT [1.00] > 2  <CR>
```

9. Place additional text.

```
ENTER A COMMAND > TP
SELECTED FONT IS: MAIN
ENTER TEXT STARTING POINT > 6,5  <CR>
ENTER A CHARACTER > THIS IS FAT.  <Esc>
```

10. Adjust the text size and slant.

```
ENTER A COMMAND > TS
CHANGE TEXT SLANT(30.000) LIMITS:-45.000 TO 45.000 > 0  <CR>
ENTER A COMMAND > TZ
CHANGE TEXT SIZE(1.000) IN > .5  <CR>
```

11. Change the font.

```
ENTER A COMMAND > FS
ENTER THE FONT NAME > COMPLEX  <CR>
FONT COMPLEX IS SELECTED
LOAD FONT NOW? (Y,N) > Y
SELECTED FONT IS: COMPLEX
```

12. Place text.

```
ENTER A COMMAND> TP
SELECTED FONT IS: COMPLEX
ENTER TEXT STARTING POINT> 6,8  <CR>
ENTER A CHARACTER> TRY THIS ONE!  <Esc>
```

13. Insert a character in a text string.

```
ENTER A COMMAND> TI
POINT TO INSERT LOCATION> SC
CLOSEST POINT TO> (Select the lower left corner of the word "ONE" in the last text
string entered.)
ENTER A CHARACTER TO INSERT> D
```

14. Delete the character just added.

```
ENTER A COMMAND> TD
POINT TO THE CHAR TO DELETE> (Select the "D" in the word "DONE".)
```

15. Replace the text in the last string entered.

```
ENTER A COMMAND> TX
SELECTED FONT IS: COMPLEX
ENTER TEXT STARTING POINT> SC
CLOSEST POINT TO> (Select the lower left corner of the word "ONE".)
ENTER A CHARACTER> TEXT <Esc>
```


16. Quit the drawing without saving.

17. Turn to Module 37 to continue the learning sequence.

<h1 style="text-align:center">Module 66
TOLERANCE</h1>

DESCRIPTION

TOLERANCE (TO) sets the size of the searching area around the screen cursor. This search area defines the space on the screen where a snap command function can occur. This area has nothing to do with the size or scale of your drawing, but relies totally on the real size as measured on the screen. In addition to affecting the various snaps, TOLERANCE plays a part in the screen selection of your drawing objects. If the object you are selecting is not within the tolerance of the cursor, Generic CADD will not find it. Commands such as OBJECT BREAK, OBJECT CHANGE, OBJECT ERASE, OBJECT MOVE, OBJECT COPY, FILLET, TRIM, EXTEND, and CHAMFER are affected by TOLERANCE.

The default value of TOLERANCE is 1/4". The largest acceptable value is 1". Once changed, the tolerance value remains in effect until you exit Generic CADD.

APPLICATIONS

In the early stages of creating a new drawing, it is easier and faster to locate points if the tolerance value is fairly large. Points are easily discernable from one another, and there is no risk of snapping to an incorrect point. Once the drawing becomes more dense, however, the TOLERANCE needs to be smaller, as it becomes difficult in the crowded drawing to get close to the point desired without possibly jumping to another point.

TYPICAL OPERATION

In this activity you change the default tolerance from 1/4" to 1".

1. Start a new drawing called "TOLERAN."

2. Change the default tolerance to 1".

```
ENTER A COMMAND> TO
CHANGE TOLERANCE TO: (0.0 - 1.0) (0.250) IN>1 <CR>
```

The tolerance is now increased.

3. Quit the drawing.

4. Turn to Module 11 to continue the learning sequence.

Module 67
TRACE SCALE /TRACE MODE
/DRAWING ALIGN

DESCRIPTION

The **TRACE SCALE, TRACE MODE,** and **DRAWING ALIGN** commands work together to define various parameters when you use a digitizer to copy an existing drawing into a Generic CADD file. Each command operates only if you use a digitizer for a pointing device. The commands are described below, with each corresponding two-letter command in parentheses.

TRACE MODE (TM) allows you to use a digitizer to trace a drawing into a Generic CADD drawing file. This command is a toggle, going in and out of TRACE MODE. The Generic CADD default is TRACE MODE in the off position. While in the on position, you can trace on the digitizer to locate points rather than selecting points on the screen.

TRACE SCALE (RZ) allows you to set the scale of the drawing you want to trace. If you are tracing for the first time, use the DRAWING ALIGN command first to begin the correct setup. After selecting the command, enter the desired scale at the prompt. TRACE SCALE is in effect only while TRACE MODE is toggled to the on position. This setting remains in effect until you change the value.

DRAWING ALIGN (DA) allows you to set the parameters necessary to begin tracing a drawing into a Generic CADD drawing file. Begin by firmly taping the drawing you want to trace to the digitizer. After selecting the command, you are prompted for the correct TRACE SCALE. As with scale values in the plotting functions, the scale is set as a ratio, with the first number as a value of one. The second number is the proportional number. A value of .5 is a scale of half size, while a value of 2 is double the original size. Remember that with architectural drawings, set all values first to inches. Thus a 1/8" = 1'0" scale is set as 1:96. Refer to the plotting module if you have further questions about scale values. If you have not begun a drawing, after selecting the desired scale, Generic CADD places you in the TRACE MODE and you can begin tracing the drawing. If you already have a drawing in progress, enter a reference point on the screen. Select the lower left corner of the screen, and use the NP snap mode when you select the point. Then choose the corresponding point on the drawing. This point is the reference point from which all other points are scaled. If you have not yet selected a tracing scale, you must do so now. Select a point on the screen away from the reference point, then select the corresponding point on the drawing. Generic CADD calculates the scale and displays the value on the sreen prompt line. Type Y to accept the displayed scale, or enter the desired scale. Generic CADD then puts you in TRACE MODE so that you may continue tracing the drawing.

APPLICATIONS

DRAWING ALIGN, TRACE SCALE, and TRACE MODE allow you to create drawing files of existing drawings quickly and easily. This option is especially useful in remodeling work, where the original drawing already exists, yet you need a background drawing in Generic CADD to show changes to the original. Digitizing is also a quick way to enter many plans for the facilities management environment.

TYPICAL OPERATION

No example is included.

Turn to Module 71 to continue the learning sequence.

Module 68
TRIM

DESCRIPTION

TRIM (RM) trims a selected object to meet cleanly with another. Objects that trim are lines and arcs. Lines, arcs, and circles can be trimmed to. Objects that are crossing can be trimmed as well as objects that do not quite meet. When selecting the object to trim, you must identify the object by choosing a point on the portion of the object that you want to keep. If Generic CADD finds no object to trim to, it trims the first selected line to a point perpendicular to the point you wanted to trim to. With this capability, Generic CADD trims a line to any chosen length.

APPLICATIONS

Like all the Generic CADD editing and trimming functions, TRIM is critical to producing a concise and correct drawing. Speed of drawing entry is enhanced, as you know that linework corrections can be made with TRIM.

TYPICAL OPERATION

In this exercise you draw and trim several objects.

1. Start a new drawing called "TRIM."

2. Draw two lines.

```
ENTER A COMMAND > L1
ENTER START POINT > > 3,3  <CR>
ENTER NEXT POINT > 7,11  <CR>
ENTER NEXT POINT > PU
ENTER A COMMAND > L1
ENTER START POINT > > 3,12  <CR>
ENTER NEXT POINT > 11,5  <CR>
ENTER NEXT POINT > PU
```

3. Copy the lines twice.

```
ENTER A COMMAND > WC
PLACE WINDOW > (Place a window around both lines.)
ENTER A REFERENCE POINT > 6,10 <CR>
ENTER NEW REFERENCE POINT OR OFFSET > 16,10  <CR>
ENTER NUMBER OF COPIES (1-99) > 2  <CR>
```

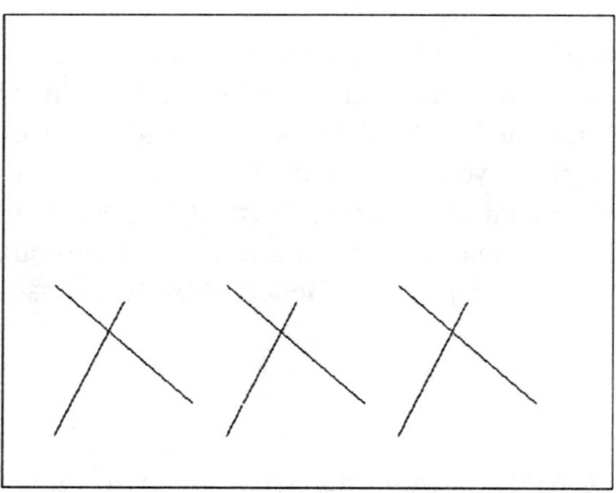

4. Trim the first set of lines.

NOTE

The first object selected is the one trimmed. Select a point on the portion of the object you want to retain.

```
ENTER A COMMAND > RM
ENTER A POINT ON THE OBJECT TO TRIM > 4,11  <CR>
SECOND OBJECT > 4,5 <CR>
```

5. Trim the center set of lines.

```
ENTER A COMMAND > RM
ENTER A POINT ON THE OBJECT TO TRIM > 17,11  <CR>
SECOND OBJECT > 14,11 <CR>
```

6. Trim the third set of lines.

```
ENTER A COMMAND >  RM
ENTER A POINT ON THE OBJECT TO TRIM >  25,7 < CR >
ENTER SECOND OBJECT >  24,11 < CR >
```

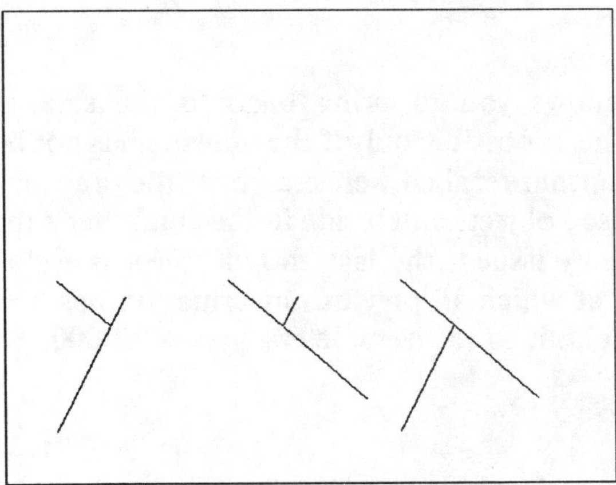

7. Quit the drawing without saving.

8. Turn to Module 29 to continue the learning sequence.

<h1 style="text-align:center">Module 69
UNERASE</h1>

DESCRIPTION

UNERASE (UE) allows you to bring back to the screen objects that were previously erased. This is possible only if the drawing has not been saved or packed since the objects you want recalled were erased. If the drawing has not been saved or packed, these erased objects still reside in the computer's memory. As each UE command is repeatedly issued, the last erased object is restored to screen, until you reach the point at which all previous information has been saved or packed. The Generic CADD limit to recoverable erasures is 32,000.

APPLICATIONS

UNERASE acts like an instant correction for any erase mistakes you may make. You may use WINDOW ERASE and window too many objects, or you may use OBJECT ERASE and select the wrong object. Whatever the case, UNERASE corrects your mistake.

TYPICAL OPERATION

In this session you draw several objects, erase them, then restore them to the screen.

1. Start a new drawing called "UNERASE."

2. Draw two rectangles.

```
ENTER A COMMAND> RE
ENTER A CORNER OF RECTANGLE> 5,5   <CR>
ENTER NEXT CORNER OF RECTANGLE> 18,17 <CR>
ENTER A COMMAND> RE
ENTER A CORNER OF RECTANGLE> 6,10   <CR>
ENTER NEXT CORNER OF RECTANGLE> 22,12   <CR>
```

3. Draw a circle.

```
ENTER A COMMAND> C2
ENTER CENTER OF CIRCLE> 24,8 <CR>
ENTER A POINT ON CIRCLE> 30,8  <CR>
```

4. Draw another rectangle.

```
ENTER A COMMAND> RE
ENTER A CORNER OF RECTANGLE> 12,12  <CR>
ENTER NEXT CORNER OF RECTANGLE> 14,14  <CR>
```

5. Draw a series of lines.

```
ENTER A COMMAND> L1
ENTER START POINT> > 14,18  <CR>
ENTER NEXT POINT> 16,22  <CR>
ENTER NEXT POINT> 22,12 <CR>
ENTER NEXT POINT> PU
```

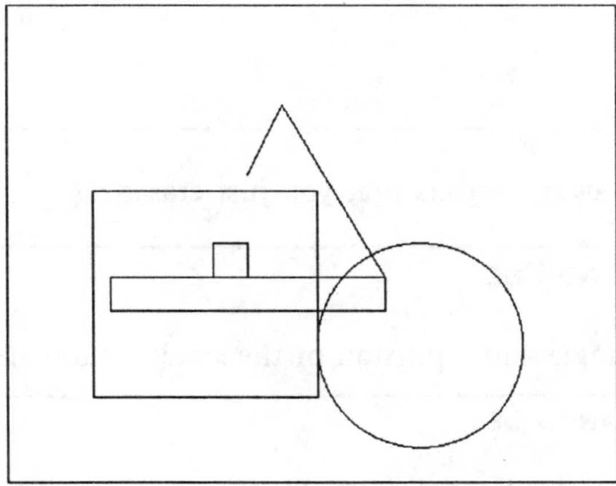

6. Erase the circle.

```
ENTER A COMMAND> OE
ENTER A POINT ON THE OBJECT TO ERASE> (Select a point on the perimeter of the circle.)
```

7. Erase a segment of the small square.

```
ENTER A COMMAND> OE
ENTER A POINT ON THE OBJECT TO ERASE> (Select the top segment of the small square.)
```

8. Erase several objects within a windowed area.

ENTER A COMMAND > **WE**
PLACE WINDOW > (Select two diagonal points to define a windowed area around the large rectangle.)

9. Refresh the screen.

ENTER A COMMAND > **RD**

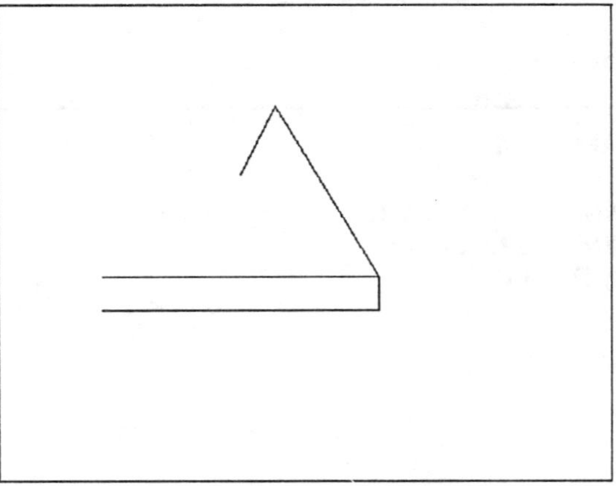

10. Unerase the drawing objects that you just erased.

ENTER A COMMAND > **UE**

The large rectangle and a portion of the small square are redrawn.

ENTER A COMMAND > **UE**

The small square top segment is redrawn.

ENTER A COMMAND > **UE**

The circle is redrawn.

ENTER A COMMAND > **UE**
NOTHING TO ERASE!

11. Quit the drawing without saving.

12. Turn to Module 49 to continue the learning sequence.

Module 70
UNITS

DESCRIPTION

The units commands are used to specify the kinds of conventions (feet, inches, meters, etc.) desired for distances, dimensions, grids, text, and displays in your drawing.

Once set at the onset of drawing development, the selected unit should remain in place until completion of the drawing. The default setting, or the one that is in effect when you enter Generic CADD, is feet and inches, with portions of inches displayed in decimal format.

Generic CADD offers numerous unit options. Each option is a toggle. A toggle, by definition, alternately turns on and off. Once a particular option is toggled on, it remains in effect for all additional work on the drawing. The following gives a description of each unit command, and the corresponding two-letter keyboard command is included in parentheses.

METERS (MT) Allows entry and display of coordinates in meters. Remember that this toggle also affects the manual entry and measure commands. Fractional portions of meters are shown in decimal format, with the number of decimal places as specified in the DECIMAL VALUE (DV) command.

CENTIMETERS (MC) Allows entry and display of coordinates in centimeters. Fractional portions of centimeters are shown in decimal format, with the number of decimal places as specified in the DECIMAL VALUE (DV) command.

MILLIMETERS (MM) Allows entry and display of coordinates in millimeters. Fractional portions of millimeters are shown in decimal format, with the number of decimal places specified in the DECIMAL VALUE (DV) command.

DECIMAL FEET (FT) Allows entry and display of coordinates in feet. Fractional portions of feet are displayed in decimal format, with the number of decimal places as specified in the DECIMAL VALUE (DV) commmand.

FEET AND INCHES (FI) Allows entry and display of coordinates in feet and inches. Fractional portions of feet are in inches. Fractional portions of inches are in decimal or fractional format, depending upon whether DECIMALS or FRACTIONS is currently selected. The system default is decimals.

INCHES (IN) Allows entry and display of coordinates in inches. Fractional portions of inches are in decimal or fractional format, depending upon whether DECIMALS or FRACTIONS is currectly selected.

FRACTIONS (FR) Allows display of inches in a fractional format. Decimal fractions of inches is the default when you enter Generic CADD. Typing FR toggles the fractional inch display to fractions.

FRACTIONAL VALUE (FV) Controls the accuracy of fractions as they are displayed in the coordinate display. When FV is toggled on, a list of denominators is shown for your selection. Type the value you desire. The default is 1/16.

DECIMALS (DE) Allows display of portions of inches in a decimal format. DECIMAL is the system default. You select the number of decimal places shown with the DECIMAL VALUE (DV) command.

DECIMAL VALUE (DV) Allows control of the number of places that decimal values are shown. The range is zero to eight places. The default is three decimal places.

ARC-ANGLE MINUTES (AM) Allows the angle display format to be in minutes. This format includes degrees, minutes, and seconds, with the information displayed in the DD:MM:SS format. Unlike most of the other units commands, ARCMINUTES is for display only. Degrees, minutes, and seconds must be changed to decimal format for manual entry.

ARC-ANGLE DEGREES (AD) Allows the specification and display of angles in degrees. The total number of decimal spaces allowed is controlled with the DECIMAL VALUE(DV) command.

APPLICATIONS

Drawings are created in real-world size in Generic CADD. However, the system must know the units you want to use when specific distances or dimensions are entered or displayed.

TYPICAL OPERATION

In this exercise you change the default units from decimal portions of feet and inches to fractional portions in 1/8" increments.

1. Start Generic CADD. Type **CADD** and press **Return** at the DOS prompt. Press **Return** again at the Generic CADD title page.

2. Start a new drawing called "UNITS."

```
ENTER A DRAWING FILE NAME> UNITS  <CR>
IS THIS A NEW DRAWING (Y, N)> Y
```

3. Set the display of portions of inches to fractions.

```
ENTER A COMMAND> FR
DISPLAY IN FRACTIONS.
```

4. Set the fractional value to 1/8".

```
ENTER A COMMAND> FV
SET FRACTIONS (2,4,8,16,32,64) (16)  8  <CR>
```

5. Draw a line.

NOTE
When entering exact dimensions, use a space to separate inches from portions of inches.

```
ENTER A COMMAND> L1
ENTER START POINT> 4,4  <CR>
ENTER NEXT POINT> 1'2 1/2", 4  <CR>
ENTER NEXT POINT> PU
```

6. Measure the line.

```
ENTER A COMMAND> MD
```

7. Locate the cursor near the left line endpoint.

```
ENTER STARTING POINT> NP
```

8. Locate the cursor near the right endpoint.

```
ENTER NEXT POINT (ESC or PENUP TO QUIT) > NP
DISTANCE = 0' 10 1/2"
ENTER NEXT POINT (ESC or PENUP TO QUIT) > PU
```

9. Quit the drawing without saving.

```
ENTER A COMMAND > QU
SAVE CURRENT DRAWING (Y or N) > N
"C" TO CONTINUE
"Q" TO QUIT > Q
```

10. Turn to Module 33 to continue the learning sequence.

Module 71
VIDEO MENU

DESCRIPTION

The video menu is the group of on-screen commands to the right of the drawing area. Generic CADD automatically loads the default menu called LEVEL3.MNU for Generic CADD Level 3, LEVEL2.MNU for Level 2 versions, and LEVEL1.MNU for Level 1 versions. You can customize this menu to rearrange or rename the commands in an order that is more appropriate to your type of work. In addition, you can choose to display a video menu or remove it from view, leaving more room to display your drawing. The following commands are available to manipulate any custom menus that you create. Each corresponding two-letter command is in parentheses.

LOAD VIDEO MENU (LV) loads a previously created menu from the disk. At the prompt, enter the name of the .MNU file. Give the complete drive and directory if necessary. If the previous menu has not been erased from the screen with the DELETE/CLEAR MENU command, the new menu is added to the end of the existing menu. When you load a digitizer menu on top of a video menu or load a video menu on top of a digitizer menu, the screen is automatically cleared. Generic CADD does not allow both types of menus to be used at the same time.

DELETE/CLEAR MENU (VX) clears the screen of the current video menu in preparation for loading a new menu to the screen. The menu is cleared after initiating the command. When you load a digitizer menu on top of a video menu or load a video menu on top of a digitizer menu, the screen is automatically cleared. Generic CADD does not allow both types of menus to be used at the same time.

NEW MENU clears the existing menu and loads a specified menu to the screen. There is no two-letter command for this command. To issue from the keyboard, use the DELETE/CLEAR MENU and the LOAD VIDEO MENU successively. Select the UTILITIES command from the on-screen root menu, then choose the NEW VIDEO

MENU command. NEW MENU is actually a combination of the LOAD VIDEO MENU and the DELETE/CLEAR MENU commands.

DISPLAY MENU (VM) toggles the video menu on and off from view. The commands can be entered from the keyboard, so the video display is not needed. The default is DISPLAY MENU on. To toggle to the off position, select the command. To toggle on again, select the command again.

APPLICATIONS

A computer aided design and drafting software package works best when it works exactly the way you do. Customization is critical, as no CAD package can fully answer everyone's needs. Through the video commands, commands can be altered, renamed, or deleted to represent those which you put to use. Access to commands can be simpler and more specific. Toggling the DISPLAY MENU to the off position creates more drawing screen area for your drawing.

TYPICAL OPERATION

In this activity you delete and reload the default on-screen video menu.

1. Start a new drawing called "VIDEO."

2. Erase the existing video menu.

```
ENTER A COMMAND>  VX
```

The video menu is erased from view.

3. Load a new menu. Since you have created no other menu to load, reload the default menu.

```
ENTER A COMMAND>  LV
ENTER THE MENU FILE NAME>  LEVEL 3.
```

The default menu is reloaded.

4. Erase and reload the default menu simultaneously.

> ENTER A COMMAND > (Select the UTILITIES command from the on-screen ROOT
> menu with your pointing device.)
> ENTER A COMMAND > (Select the NEW VID MENU command from the UTIITIES
> submenu.)
> ENTER THE MENU FILE NAME > **LEVEL3** <**CR**>

The video menu is restored.

5. Toggle the video menu off.

> ENTER A COMMAND > **VM**
> DISPLAY MENU IS OFF

6. Toggle the video menu on again.

> ENTER A COMMAND > **VM**
> DISPLAY MENU IS ON

7. Quit the drawing.

8. Turn to Module 40 to continue the learning sequence.

Module 72
WINDOW MIRROR

DESCRIPTION

WINDOW MIRROR (WI) allows you to make a mirror image of a windowed object or group of objects. The mirror is created about a selected axis point in any of eight directions. The axis point can be anywhere, from on the object itself to a distance away. The available directions are up, down, left, right, and the four corresponding diagonals. After identifying the object to be mirrored, select the axis point, then indicate the direction of the mirror by selecting a point on the screen. As in all copy functions, the original remains in place after the copy appears. Text mirrors just like any other graphic object, so be careful you do not include text in a selected mirror window.

APPLICATIONS

Mirror images are a great benefit to the drafter. Some commonly used applications include mirroring of adjacent toilet rooms, duplicating the fixtures; mirroring of offices or even entire apartment units. Many mechanical parts are symmetrical about at least one axis. Draw only half and mirror the balance.

Your may not need an exact mirror, but it is easy to create a mirror image and edit the mirror as needed. WINDOW MIRROR can save a lot of time.

TYPICAL OPERATION

In this exercise you draw a table and chairs and create a grouping by mirroring twice in succession.

1. Start a new drawing called "MIRROR."

2. Draw a circle for the table.

```
ENTER A COMMAND >  C2
ENTER CENTER OF CIRCLE >  7,7   <CR>
ENTER A POINT ON CIRCLE >  7,10 <CR>
```

3. Draw a rectangle for the chair.

```
ENTER A COMMAND > RE
ENTER A CORNER OF RECTANGLE > 6,11 <CR>
ENTER NEXT CORNER OF RECTANGLE > 8,13  <CR>
```

4. Copy the chair nine times radially.

```
ENTER A COMMAND > RC
PLACE WINDOW > (Use the screen cursor to place a window around the chair.)
ENTER AN AXIS POINT > 7,7  <CR>
ENTER TOTAL DEGREES TO SPAN > 360  <CR>
ENTER NUMBER OF ITEMS IN SPAN > 9  <CR>
```

5. Mirror the single table with chairs to create two sets.

```
ENTER A COMMAND > WI
PLACE WINDOW > (Use the cursor to place a window around the table and chairs.)
ENTER AN AXIS POINT > 14,7  <CR>
ENTER DIRECTION OF MIRROR (OUTSIDE OF WINDOW) > (Select a point on the
screen to the right).
```

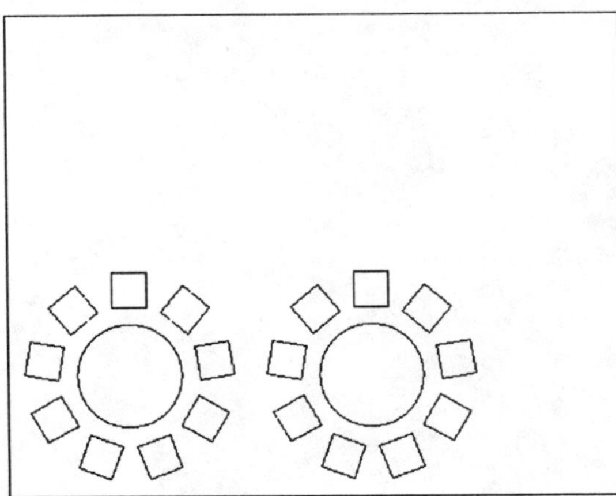

6. Mirror the two tables with chairs to create four sets.

```
ENTER A COMMAND > WI
PLACE WINDOW (Use the cursor to place a window around both tables and chairs.)
ENTER AN AXIS POINT > 14,14  <CR>
ENTER DIRECTION OF MIRROR (OUTSIDE OF WINDOW) > (Select a point at the top
of the screen.)
```

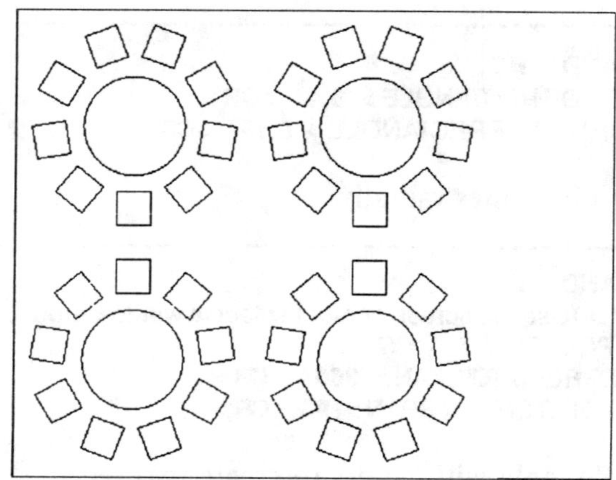

7. Quit the drawing without saving.

8. Turn to Module 74 to continue the learning sequence.

Module 73
WINDOW RESCALE

DESCRIPTION

WINDOW RESCALE (WZ) allows the size and proportion of a windowed object to be altered. The X dimension and the Y dimension can be scaled to different values. Either fractional or decimal values are accepted. The current value is shown in parentheses at the X and Y scale prompt. The current value of an unscaled object is one. After identifying the object or objects by choosing a windowed area, a reference point must be selected. As in the WINDOW ROTATE command, the reference point or axis point is the only point that stays in the same position during the rescaling process. All other points of the selected object are scaled in relation to this selected point. Entry of negative scales is accepted, although not commonly used. Negative scale values create a mirror version of the original, which sometimes appears as though the object has been turned inside out.

APPLICATIONS

WINDOW RESCALE allows you to create objects and copy and rescale them rather than recreating a differently proportioned object. This approach saves time in generating a drawing. For example, a 36" x 72" desk can quickly become a 36" x 108" worksurface with WINDOW RESCALE.

TYPICAL OPERATION

In this session, you draw several objects and rescale them.

1. Start a new drawing called "RESCALE."

2. Draw a rectangle.

```
ENTER A COMMAND> RE
ENTER A CORNER OF RECTANGLE> 12,6  <CR>
ENTER NEXT CORNER OF RECTANGLE> 22,8  <CR>
```

3. Resize the rectangle.

```
ENTER A COMMAND> WZ
PLACE WINDOW> (Place a window to totally contain the rectangle.)
ENTER A REFERENCE POINT> 12,6  <CR>
ENTER NEW X SCALE (1.00)> 1.5  <CR>
```

NOTE

After you enter a new X scale value, the Y scale value prompt default assumes this number. Generic CADD gives you the option to change it.

```
ENTER NEW Y SCALE (1.50)> 3  <CR>
```

4. Draw a circle.

```
ENTER A COMMAND> C2
ENTER CENTER OF CIRCLE> 18,18  <CR>
ENTER A POINT ON CIRCLE> 18,16  <CR>
```

5. Resize the circle.

NOTE

When you rescale a circle or arc and enter different values for X and Y, the objects usually take on the scale factor value entered for the Y scale value only. It may be necessary to use curves to create the desired object rather than attempt to rescale circles and arcs in different proportions.

```
ENTER A COMMAND> WZ
PLACE WINDOW> (Place a window around the circle.)
ENTER A REFERENCE POINT> 18,18
ENTER NEW X SCALE (1.00)> 2  <CR>
ENTER NEW Y SCALE (2.00)> 2  <CR>
```

6. Quit the drawing without saving.

7. Turn to Module 65 to continue the learning sequence.

Module 74
WINDOW ROTATE

DESCRIPTION

WINDOW ROTATE (WR) allows you to turn or rotate any object or objects within a selected window. After the item or items are identified, select the axis point. This is the single point that remains in the same location after the item is rotated. In other words, the axis point is the point about which the selected items rotate. It may be on the objects or off a distance from them. Only objects completely within the selected window are rotated. At the angle prompt, three options for entering the angle are available. You can enter the desired angle if known; type A for angle to define the angle on the screen with a basepoint and a ray point; or type V for vertex to define the angle on the screen with a basepoint and two ray points. Angles are measured from the horizontal position in a counterclockwise rotation, beginning with the first ray selected and ending with the second ray selected. A 360-degree entry rotates the objects completely around, so there is no visual difference to the rotated version, while a 180-degree entry turns the object upside down. Negative degree entries are accepted. Thus, -45 degrees is equal to 315 degrees.

APPLICATIONS

WINDOW ROTATE is a commonly used editing command. Sometimes, it is easier to initially draw an object in the horizontal/vertical position, then rotate it into the correct position than draw it in the angled position first.

TYPICAL OPERATION

In this exercise you create objects, then rotate them.

1. Start a new drawing called "ROTATE."

2. Draw two rectangles.

```
ENTER A COMMAND> RE
ENTER A CORNER OF RECTANGLE> 16,2  <CR>
ENTER NEXT CORNER OF RECTANGLE> 18,26  <CR>
ENTER A COMMAND> RE
ENTER A CORNER OF RECTANGLE> 13,19  <CR>
ENTER NEXT CORNER OF RECTANGLE> 20,20  <CR>
```

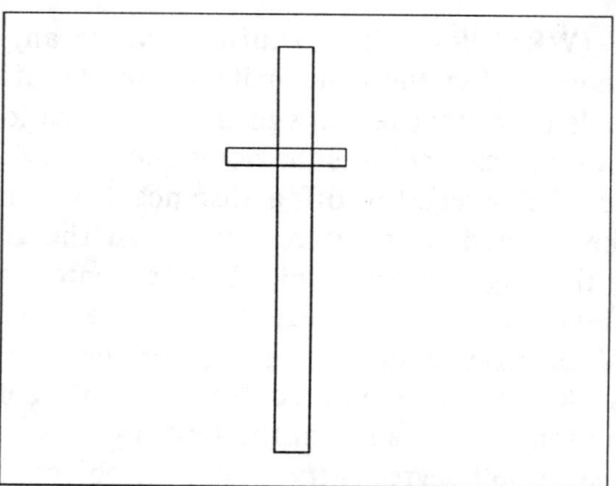

3. Rotate the rectangles.

```
ENTER A COMMAND> WR
```

NOTE

Only objects totally within a windowed area are rotated.

```
PLACE WINDOW> (Place a window to totally contain both rectangles.)
ENTER AN AXIS POINT> 17,14  <CR>
```

NOTE

Generic CADD accepts both negative and positive angles.

```
ENTER THE ANGLE> 45  <CR>
```

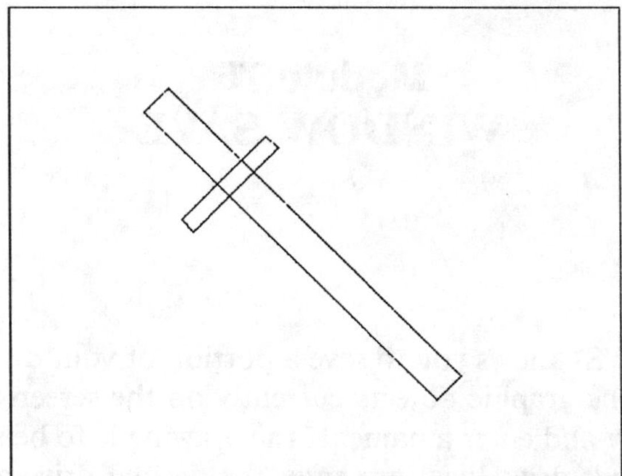

4. Quit the drawing without saving.

5. Turn to Module 75 to continue the learning sequence.

Module 75
WINDOW SAVE

DESCRIPTION

WINDOW SAVE (WS) allows you to save a portion of your drawing as a separate drawing file. Only the graphic objects currently on the screen view are saved. To save, place a window and enter a name. If the drawing is to be saved to a location other than the default drive location, enter the desired drive and path also. The name is limited to a maximum of eight characters.

APPLICATIONS

WINDOW SAVE is used to save a drawing file consisting of only a portion of your original drawing. The saved window is useful for recording several design variations during the design process. Each window may be loaded onto the screen as a separate drawing. Saved windows can also be added to other drawings, using the DRAWING LOAD command. Using this method, parts of one drawing can be used in other drawings, again saving the time needed to redraw them.

TYPICAL OPERATION

In this activity you create a drawing and save a view to the default drive.

1. Begin Generic CADD and reload the SAMPLE drawing to the screen.

2. Save a windowed area.

```
ENTER A COMMAND > WS
PLACE WINDOW > (Select a window containing the desk and the side chair.)
SAVE FILE: (SAMPLE.DWG) > SAMPLE2   <CR>
```

3. Clear the screen.

```
ENTER A COMMAND > DX
!!!WARNING!!!
DO YOU REALLY WANT TO ERASE THE DRAWING (Y,N) > Y
```

4. Reload SAMPLE2 to the screen.

```
ENTER A COMMAND> DL
ENTER A DRAWING FILE NAME> SAMPLE2  <CR>
RENAME WORKING DRAWING? (Y/N)> Y
WORKING FILENAME (SAMPLE2.DWG)>  <CR>
ENTER AN INSERT ORIGIN>  <CR>
PRESS RETURN FOR 0,0 ORIGIN
```

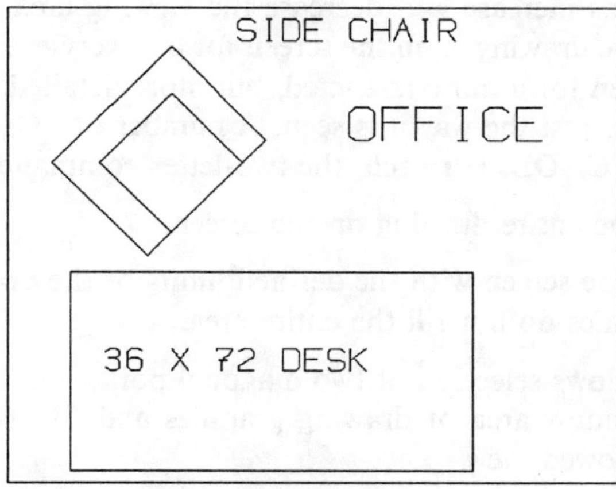

5. Zoom back to see that only the desk and chairs are part of the drawing.

```
ENTER A COMMAND> ZB
ENTER CENTER OF ZOOM> (Select a point in the screen center.)
```

6. Quit the drawing without saving.

7. Turn to Module 73 to continue the learning sequence.

Module 76
ZOOMS

DESCRIPTION

The zoom commands increase and decrease the viewing area of the drawing on the screen. The entire drawing is on the screen for an overview, or a small portion of the drawing is seen for a more restricted, but more detailed view. The drawing itself is not changed, just the way it is seen. A number of ZOOM commands are included in Generic CADD. For each, the two-letter command is in parentheses.

ALL (ZA) Shows the entire drawing on the screen.

LIMITS (ZL) Fills the screen with the defined limits of the drawing area, even if graphics do not fill the entire area.

WINDOW (ZW) Allows selection of two diagonal points on the screen to define a window area of drawing graphics and fills the screen with the windowed view.

VALUE (ZM)   Allows a scale value to be defined to show the screen graphics at a proportion of their real size.

VIEW (ZV)   Restores to the screen a view previously defined in the NAME VIEW command.

PREVIOUS (ZP) Displays the drawing area view previously on the drawing screen.

UP (ZU)   Moves the view up into the drawing, allowing more detail to be seen more clearly.

BACK (ZB)   Moves the view farther away from the drawing, allowing more of the drawing to appear on the screen.

PAN (PA)   Slides the view across the drawing. The zoom factor is not altered.

REDRAW DISPLAY (RD) Refreshes the screen view by redrawing the screen with the same view.

BACKWARDS REDRAW (BR) Refreshes the screen view by redrawing the drawing view in the reverse order in which it was originally drawn.

For a lengthy redraw, press any key to stop the redraw when the ojects you need are on the screen.

NAME VIEW (NV) Allows a current screen view to be saved with a name for recalling to the screen for later reference.

APPLICATIONS

The size and resolution of most monitors make it difficult to view and create large portions of a drawing at once and still be able to see the detail. The zoom commands enable a closer view of a portion of the drawing, so that additional detail may be added of modified more easily.

The zoom commands have no effect on the dimensions of the drawing, only the screen display.

ZOOM ALL is helpful when an overview of the entire drawing is needed. ZOOM LIMITS shows where the drawing graphics are located in relation to the limits that have been set.

ZOOM PREVIOUS is helpful to repeatedly zoom in to edit or examine a detail and return to a larger view to see the effect of the changes.

ZOOM WINDOW selects quickly the exact view desired to fill the screen. ZOOM WINDOW is usually faster than the ZOOM UP command if it is a long way to zoom into the drawing. ZOOM UP has a predefined zoom amount built into the command to make objects in each successive view twice as large as in the previous view. You must ZOOM UP several times to get the same view available with a single ZOOM WINDOW command.

ZOOM BACK is used to pull your view away from the drawing. The amount of zoom is preset, making objects in each successive ZOOM BACK view half as large as in the previous view. With a highly zoomed-in view on the screen, use ZOOM BACK several times to see the entire drawing. The ZOOM ALL command is usually the faster way to accomplish this task.

The PAN command allows movement across the drawing when another view is needed, but the level of detail showing is appropriate.

REDRAW DISPLAY is used to refresh or redisplay the screen view at its current zoom. This command will clear up any misconceptions about the way a line or object appears on the screen.

BACKWARDS REDRAW also redraws the screen, but in the reverse order in which the items were originally drawn. If a recently drawn object on a large drawing must be edited, BACKWARDS REDRAW can save time if the redraw is stopped when the object appears.

NAME VIEW saves a view with a name for later recall to the screen. NAME VIEW is useful for drawings on which there is continual movement back and forth between several views. As the drawing progresses, named views can be overwritten to name a new view.

ZOOM VIEW allows the screen recall of a view saved in NAME VIEW. Faster than using ZOOM WINDOW or ZOOM BACK and ZOOM UP several times, ZOOM VIEW moves instantly to the desired view.

TYPICAL OPERATION

In this exercise you practice the ZOOM commands by drawing several figures and changing the display area.

1. Start Generic CADD. Type **CAD** and press **Return** at the DOS prompt. Press **Return** at the Generic Cadd Title page.

2. Start a new drawing called "ZOOM."

```
ENTER A DRAWING FILE NAME > ZOOM   <CR>
IS THIS A NEW DRAWING (Y,N) > Y
```

3. Draw a rectangle.

```
ENTER A COMMAND >  RE
ENTER A CORNER OF RECTANGLE >  2,2   <CR>
ENTER NEXT CORNER OF RECTANGLE >  18,12   <CR>
```

4. Draw a circle.

```
ENTER A COMMAND >  C2
ENTER CENTER OF CIRCLE >  16,10   <CR>
ENTER A POINT ON CIRCLE >  8,16   <CR>
```

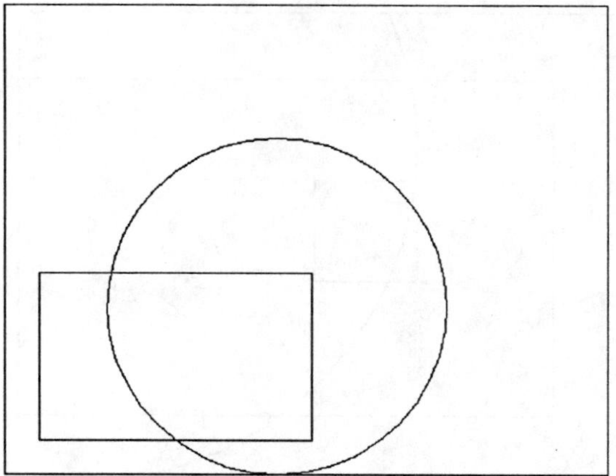

5. Now Zoom into your drawing.

```
ENTER A COMMAND> ZU
ENTER CENTER OF ZOOM> 9,7  <CR>
```

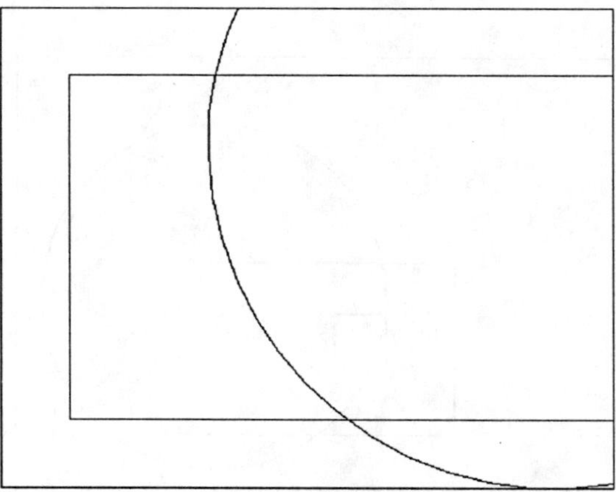

6. Draw another smaller rectangle in the zoomed view.

```
ENTER A COMMAND> RE
ENTER A CORNER OF RECTANGLE> 6,6  <CR>
ENTER NEXT CORNER OF RECTANGLE> 9,9  <CR>
```

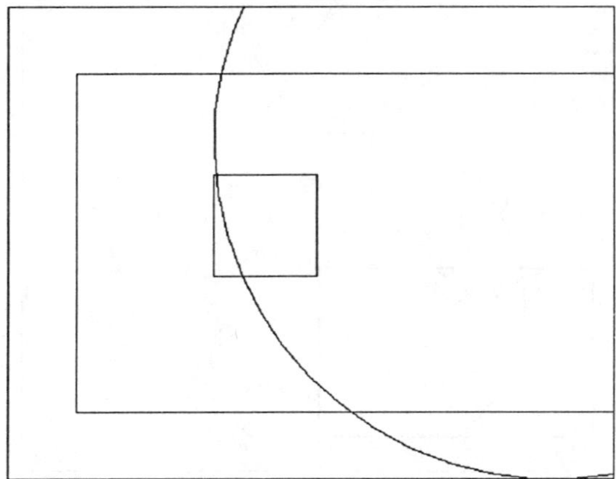

7. Zoom away from your drawing to see more of it on the screen.

```
ENTER A COMMAND> ZB
ENTER CENTER OF ZOOM > 10,10  <CR>
```

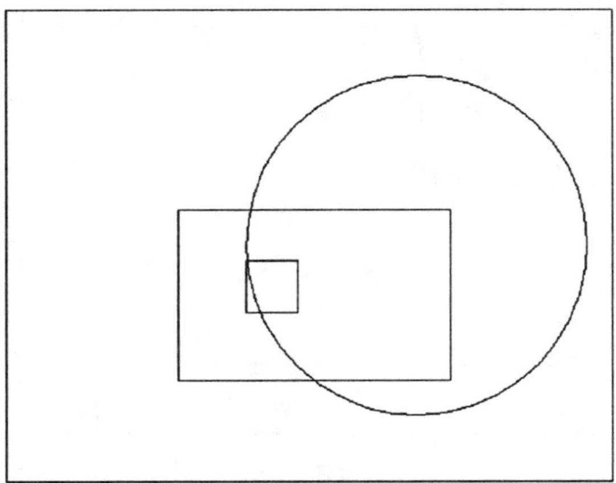

8. Now bring all the drawing into view on the screen.

```
ENTER A COMMAND> ZA
```

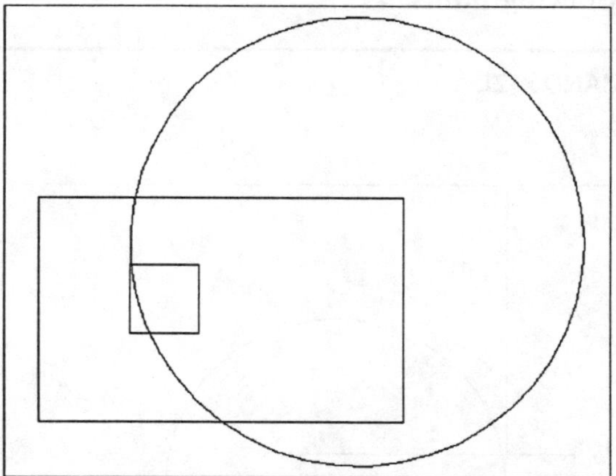

9. Pan or move across your drawing to the lower left.

```
ENTER A COMMAND > PA
ENTER NEW CENTER OF SCREEN > 4,4  <CR>
```

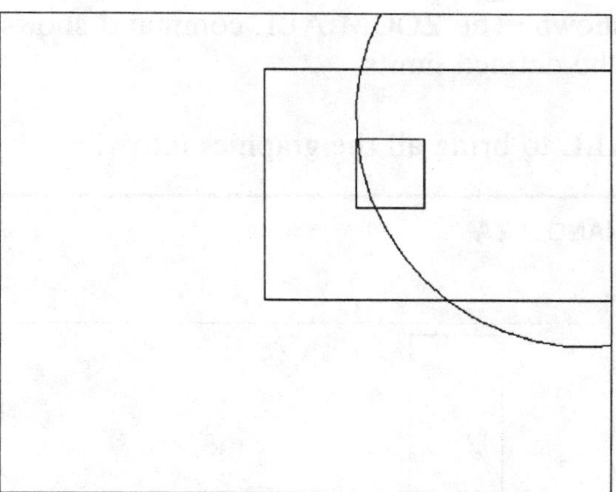

10. Add another rectangle.

```
ENTER A COMMAND > RE
ENTER A CORNER OF RECTANGLE > 0,0  <CR>
ENTER NEXT CORNER OF RECTANGLE > 6,30 <CR>
```

11. Zoom to the drawing limits.

ENTER A COMMAND > **ZL**

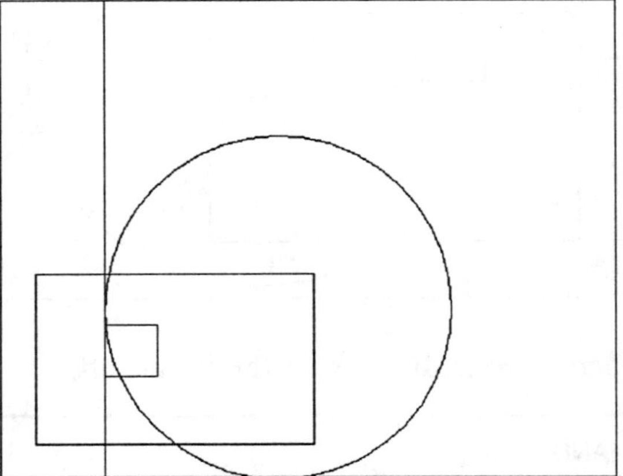

Because your drawing extends beyond the defined limits, not all of the graphics are shown. The ZOOM ALL command shows all of the drawing, regardless of the defined limits.

12. Use ZOOM ALL to bring all the graphics into view.

ENTER A COMMAND > **ZA**

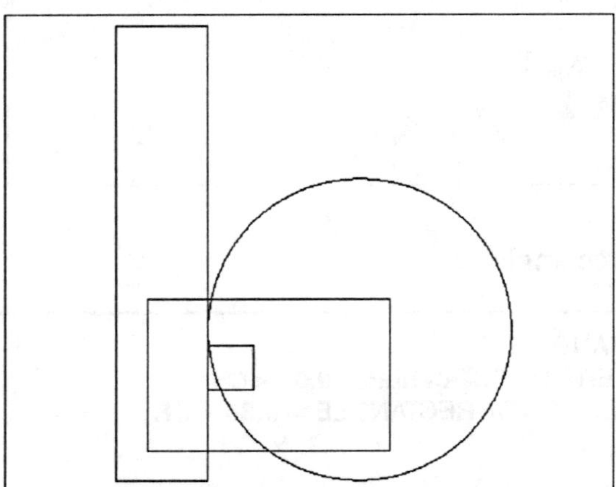

13. Quit the drawing without saving.

```
ENTER A COMMAND >  QU
SAVE CURRENT DRAWING (Y or N) >  N
"C" TO CONTINUE
"Q" TO QUIT >  Q
```

14. Turn to Module 42 to continue the learning sequence.

COMMAND REFERENCE

Command		Description
A2	TWO POINT ARC	Creates an arc from a specified center point and an endpoint.
A3	THREE POINT ARC	Creates an arc from two specified endpoints and a midpoint on the arc.
A4	FOUR POINT ARC	Creates an arc from selection of the arc center, start point, midpoint, and an endpoint.
AC	ABSOLUTE COORDINATES	Displays the coordinate location of the cursor as an X and Y distance from the drawing origin.
AD	ARC,ANGLE DEGREES	Allows the specification and display of angles in degrees.
AF	AUTOFILLET	Creates fillets between lines and double lines as they are drawn.
AL	ALL LAYERS EDIT	Allows all layers to be edited if toggled to the on position.
AM	ARC,ANGLE MINUTES	Allows the angle display format to be in minutes.
AT	ARROW TYPE	Selects among six available line terminators for dimensioning.
AW	ARROW MODE	Toggles between open and closed arrowheads for dimensioning.
AX	ANGLE DIMENSION	Dimensions the angle between two selected lines.
BE	BEZIER EDIT	Allows editing of two adjacent Bezier curves at once.
BP	BASEPOINT	Selects the points for the drawing basepoint.
BR	BACKWARD REDRAW	Refreshes the screen view by redrawing the drawing view in the reverse order in which it was originally drawn.
BV	BEZIER CURVE	Creates a smooth curve defined by a number of tangent lines of a minimum of three points.
C2	TWO POINT CIRCLE	Creates a circle by selection of a center point and a perimeter point.
C3	THREE POINT CIRCLE	Creates a circle by selection of three perimeter points.

Command		Description
CA	CHAMFER DISTANCE	Sets the distance between the intersection of two selected lines and the point where each line is chamfered in the CHAMFER command.
CC	COMPONENT CREATE	Makes components of selected objects.
CD	COMPONENT DUMP	Saves all at once all the components currently defined on a drawing.
CE	COMPONENT EXPLODE	Returns a component into the graphics from which it was originally created.
CG	COMPONENT DRAG	Allows viewing a component as a ghosted image as it is placed on a drawing.
CH	CHAMFER	Creates a line between two selected non-parallel lines.
CI	COMPONENT IMAGE	Places the graphics used to create a component on a drawing without bearing the status of a component.
CK	CURSOR COLOR	Sets the color of the drawing screen cursor.
CL	COMPONENT LOAD	Brings a component to a specified drawing file for placement on the drawing.
CM	CURSOR MOVEMENT	Controls the movement of the cursor if the arrow keys on the keyboard are used as a pointing device.
CN	COMPONENT REPLACE	Allows replacement of all specified placed components with another component.
CO	COMPONENT LIST ON/OFF	Toggles on and off the visibility of the component list on the menu.
CP	COMPONENT PLACE	Places a previously saved component on a drawing.
CR	COMPONENT ROTATION	Defines the angle at which a component is placed.
CS	COMPONENT SAVE	Saves the definition of a component to a specified disk.
CU	CURSOR SIZE	Sets the size of the drawing screen cursor.
CV	COMPLEX CURVE	Creates a smooth curve by the selection of a minimum of three points through which the curve is fitted.
CX	COMPONENT REMOVE	Removes all placements of a specified component from a drawing.
CZ	COMPONENT SCALE	Alters the scale of a component before it is placed.
DA	DRAWING ALIGN	Sets the parameters needed prior to tracing a drawing into a drawing file using a digitizer.

Command		Description
DC	DELTA COORDINATES	Displays the coordinates of the cursor as an X and Y distance in relation to the previously selected point.
DE	DECIMALS	Allows display of portions of inches in a decimal format.
DF	DISPLAY FILL	Toggles on and off the visibility of placed area fills.
DG	DRAWING CHANGE	Alters several features of objects that are already on the drawing.
DH	DISPLAY HATCH	Toggles on and off the visibility of placed hatch patterns.
DK	DISPLAY COLOR	Sets the color of the screen display text.
DL	DRAWING LOAD	Loads a selected drawing onto the screen.
DO	DRAWING REORIGIN	Changes the origin of the drawing.
DP	DRAWING PLOT	Plots the current drawing.
DR	DRAWING ROTATE	Rotates all objects within an entire drawing to a specified angle.
DS	DRAWING SAVE	Saves a drawing to disk.
DV	DECIMAL VALUE	Controls the number of places that decimal values are shown.
DX	DRAWING ERASE	Deletes all graphics from the screen.
DZ	DRAWING RESCALE	Changes the scale of all objects on the drawing.
ED	ERASE LAST DIMENSION	Removes the last single dimension drawn.
EL	ERASE LAST	Removes the last item drawn from the drawing.
EP	ELLIPSE	Creates an ellipse from a specified length and location of the major and minor axis.
FA	FAST ARCS ON/OFF	Speeds the drawing display by displaying arcs and circles with a lower resolution.
FF	FITTED FILL	Fills areas defined by objects with poorly defined corners.
FH	FITTED HATCH	Hatches areas defined by objects with poorly defined corners.
FI	FEET AND INCHES	Allows entry and display of coordinates in feet and inches.
FK	FILL COLOR	Specifies the color of filled areas on a drawing.
FL	FILLET	Creates an arc between two non-parallel lines or two arcs.
FR	FRACTIONS ON/OFF	Allows display of inches in a fractional format.
FS	FONT SELECT	Selects the lettering style for on-screen text.
FT	DECIMAL FEET	Allows entry and display of coordinates in feet.
FV	FRACTIONAL VALUE	Controls the accuracy of fractions as they are displayed in the coordinate display.

Command		Description
GC	COMPONENT SNAP	Snaps to the points within a component.
GR	GRID ON/OFF	Toggles the screen grid display on and off.
GS	GRID SIZE	Sets the distance between grid points.
HK	HATCH COLOR	Specifies the color of hatch patterns to be placed.
HN	HATCH NAME	Allows the naming of the hatch pattern to be placed.
HR	HATCH ROTATE	Rotates a hatch pattern as it is placed.
HZ	HATCH SCALE	Changes the scale of hatch patterns to be placed.
IL	IMAGE LOAD	Loads a previously saved image file.
IN	INCHES	Allows entry and display of coordinates in inches.
IS	IMAGE SAVE	Saves a pixel image of the drawing screen as a .GX2 file.
KT	CLEAN CORNER	Trims all lines in an intersection created with two sets of parallel lines.
L1	STRAIGHT LINE	Draws a single straight line.
L2	DOUBLE LINE	Draws two parallel lines simultaneously.
LB	LOAD BATCH FILE	Loads and executes a selected batch file.
LD	LOAD DIGITIZER MENU	Loads a digitizer menu file.
LE	DIMENSION LEADER	Creates a leader line pointing from one object to another.
LF	LETTER FONT	Selects the font used in dimensioning.
LH	LETTER SIZE	Sets the text height used in dimensioning.
LK	LINE COLOR	Sets an on-screen color to be associated with lines or objects.
LL	SHOULDER LENGTH	Controls the length of the horizontal portion of the leader line in the DIMENSION LEADER command.
LP	LETTER PLACEMENT	Allows a choice between placing dimension text above or into the dimension line.
LR	LETTER DIRECTION	Determines the text alignment in relation to the dimension line.
LS	LIMITS	Establishes the drawing sheet boundaries.
LT	LINE TYPE	Allows selection of a variety of predefined linetypes.
LV	LOAD VIDEO MENU	Loads a previously created video menu from the disk.
LW	LINE WIDTH	Allows selection of eleven different line widths.
LX	LINEAR DIMENSION	Dimensions horizontal, vertical, and angled lines on a drawing.

Command		Description
LZ	LINE SCALE	Sets the interval at which a line pattern repeats.
MA	MEASURE ANGLE	Measures an angle between any two selected points.
MB	MANUAL ENTRY OFFSET BASEPOINT	Allows all coordinates entered to be referenced from the selected basepoint.
MC	CENTIMETERS	Allows entry and display of coordinates in centimeters.
MD	MEASURE DISTANCE	Measures the distance between any two selected points.
MM	MILLIMETERS	Allows entry and display of coordinates in millimeters.
MO	MANUAL ENTRY OFFSET ORIGIN	Allows entry of a point to be offset from the drawing origin.
MP	MOVE POINT	Moves any selected point on an object.
MR	MANUAL ENTRY OFFSET RELATIVE	Allows entry of a point to be a specified distance from the last point entered.
MT	METERS	Allows entry and display of coordinates in meters.
MV	MEASURE AREA	Calculates the area of a selected figure.
NL	NEAREST LINE SNAP	Snaps the cursor to the nearest line.
NP	NEAREST POINT SNAP	Snaps the cursor to the nearest point.
NV	NAME VIEW	Allows a current screen view to be saved with a name for later recall.
OB	OBJECT BREAK	Removes a section of an existing object between any two selected points.
OC	OBJECT COPY	Allows creation of up to 100 copies of a single specified object.
OE	OBJECT ERASE	Allows erasing of a single specified object.
OF	OBJECT FILL	Allows selection of objects to fill by identifying each boundary separately.
OG	OBJECT CHANGE	Allows changing of the line type, line width, line color, and layer of a selected object.
OH	OBJECT HATCH	Allows selection of objects to hatch by identifying each boundary separately.
OM	OBJECT MOVE	Allows a single object to be identified and moved to a new location.
OR	ORTHO MODE	When toggled on, allows you to draw perfectly straight vertical or horizontal lines.
OT	OVERRIDE TEXT	Toggles between the automatic creation of dimension text and manual entry of the text.
P1	DRAWING PATH	Controls where Generic CADD saves or retrieves drawings.

	Command	Description
P2	COMPONENT PATH	Allows changing of the disk and directory where components are stored.
P3	FONT PATH	Allows specification of the drive and directory where Generic CADD looks for and saves fonts.
PA	PAN	Slides the view across the drawing, without altering the zoom factor.
PC	CONSTRUCTION POINTS	When toggled on, displays small x-shaped graphics representing points selected on the screen.
PD	PACK DATA	Removes erased objects from memory.
PF	PROXIMITY FIXED	Determines where dimension lines are placed in relation to the points being dimensioned.
PM	DIGITIZER ACTIVE AREA	Defines the area on the digitizer to use for pointing on the drawing screen.
PO	STANDARD POINT	Places small cross shaped graphics as needed for reference.
PR	REFERENCE POINTS	Toggles the visibility of component reference points on and off.
PS	STANDARD POINTS	Toggles on and off the display of standard points.
PT	POLAR COORDINATES	Displays the coordinates of the cursor as a distance and angle from the previously selected point.
PU	PEN UP	Stops the drawing mode of single or double lines.
QU	QUIT	Exits Generic CADD.
RB	RUBBER BANDING	Toggled on, pulls a stretching line behind the moving cursor.
RC	RADIAL COPY	Allows copying of a windowed object in a circular pattern.
RD	REDRAW DISPLAY	Refreshes the screen view by redrawing the screen with the same view.
RE	RECTANGLE	Draws a rectangle by selection of two diagonal points.
RF	FILLET RADIUS	Sets the radius of the arc used in the FILLET command.
RM	TRIM	Trims a selected object to meet cleanly with another.
RP	REGULAR POLYGON	Creates an equal sided and equal angled geometric figure of a specified number of sides.
RT	RETURN TO GENERIC CAD	Returns to the Generic CADD menu from DOTPLOT.

Command		Description
RZ	TRACE SCALE	Sets the scale of the drawing traced in the TRACE MODE command.
SA	PARALLEL SNAP	Allows a line to be drawn parallel to an existing line.
SB	SAVE BATCH FILE	Saves a drawing file as a batch file.
SC	CLOSEST POINT SNAP	Snaps the cursor to the closest entity point.
SD	SELECT DIGITIZER AREA	Enables up to ten digitizer menus to be active simultaneously.
SF	SCREEN FLIP	Displays a text screen with current detailed information about the status of the current drawing.
SG	SNAP TO GRID	When toggled on, allows the cursor to locate only on the grid points currently defined on the screen.
SI	INTERSECTION SNAP	Snaps the cursor to the intersection of two entities.
SK	DIMENSION COLOR	Selects the on-screen color for dimension lines, line terminators, and text.
SL	STAUTS LINE	Toggles the on-screen status line on and off.
SM	MIDPOINT SNAP	Snaps the cursor to the midpoint of a selected line.
SN	ARC CENTER SNAP	Snaps the cursor to the center of a selected circle or arc.
SO	SOLID LINE	Creates solid infill in double lines.
SP	PERPENDICULAR SNAP	Allows a line to be drawn perpendicular to an existing selected line.
SX	ARC TANGENT SNAP	Snaps the cursor to the tangent point of a selected circle or arc.
TA	TEXT ASPECT	Controls the width of each text character.
TC	TEXT CREATE/EDIT	Allows definition of text characters to create a unique font style.
TD	TEXT DELETE	Deletes specified characters in a string of text.
TF	FAST TEXT	Allows all drawing text to be temporarily turned off from view.
TH	DOUBLE WIDTH	Allows the setting of the separation distance between parallel lines in the DOUBLE LINE command.
TI	TEXT INSERT	Inserts new characters in an existing text string.
TK	TEXT COLOR	Sets the on-screen color of drawing text.
TM	TRACE MODE	Allows use of a digitizer to trace a drawing into a drawing file.

Command		Description
TO	TOLERANCE	Sets the size of the searching area around the screen cursor.
TP	TEXT PLACE	Places text on a drawing.
TR	TEXT ROTATION	Sets the rotation of text as it is placed on the drawing.
TS	TEXT SLANT	Controls the slant of each character in a text string.
TV	FAST TEXT VIEW	Allows selection of specified text to be viewed, even though FAST TEXT is toggled to the on position.
TX	TEXT REPLACE	Allows replacement of existing characters in a text string.
TZ	TEXT SIZE	Sets the on-screen height of drawing text.
UD	DIMENSION DIRECTION	Selects the direction of a dimension.
UE	UNERASE	Restores to the screen objects that were previously erased.
UL	DIMENSION LAYER	Determines the layer on which the dimensions are placed.
UM	DIMENSION MODE	Gives a choice between the three dimension modes — single, partitioned, or cumulative.
VM	VIDEO MENU	Toggles the display of the video menu on and off.
VX	DELETE/CLEAR VIDEO MENU	Clears the screen of the current video menu in preparation for loading a new menu to the screen.
WC	WINDOW COPY	Allows creation of up to 99 copies of a windowed group of objects.
WE	WINDOW ERASE	Erases all identified objects within a specified window.
WF	WINDOW FILL	Fills all objects within a windowed area solid.
WG	WINDOW CHANGE	Changes the line type, line width, line color, and layer of a windowed group of selected items.
WH	WINDOW HATCH	Selects a group of objects within a window to infill with a selected hatch pattern.
WI	WINDOW MIRROR	Creates a mirrored image of a windowed object or objects.
WM	WINDOW MOVE	Allows a series of objects to be moved.
WR	WINDOW ROTATE	Rotates objects within a selected window.
WS	WINDOW SAVE	Saves a portion of a drawing as a separate drawing file.
WT	WINDOW TEXT	Allows creation of new font characters from objects already on the drawing screen.

Command		Description
WZ	WINDOW RESCALE	Alters the size and proporton of a windowed object.
XD	EXIT TO DOTPLOT	Enters DOTPLOT directly from Generic CADD.
XL	EXTENSION LENGTH	Sets the length of the dimension extension lines.
XO	EXTENSION OFFSET	Controls the distance between the dimension extension lines and the points being dimensioned.
XS	EXTENSION STRETCH	Toggles between variable and fixed length extension lines in dimensioning.
XT	EXTEND	Lengthens or extends a selected object to meet another.
YC	LAYER CURRENT	Sets the current drawing layer.
YD	LAYER DISPLAY	Sets the layers which are viewed on the screen.
YG	LAYER CHANGE	Allows modification of certain characteristics of all objects on a specified layer.
YH	LAYER HIDE	Turns off from view a selected layer.
YL	LAYER LOAD	Loads a previously saved drawing onto a single selected layer.
YR	LAYER ROTATE	Rotates all objects on a selected layer.
YS	LAYER SAVE	Saves all information on a selected layer to a separate drawing file.
YX	LAYER ERASE	Erases all information on a specified layer.
YZ	LAYER RESCALE	Rescales all objects on a selected layer.
ZA	ZOOM ALL	Shows the entire drawing on the screen.
ZB	ZOOM BACK	Moves the screen view farther away from the drawing.
ZL	ZOOM LIMITS	Fills the screen with the defined limits of the drawing area.
ZM	ZOOM VALUE	Allows a scale value to be defined to show the screen graphics at a proportion of their real size.
ZP	ZOOM PREVIOUS	Displays the drawing area view previously on the drawing screen.
ZU	ZOOM UP	Moves the screen view up from the current view.
ZV	ZOOM VIEW	Restores to the screen a view previously saved in the NAME VIEW command.
ZW	ZOOM WINDOW	Fills the screen with all the graphics in a selected window.

Appendix B
TERMS AND DEFINITIONS

Term	Definition
Chamfer	An angled line cutting off the corner of two intersecting lines.
Character	A letter, number, punctuation mark, space, or symbol displayed on the screen in a string of text.
Circumference	The boundary line of a closed figure, usually a circle.
Concentric	Having a common center point.
Coordinate	One of a set of numbers that determines the location of a point.
Default	A predetermined setting that is normal mode when Generic CADD is turned on.
Diameter	A straight line which passes through the center of a circle, connecting two opposite points on the circumference.
Digitizer	A hardware device for tracing drawings into a computer file.
Dimension Lines	The line that connects two extension lines and indicates the length or angle of the object being dimensioned.
Drive	An electromechanical device used to read and write information to and from a magnetic disk. A disk may be removable or fixed.
Extension Lines	Lines in dimensioning which extend from the object or point being measured to the dimension line. Also called witness lines.
Extension Offset	The distance the extension lines are offset from the points being measured.
Fillet	An arc inserted between two intersecting lines.
Font	Text lettering style.
Function Keys	The keys F1 through F10 (or F12) located on a computer keyboard. These keys are often assigned special functions.
Hardware	The equipment components that make up a computer system.
Hatch	A pattern of infill for an object, usually made of a series of lines, such as cross-hatch, bricks, etc.
Intersection	The common point of two crossing figures.

Term	Definition
Leader	A line with an arrow that points to an object and is usually accompanied by a string of explanatory text.
Line terminator	A special symbol that ends a leader or dimension line, usually an arrow, a dot, or a slash mark.
Major axis	The longest axis of an ellipse.
Memory	A computer's temporary storage area. Also referred to as RAM or random access memory. Information stored in memory is lost when the power is turned off. Computer programs are usually loaded and reside in a computer's memory during program execution.
Minor axis	The shortest axis of an ellipse.
Orthogonal	Pertaining to or composed of right angles.
Path	Often used in place of the term filepath or file directory.
Perimeter	The length of an object's boundary.
Pixel	A point of light on the drawing screen. Several pixels create an object, depending upon the screen resolution.
Plot	Transfer a drawing on the screen to paper, using a plotter.
Polygon	A closed figure with three or more sides.
Radius	A line segment joining the center of a circle with a point on the circumference.
RAM	Ramdom Access Memory. See Memory.
Root Directory	The initial, or top directory, usually found on the hard disk.
Rubber band	A line attached to the cursor that is pulled behind as a drawing is made. Allows viewing of a point location before the point is actually placed.
Software	The programs (computer instructions) and data files that reside on magnetic media, paper, or in computer hardware.
Status Line	The lines of information that appear at the bottom of the Generic CADD drawing screen, providing information about the current drawing and the current command.
Subdirectory	A directory, or filepath, that is subordinate to a higher level directory.
Toggle	Functions that can be turned on or off by the same key sequence. ORTHOGONAL MODE and GRID ON/OFF are toggles.
Tolerance	The search area around the screen cursor. the tolerance setting affects the snap commands.

Appendix C
DRAWING EXAMPLES

Try your expertise at the following drawings!

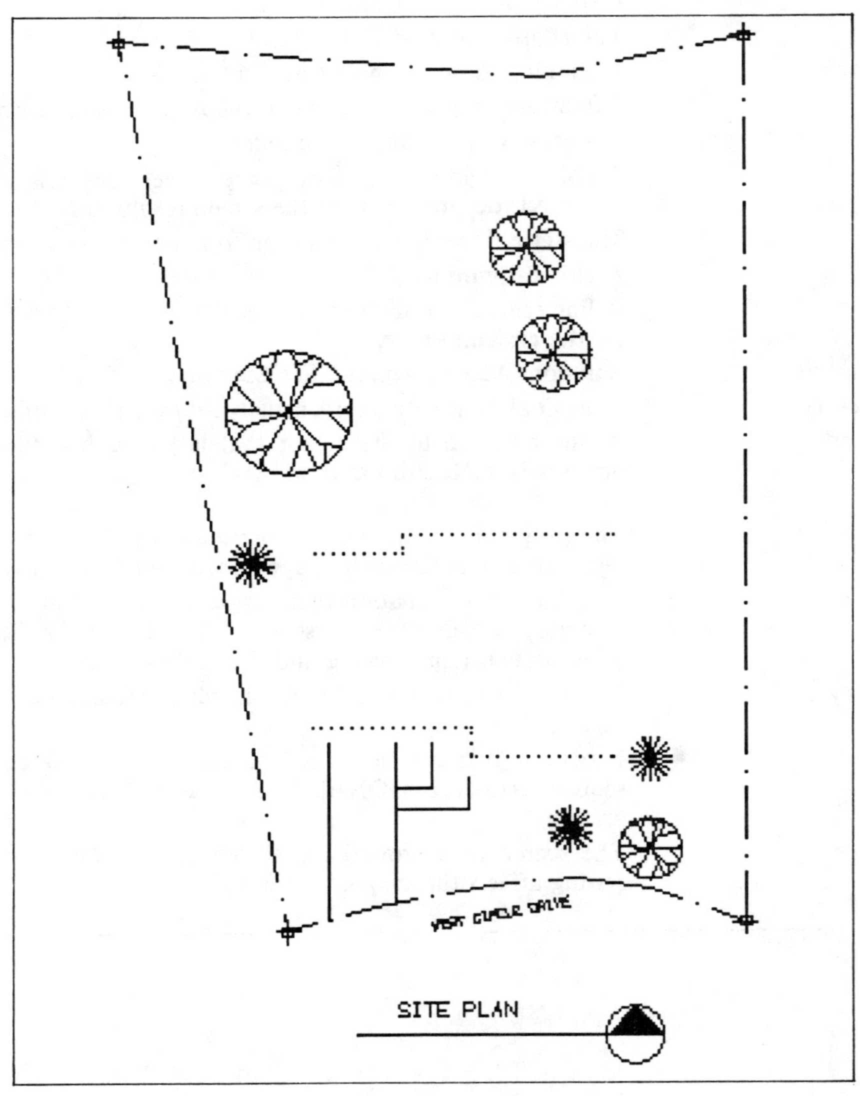

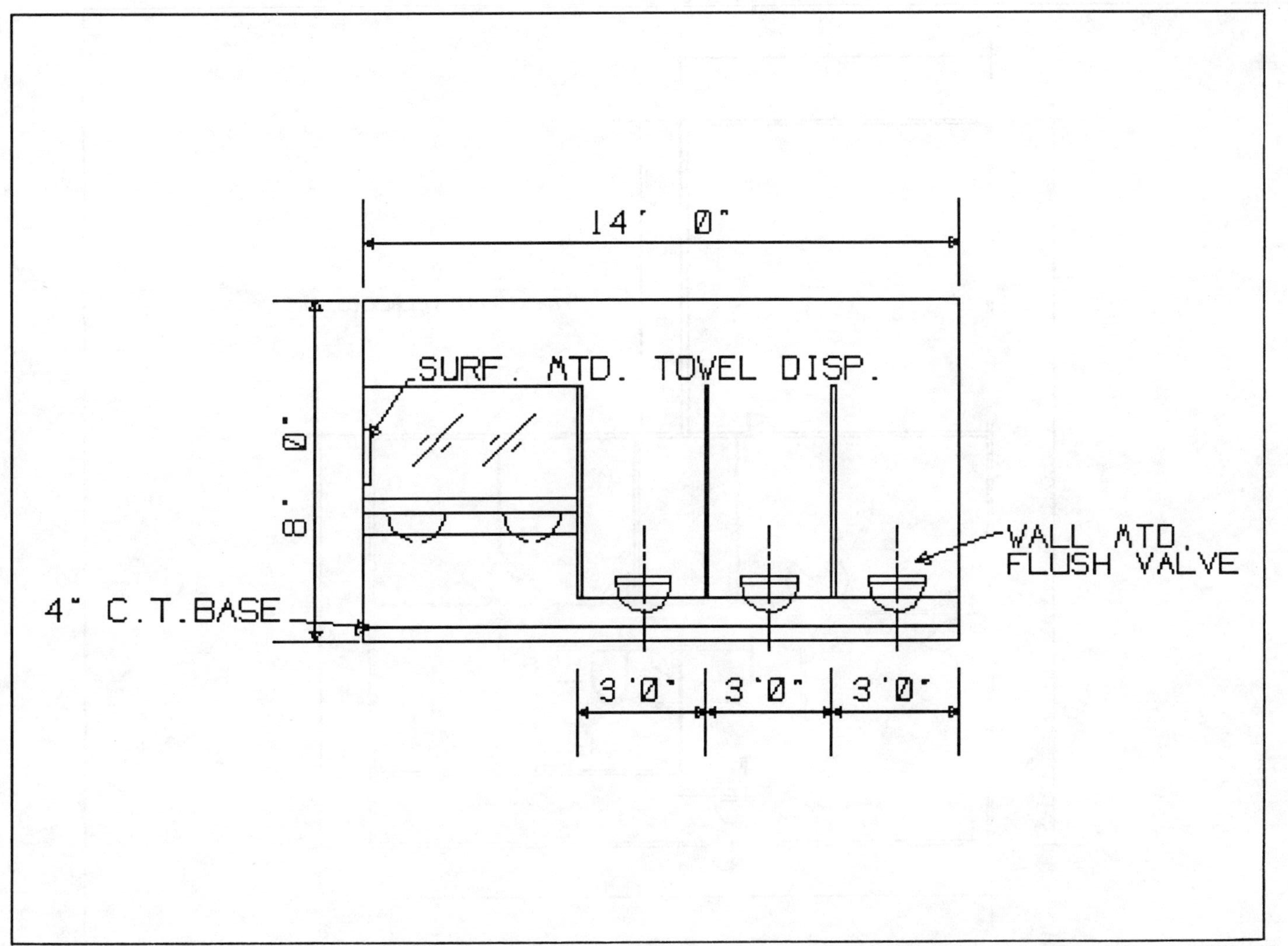
14' 0"
SURF. MTD. TOWEL DISP.
8' 0"
WALL MTD.
FLUSH VALVE
4" C.T.BASE
3'0"
3'0"
3'0"

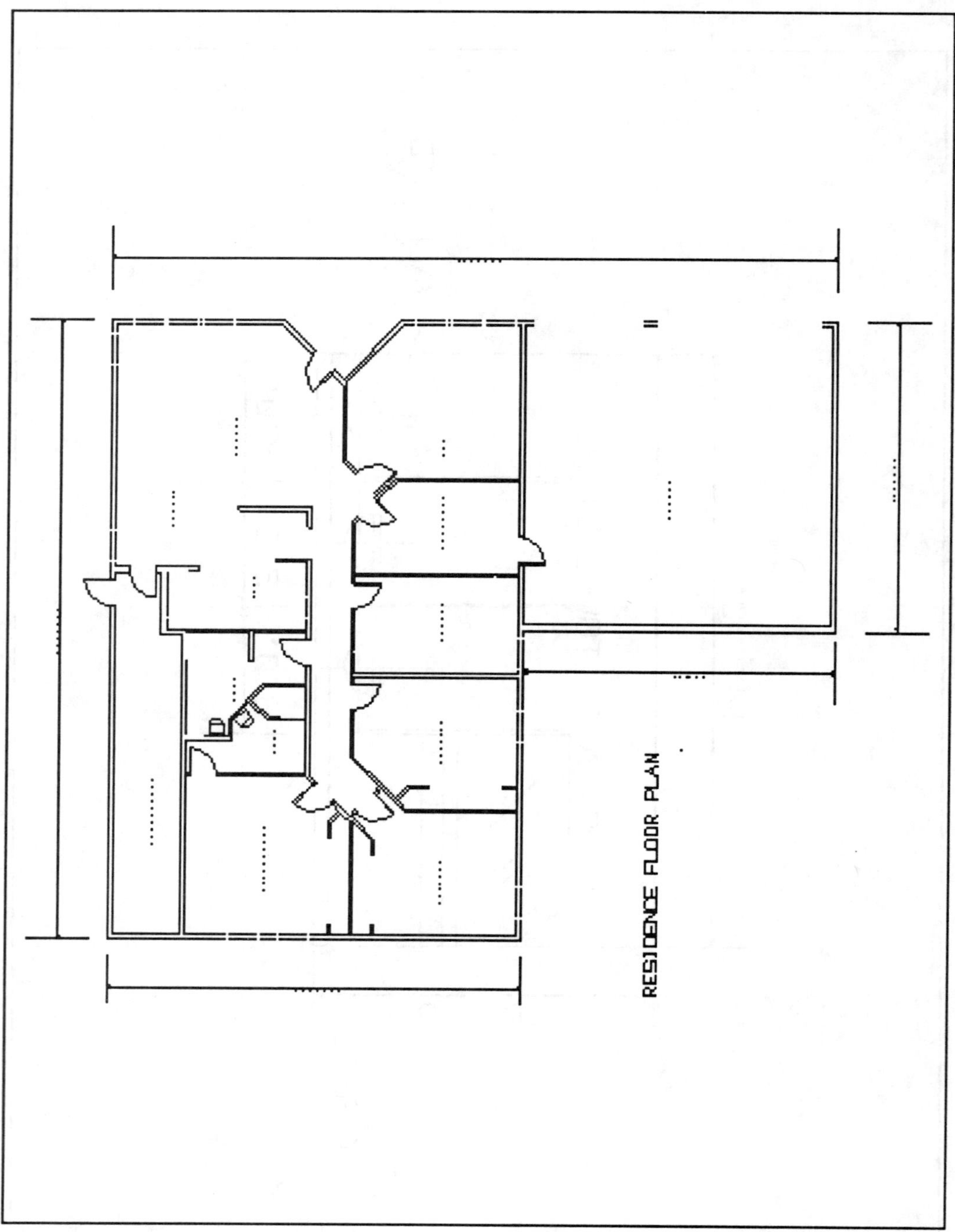

RESIDENCE FLOOR PLAN

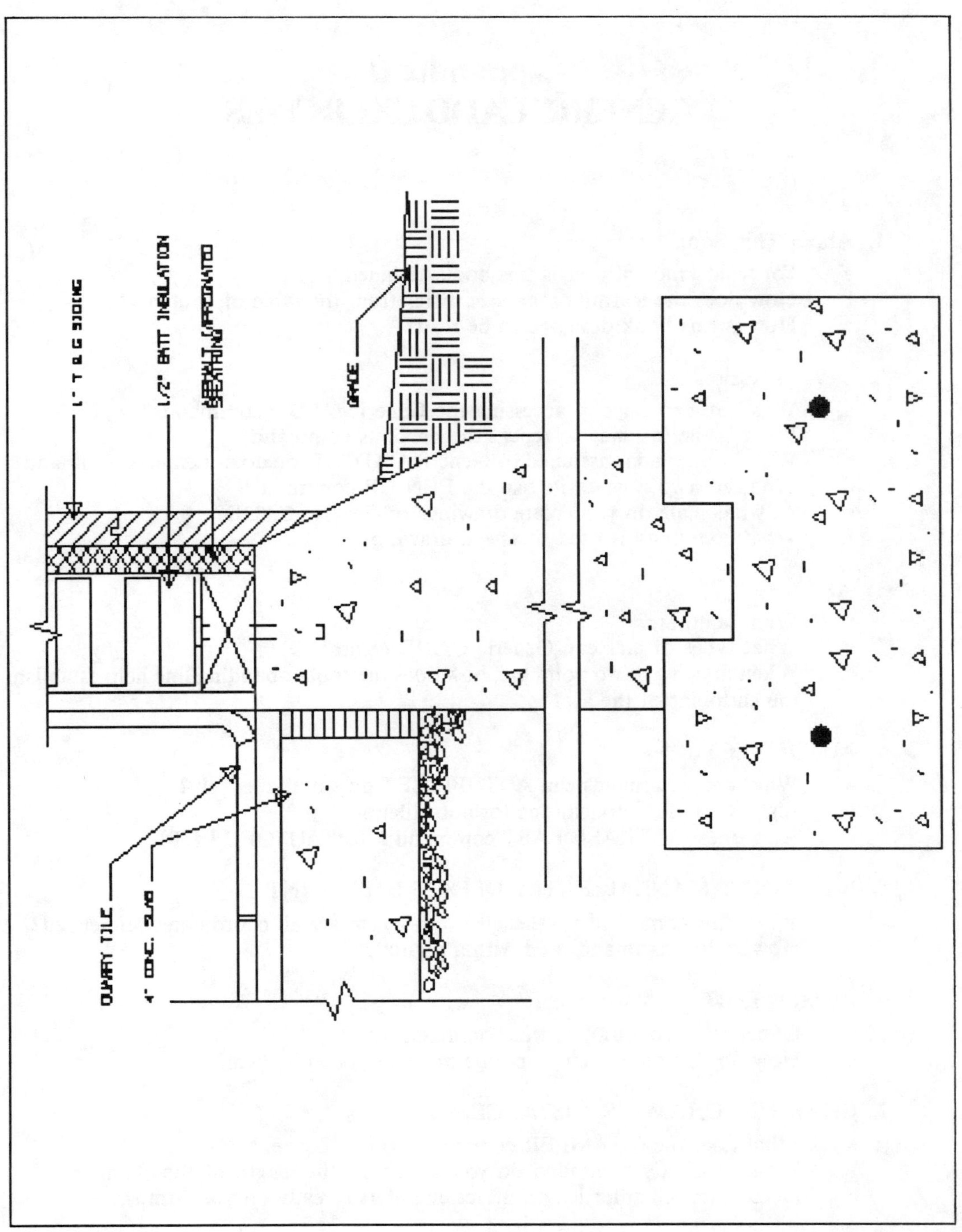
1" T & G SIDING
1/2" BATT INSULATION
BREATHING (IMPREGNATED)
GRADE
QUARRY TILE
4" CONC. SLAB

Appendix D
GENERIC CADD EXERCISES

1. About This Book

    a.   For what kinds of user is this book designed?
    b.   How does the learning sequence differ from the table of contents?
    c.   How is this book designed to be read?

2. Sample Session

    a.   What are two ways of accessing the Generic CADD commands?
    b.   What is the fast way to repeat the previous command?
    c.   What command is assumed by Generic CADD if you do not enter a command?
    d.   What are two ways to invoke the PEN UP command?
    e.   At what scale do you create drawings in Generic CADD?
    f.   What command is used to save a drawing?

3. ARC

    a.   What is an arc?
    b.   What types of arcs can Generic CADD create?
    c.   When drawing a two point arc, how does the rubber banding line help establish the endpoint of the arc?

4. AUTOFILLET

    a.   What two commands can AUTOFILLET do simultaneously?
    b.   List five useful applications for autofilleting.
    c.   How does the ERASE LAST command affect AUTOFILLET?

5. BASEPOINT/MANUAL ENTRY OFFSET BASEPOINT

    a.   When this command is selected, from where are all coordinates referenced?
    b.   How is this command used with a digitizer?

6. BEZIER EDIT

    a.   Under what condition is this command used?
    b.   How do you see the curve points move as you edit them?

7. CHAMFER/CHAMFER DISTANCE

    a.   What does the CHAMFER command do to a corner?
    b.   What two-letter command do you use to set the length of the chamfer?
    c.   Does a new chamfer length affect chamfers already on your drawing?

8. **CIRCLE**
   a.   What are the ways Generic CADD creates circles?
   b.   Which would you use if you knew the diameter of the desired circle?
   c.   How would you draw several concentric circles?

9. **CLEAN CORNER**
   a.   What types of intersections does this command correct?
   b.   CLEAN CORNER is usually used in conjunction with what command?
   c.   Under what condition will Generic CADD give you the "Object not found" error message?

10. **COMPONENTS**
    a.   How does Generic CADD interpret a component?
    b.   What command is used to return a component to its original graphic status?
    c.   What snap mode will allow you to snap to any construction point of a component?
    d.   What is the largest, single advantage of using components?

11. **CONSTRUCTION POINTS**
    a.   Do construction points always appear on your drawing?
    b.   What is meant by a toggle?

12. **CURSOR COLOR/CURSOR SIZE/CURSOR MOVEMENT**
    a.   What is the default cursor size value?
    b.   Is the CURSOR MOVEMENT command used when you use a mouse as a pointing device?
    c.   What are two ways to choose the cursor color?

13. **CURVES**
    a.   What is the minimum number of points needed to create a curve?
    b.   What two curve types can Generic CADD create?

14. **DIGITIZER**
    a.   For what do you use the digitizer?
    b.   What are the three available digitizer control commands?

15. **DIMENSIONS**
    a.   How does Generic CADD know the dimension of a line you have drawn?
    b.   What are the three dimensioning modes?
    c.   How do you control the dimension layer and color?
    d.   How do you choose the line terminator for the dimensioning?
    e.   What commands control the dimension extension lines?

16. DIMENSION TEXT
    a.   How are dimensional text size and font defined?
    b.   What command controls the location of the text within or above the dimension line?
    c.   Which command do you use if the dimension text you want is different from the dimension Generic CADD actually measures?

17. DISPLAY COLOR
    a.   What command controls the screen color of the Generic CADD menu?
    b.   How is the grid color set?
    c.   Why might you want to change the screen menu color?

18. DISPLAY COORDINATES
    a.   What are the three ways coordinates are calculated and displayed?
    b.   What is the difference among these three options?
    c.   How do you move from one coordinate display to another?

19. DOUBLE LINE/DOUBLE WIDTH
    a.   Which command sets the thickness of a double line?
    b.   What are some examples of how you might use double lines?
    c.   How do you control where Generic CADD draws the double lines in relation to where you draw the line with the cursor?
    d.   How do you edit double line intersections?

20. DOTPLOT
    a.   How do you send a plot to a printer?
    b.   What command takes you directly from Generic CADD into DOTPLOT?
    c.   What command returns you from DOTPLOT to Generic CADD?
    d.   What are the three ways to scale or view your drawing and plot?
    e.   What is the scale ratio for a $1/4" = 1'0"$ plot?
    f.   When would you use DOTPLOT rather than generate a pen plot?

21. DRAWING CHANGE/ROTATE/RESCALE/REORIGIN
    a.   How can you change the linetype of all the lines on a specified layer?
    b.   Which command rotates the entire drawing?

22. DRAWING ERASE
    a.   When is DRAWING ERASE most commonly used?
    b.   Is information on layers currently hidden erased when this command is used?
    c.   When DRAWING ERASE is used is the drawing removed from the hard drive?

23. DRAWING LOAD
    a.   Under what condition is it necessary to clear the drawing screen before issuing the DRAWING LOAD command?

b. Explain how Generic CADD uses DRAWING LOAD to create composites of several previously created drawings.

c. How do drawings align when loaded on top of one another?

24. DRAWING PATH

a. Explain how you use DRAWING PATH to control the saved location of a drawing.

b. What process would you use to save a drawing to the A floppy drive?

c. What is the default drawing path?

d. If Generic CADD is unable to find a drawing you created earlier, what are the possible reasons?

25. DRAWING PLOT

a. What hardware is used to produce a drawing plot?

b. What are the only limitations on the paper size you choose?

c. What scale options are available?

d. How does Generic CADD determine which lines to plot with which pens in the plotter?

e. Can Generic CADD plot any portion of the drawing not shown in the current screen view?

f. How do you save a plot to a disk rather than sending it to the plotter?

g. What are the advantages and disadvantages of saving a plot to disk?

26. DRAWING SAVE

a. How is a drawing saved to the hard drive?

b. How is a drawing saved to the floppy frive?

c. Why save a drawing to the hard drive?

d. How often should you save?

e. How do you create different versions of the same drawing?

27. ELLIPSE

a. What two ellipse types does Generic CADD offer?

b. What are the advantages and disadvantages of each type?

28. ERASE LAST

a. How does ERASE LAST work?

b. How many times can you use this command in a row?

29. EXTEND

a. How is EXTEND different from the TRIM command?

b. How does EXTEND function to shorten a line?

30. FAST ARCS ON/OFF
    a. What is the purpose of this command?
    b. What are the viewing disadvantages when this command is toggled to the on position?

31. FILL
    a. What are the advantages of using FILL?
    b. Why is it good to have the fill off during some drawing sessions?
    c. Which command controls the color of the fill?
    d. Which command controls the display of the fill?

32. FILLET/FILLET RADIUS
    a. What is a fillet?
    b. How is the fillet radius defined?
    c. What happens to two selected lines when the fillet radius is set to zero?

33. GRIDS
    a. What is the purpose of the grids?
    b. Why doesn't a small grid display completely when you are zoomed away from your drawing?
    c. What command controls the grid color?
    d. Does the grid ever plot?

34. HATCH
    a. For what are hatch patterns used?
    b. Name four of the hatch patterns included with Generic CADD.
    c. What is the name extension of hatch patterns?
    d. What is the fastest way to erase a large hatched area?
    e. Why is it good to have the hatch display off during some drawing sessions?

35. IMAGE SAVE/IMAGE LOAD
    a. What is an image file?
    b. Why are they used?
    c. What is the name extension of all image files?
    d. Can image files be modified?
    e. Why does an image file usually load more quickly than a drawing file?

36. LAYERS
    a. How many layers are available in Generic CADD?
    b. What are the advantages of using numerous layers in a drawing?
    c. List and define three layer commands.
    d. Where on the screen is the current layer displayed?
    e. Which command turns off a selected layer?
    f. Is the ALL LAYERS EDIT default toggle on or off? Why?

37. **LEADER/SHOULDER LENGTH**
    a. What sequence of functions does this command perform?
    b. What controls the size of the arrowhead?
    c. How do you add the text notes?

38. **LIMITS**
    a. What does the LIMITS command do?
    b. What two ways can you convey to Generic CADD the size of the limits you want?
    c. Will ZOOM LIMITS always bring your entire drawing into view? Why or why not?
    d. Which coordinate is always held as entered when entering the limit boundaries?

39. **LINES**
    a. What are the four line commands?
    b. What is the Generic CADD default for each?
    c. Why is it helpful to change the line color as you draw?
    d. Under what hardware restraints is it necessary to use LINE WIDTH?

40. **LOAD BATCH FILE/SAVE BATCH FILE**
    a. What is the purpose of batch files?
    b. What extension is automatically given to a saved batch file?
    c. Name two examples of useful batch files.

41. **MANUAL ENTRY OFFSET ORIGIN**
    a. What does this command do?
    b. Why is it natural that this setting is the Generic CADD default?
    c. When in this mode, from what point are all added points determined?

42. **MANUAL ENTRY OFFSET RELATIVE**
    a. What does this command do?
    b. From what point is each sucessive point determined?
    c. Under what conditions is this command needed?

43. **MEASURE**
    a. Why is it helpful to find the dimensions of certain elements of your drawing?
    b. What three types of measurements can Generic CADD perform?
    c. Why is it important to use the snap commands when measuring?

44. **MOVE POINT**
    a. What is a point in relation to the MOVE POINT command?
    b. Name three instances where you would need this command.
    c. At which point does a circle move with this command?

45. OBJECT BREAK

    a.   Explain the function of the OBJECT BREAK command.

    b.   Name two common instances in which you would need this command.

    c.   From your experience, explain how a circle is broken, depending upon how the points are selected.

46. OBJECT CHANGE/WINDOW CHANGE

    a.   Why is this command helpful?

    b.   What attributes of an object or objects can be changed?

47. OBJECT COPY/WINDOW COPY

    a.   What are two ways to identify the item or items to be copied?

    b.   What is the maximum number of copies allowed at one time?

    c.   What is the copy distance?

    d.   Name five examples of common items that are most productively copied using this command.

48. OBJECT ERASE/WINDOW ERASE

    a.   What are the two ways to identify the item or items to be erased?

    b.   How does this command differ from ERASE LAST?

49. OBJECT MOVE/WINDOW MOVE

    a.   What are the two ways to identify the item or items to be moved?

    b.   Explain what is meant by the option of stretching straight lines as you move.

    c.   Give an example of when you would choose to stretch the identified straight lines and when you would not.

50. ORTHOGONAL MODE

    a.   What does drawing in orthogonal mode mean?

    b.   What special type of command is ORTHOGONAL MODE?

    c.   Why is it not good to guess at drawing a straight line on the screen?

51. PACK DATA

    a.   What happens as Generic CADD removes data from your drawing?

    b.   What does PACK DATA then do?

    c.   How does this command affect the UNERASE command?

52. PEN UP

    a.   Explain the function of the PEN UP command.

    b.   In most cases, what is the substitute command for PEN UP?

    c.   Why is this command not used in the TEXT PLACE command?

53. QUIT

    a.   What does the QUIT command do?
    b.   Does the QUIT command save your drawing?
    c.   When is QUIT most helpful?

54. RADIAL COPY

    a.   What does RADIAL COPY do?
    b.   How is it different from OBJECT COPY?
    c.   Give examples of three graphics that are created more easily with RADIAL
         COPY.

55. RECTANGLE

    a.   How many points define a rectangle?
    b.   Generic CADD sees a rectangle as made up of how many lines?
    c.   Would you use OBJECT ERASE or WINDOW ERASE to delete a rectangle
         most easily?

56. REFERENCE POINTS

    a.   What special type of command is REFERENCE POINTS?
    b.   How do REFERENCE POINTS relate to components?
    c.   When REFERENCE POINTS is toggled to the on position, how do reference
         points appear?
    d.   Why are REFERENCE POINTS helpful?

57. REGULAR POLYGON

    a.   What is the minimum number of sides to a polygon?
    b.   What is the maximum number of sides to a Generic CADD polygon?
    c.   List the three items that must be given to Generic CADD to create a polygon.

58. RUBBER BANDING

    a.   What is a rubber band in Generic CADD?
    b.   Why is a rubber band helpful when drawing?
    c.   What is the default toggle position of RUBBER BANDING in Generic CADD?

59. SCREEN FLIP

    a.   Explain what the SCREEN FLIP command does.
    b.   Why is it helpful to view the drawing status in SCREEN FLIP?
    c.   What types of information is shown with the DISPLAY DRAWING STATUS
         option?

60. SNAPS

    a.   What is the purpose of the snap options?
    b.   What does PERPENDICULAR SNAP do?
    c.   What does CLOSEST POINT snap do?

    d.   What does INTERSECTION snap do?

    e.   Give an example of when you might use each snap option available.

61. **SOLID LINES**

    a.   What do SOLID LINES do?

    b.   How many double line segments must be drawn before Generic CADD fills the lines solid?

    c.   Which command controls the color of the infill?

    d.   Which command controls the display of the infill?

62. **STANDARD POINTS**

    a.   A standard point appears on your drawing as what shape?

    b.   What special command type is STANDARD POINTS?

    c.   Under what condition do STANDARD POINTS plot?

    d.   What are common reasons to use STANDARD POINTS?

63. **STATUS LINE**

    a.   What is the status line?

    b.   What does STATUS LINE do?

    c.   What information about your drawing does the status line reveal?

    d.   Under what conditions would you find it necessary to turn off the status line?

64. **STRAIGHT LINE**

    a.   For what is STRAIGHT LINE used?

    b.   Explain the three ways to draw a line on the screen.

    c.   How does Generic CADD see a line?

65. **TEXT**

    a.   What does the TEXT command allow you to do?

    b.   What is the default text font?

    c.   How do you choose the text color on the screen?

    d.   Explain the function of TEXT REPLACE.

    e.   In TEXT PLACE, what does the small line that appears on the screen represent?

    f.   When is the use of FAST TEXT appropriate?

    g.   What happens if you press PU at the end of a text string?

66. **TOLERANCE**

    a.   What does the TOLERANCE command set?

    b.   Does the setting relate to the scale of your drawing, the size of your drawing, or its real size as measured on the screen?

    c.   Explain when it would be helpful to change the tolerance to a larger value.

67. **TRACE MODE/DRAWING ALIGN/TRACE SCALE**
    a. For what specific hardware are these commands designed?
    b. Which command would you use to copy site plan contours onto your drawing?
    c. What are the advantages and disadvantages of tracing existing drawings into Generic CADD with a digitizer?

68. **TRIM**
    a. What is the function of the TRIM command?
    b. When selecting an object to trim, what is critical about the first point you select to identify the object?
    c. Is it possible to TRIM a circle?

69. **UNERASE**
    a. What does UNERASE allow you to do?
    b. How does saving or packing your drawing affect UNERASE?
    c. What is the limit to recoverable erasures?

70. **UNITS**
    a. What is the purpose of the UNITS command?
    b. What is the default UNITS setting?
    c. List the UNITS options that are available.

71. **VIDEO MENU**
    a. What is the video menu?
    b. What extension is automatically given to all newly created menu files?
    c. What menu is the Generic CADD default?
    d. Under what conditions would you want to design your own custom menu?
    e. When might you want to toggle DISPLAY MENU to the off position?

72. **WINDOW MIRROR**
    a. Explain the function of WINDOW MIRROR.
    b. How does Generic CADD treat text in the WINDOW MIRROR function?
    c. At what angles may mirroring be done?

73. **WINDOW RESCALE**
    a. Explain the function of WINDOW RESCALE.
    b. Can an object be rescaled in both the X and Y directions?
    c. What is the purpose of the axis point selected during WINDOW RESCALE?

74. **WINDOW ROTATE**
    a. Explain the function of WINDOW ROTATE.
    b. What is the purpose of the selected axis point?
    c. How does Generic CADD calculate angles for the rotation?

75. WINDOW SAVE
    a.   What is the function of WINDOW SAVE?
    b.   How does this command differ from IMAGE SAVE?
    c.   What is the limitation in the number of characters of the saved name?
    d.   Give three examples of parts of drawings that it would be helpful to save with WINDOW SAVE.

76. ZOOMS
    a.   The ZOOM commands have what function?
    b.   List and explain four of the most commonly used ZOOM command options.
    c.   How does ZOOM ALL differ from ZOOM LIMITS?
    d.   What affect do the zoom commands have on the actual scale of your drawing?
    e.   Explain why REDRAW DISPLAY is sometimes useful.

Other Illustrated books from Wordware Publishing, Inc.

AutoCAD Release 10

TOM BERGHAUSER and PAUL SCHLIEVE
Create, edit, and copy a variety of drawings as
easily as a word processor manipulates text. Learn
to use line types, cross-hatch patterns, layer names,
and text fonts/styles effectively. Define and modify
screen and tablet menus, components, and shape
libraries. Novice users will find that clear illustrated
examples provide the key to this Computer Aided
Drafting (CAD) based system. This book is an
excellent reference tool for drafting design experts.
It covers versions 2.17 through release 10.
1-55622-064-2 • **$23.95**
softbound • 448 pgs

AutoLISP

WILLIAM M. OLIVER
Bring the power of programming to AutoCad by
using this guide to the AutoLISP interpreter.
Graphic examples and the alphabetical listing of
commands make it easy for the beginning user to
learn and a great reference tool for the seasoned
user. You can simplify repetitive drawings and
automate complex drawing processes to allow more
time to concentrate on the design. Other features
include being able to specify points and do calcula-
tions. Teachers will find this to be a great teaching
aid.
1-55622-161-4 • **$21.95**
softbound • 320 pgs

Illustrated AutoSketch 2.0

DR. PAUL L. SCHLIEVE and
TOM BERGHAUSER
The authors of the popular Illustrated AutoCAD
bring you detailed information on this entry-level,
full functioned, precision drawing tool. This
expanded and updated AutoSketch contains more
commands than the previous version. Hands-on
activities step through the easy-to-use pull-down
menus and dialog boxes that control sophisticated
graphics manipulation functions. Details on how to
import AutoSketch drawings to AutoCAD for additional refinements are included.
1-55622-113-4 • **$21.95**
softbound • 240 pgs

Enable/OA

PETER KENT
This is your guide to better information management and greater productivity. This book
teaches you how to use Enable/OA's multitasking
features which incorporate the five essential tools of
business: word processing, database, spreadsheet,
telecommunications, and graphics. The use of
windows (up to eight at a time) is covered as well
as the use of the menu generator which allows you
to customize your system. The organization of this
book makes it a powerful tutorial and a valuable
reference.
1-55622-163-0 • **$23.95**
softbound • 750 pgs

Harvard Graphics

DAVID G. ZAHORAN
Follow the step-by-step instructions to master the
variety of options of this number one selling
business graphics software. Hands-on techniques
are used to allow beginning users to create graphs
and charts. Advanced users can use this text as a
quick reference and an indepth guide to more
involved graphic presentations. No matter who the
user, Illustrated Harvard Graphics provides simple
and effective use of the software in a non-technical
and professional manner.
1-55622-164-9 • **$21.95**
softbound • 344 pgs

Lotus 1-2-3 Release 3

JOHN MUELLER
Here is a complete, in-depth reference-tutorial for
the long-awaited Release 3 from Lotus Development Corporation. Learn how to create spreadsheets
that are three-dimensional. Specific, practical
examples show you how to organize worksheets,
consolidate templates, and create formulas within a
worksheet using Lotus' new capabilities.
1-55622-160-6 • **$21.95**
softbound • 320 pgs

Microsoft Windows 2.0

ROBERT E. WHITSITT II and
LANA K. BRYAN

This comprehensive reference/tutorial now includes the latest updates of version 2.0. Learn to work with several applications simultaneously and shift among them easily and quickly. Complete and clear descriptions of the Program Information File (PIF) Editor, Print Spooler, and Clipboard features are included. Depend on this valuable guide to master the fundamentals as well as the subtle details of this popular, new operating system.

1-55622-069-3 • **$19.95**
softbound • 304 pgs

Microsoft Word 5.0

JOHN MUELLER and WALLY WANG

Everything you need to know to use Microsoft Word 5.0 is included in this comprehensive guide. Working examples use, modify, and create Word stylesheets and provide working models that are easily adapted to your personal needs. Top-quality documents are easily achieved by following the step-by-step approach of this book. Ready access to commands and functions make this an in-depth reference tool.

1-55622-021-9 • **$21.95**
softbound • 384 pgs

Microsoft Works 1.05

ROBERT H. MARTIN

All the vital information you need to command this popular integrated software package can be found in this example-rich guide. Clear descriptions, applications, and illustrations provide thorough information on using the word processing, spread-sheet, database, and communication features. Applications are discussed in depth with adaptable examples. Build your knowledge level from scratch or expand your skills with this easy-to-use, fully annotated quick reference guide.

1-55622-061-8 • **$21.95**
softbound • 416 pgs

MS/PC-DOS 4.0
Sixth Edition

RUSSELL A. STULTZ

This complete, timesaving reference contains all the significant updates to the world's most popular operating system. The novice-to-expert DOS user is led keystroke-by-keystroke through a sequence of exercises designed to provide hands-on experience. Use the new text-based DOSSHELL to initiate powerful DOS utilities. Each command is detailed in brief, easy-to-understand modules which make this book an indispensable reference.

1-55622-111-8 • **$21.95**
softbound • 272 pgs

Novell NetWare 2.15

TIMOTHY K. McDONALD

Step-by-step techniques clearly demonstrate the fundamentals of this networking operating system from installation to operation. Master NetWare's user commands to effectively store, protect, and share company data and resources among personal computers. Learn to adapt essential software programs to NetWare's LAN for custom applications. Tips on a variety of security and printer options are included. A complete guide for effective communications between centralized personal computers. Reviewed for accuracy by Novell Corporation.

1-55622-065-0 • **$21.95**
softbound • 256 pgs

OS/2

J. EMMETT BEAM

A comprehensive source of commands for general users including a simple-to-complex learning sequence for students. Programmers will find thorough information on Assembler, Linker, and Codeview debugger utilities. Instructions on how to use the OS/2 Presentation Manager interface, the Session Manager interface, and techniques for running MS/PC-DOS within the OS/2 environment are detailed. Recommended for users of the IBM-PC AT, Personal System/2, Compaq models 286 and 386, and most other compatible microcomputers using Intel's 80286 and 80386 microprocessors.

1-55622-053-7 • **$19.95**
softbound • 264 pgs

Paradox 3.0 Volume I
Basic Menu Commands Edition
2nd Edition
DEBBIE and DOUG STONE
Explore the powerful capabilities of Paradox with
the updated information found in this book. This
excellent tutorial details Paradox rules, terms, techniques, keys, and menu options. Examples provide
models to custom design application solutions. This
book is a stand-alone reference to Paradox commands and an introductory to Volume II, the
Paradox application language (PAL) tutorial.
1-55622-158-4 • **$21.95**
softbound • 416 pgs

Paradox 3.0 Volume II
2nd Edition
DEBBIE and DOUG STONE
Maximize the power of Paradox with this updated
reference/tutorial on PAL, the Paradox programming language. Even beginning users can be up and
running after learning a few basic commands.
Hands-on activities take full advantage of this
sophisticated relational database, Paradox 3.0. This
step-by-step book is an indispensable alphabetical
reference to the commands that make this program
so versatile. An excellent accompaniment to
Volume I.
1-55622-108-8 • **$21.95**
softbound • 352 pgs

Q&A 3.0
2nd Edition
THOMAS B. CALVERT
An excellent simple-to-complex tutorial for
programming in plain English. Utilize the latest
techniques of this sophisticated business management system to gather information, create and
revise data, and generate reports. Discover the ease
of using a natural language interface, database,
word processor, filer, and report generator. Each
application is thoroughly explained with ready-to-
implement examples providing working models.
1-55622-155-X • **$21.95**
softbound • 352 pgs

Ventura 2.0
GEORGE SHELDON
All the skills, techniques, and tips needed to master
this top-selling desktop publishing program can be
found in this comprehensive tutorial reference.
Fully illustrated throughout, working examples
demonstrate the enhanced user interface and techni-
cal publishing features designed to make desktop
publishing more functional and easier to use. Step-
by-step learning begins with a blank file that you
develop into an impressive professional-quality
document. New and experienced users will find the
reference value of this book indispensable.
1-55622-104-5 • **$21.95**
softbound • 336 pages

WordPerfect 5.0
JORDAN GOLD
Taste the latest, most significant capabilities of this
top-selling word processing package. Create and
save standard formats for document elements.
Learn to size, rotate, crop, and position imported
graphics. Preview pages that use a variety of fonts,
sizes, column layouts, and graphics. New menu
structure and mnemonic command selection is completely outlined. Hands-on exercises demonstrate
the full macro language needed to create complex
macros.
1-55622-063-4 • **$19.95**
softbound • 416 pgs

WordStar Professional
Release 5
RUSSELL A. and DIANNE STULTZ
Master a host of new WordStar features including
advanced page preview, footnotes/endnotes,
windowing, TelMerge, ListMerge, and many more.
Practical hands-on activities demonstrate the new
user interface and the pull-down menus used to
initiate the latest functions. This step-by-step
learning guide is also a complete reference to the
all-new advanced document features now available
in WordStar 5.0.
1-55622-074-X • **$21.95**
softbound • 304 pgs

Business-Professional

Illustrated Novell Netware: Advanced Techniques and Applications
DR. PAUL L. SCHLIEVE AND DAVID MOLTA
This comprehensive treatment of Netware topics gives readers valuable insight into the use of Netware as an enterprise-wide connectivity platform. Beginning with an overview of the Netware software and hardware architecture, the book moves into detailed discussions of such things as database management strategies, internet working strategies for multi-server environments, and Netware network security. This book is the perfect tool for business managers, network managers, and users who have interest in this rapidly evolving field.
1-55622-169-X • **$24.95**
softbound • 320 pgs

Hawks Do, Buzzards Don't
The Complete Job-Finding Guide
GEORGE MCINTOSH
This handbook for the individual seeking a career change incorporates the proven design and techniques of a professional outplacement program into a book which is easy to read and understand. It leads the reader through a step-by-step process of self evaluation and career assessment, effective written and verbal communications, a proactive self-marketing plan, and an opportunity for long-term control of one's career. It's the next best thing to having an outplacement consultant at one's side. More than a practical workbook, readers frequently comment on the empathy and sensitivity revealed by the author in treating emotions that the job seeker regards as private and unique. The bottom line is that those who read the book feel good about themselves as their sense of self-worth and confidence is restored.
1-55622-171-1 • **$18.95**
softbound • 288 pgs

The Business Side of Writing
RUSSELL A. STULTZ
If you regard writing as a business rather than an art, this book can provide the reference information you need for a successful career in writing or publications management. These guidelines help organize and refine your approach to project planning, cost estimating, project research, financial control, development, and production. Mr. Stultz addresses the tools, techniques, methodologies, and processes to plan, manage, and automate publications development and production with emphasis on the bottom line.
1-55622-157-6 • **$15.95**
hardbound • 224 pages • 6 x 9

Investor Beware
Investigating Investments and Scams
HENRY H. ROTHENBERG
Create your own luck with this book detailing the essentials for safe investments. Avoid shady, risky, and unsuccessful investments. Learn to anticipate and interpret various investment climates and analyze a business from financial statements. The average investor will find what he needs to know about economics, financing, taxes, operating entities, and types of investments. Discover the ramifications of diversified investments such as real estate, franchises, oil and gas, gold, tax shelters, and syndications.
1-55622-055-3 • **$14.95**
softbound • 464 pgs • 6 x 9

Business Emotions
A New Business Concept
RICHARD M. CONTINO
Revolutionize your thinking, conditioning, and approach. Learn why emotions are a controlling factor in every success and failure situation. This practical book will guide you through the maze of hidden psychological issues in a simple and straightforward manner. Achieve predictable, positive, and immediate results. The author introduces unique concepts in and practical techniques for emotional awareness, self-analysis, and effective business functioning.
1-55622-058-8 • **$14.95**
softbound • 184 pgs • 6 x 9

Other Books from Wordware Publishing, Inc.

Artificial Intelligence
Illustrated VP-Expert

Business-Professional Books
Business Emotions
The Business Side of Writing
Consulting Handbook for the High-Tech Professional
Hawks Do, Buzzards Don't
How to Develop Company Policies
How to Win Pageants
Innovation, Inc.
Investor Beware
MegaTraits
Occupying the Summit
Steps to Strategic Management

Computer Aided Drafting
Illustrated AutoCAD (Release 9)
Illustrated AutoCAD (Release 10)
Illustrated AutoLISP
Illustrated AutoSketch 2.0
Illustrated GenericCADD Level 3

Database Management
The DataFlex Developer's Handbook
Illustrated dBASE II (2nd Ed.)
Illustrated dBASE III Plus
Illustrated dBASE IV
Illustrated Paradox Volume I 3.0 (2nd Ed.)
Illustrated Paradox Volume II 3.0 (2nd Ed.)

Desktop Publishing
Achieving Graphic Impact with Ventura 2.0
Desktop Publisher's Dictionary
Illustrated PFS:First Publisher 2.0
Handbook of Desktop Publishing
Illustrated Interleaf
Illustrated PageMaker 3.0
Illustrated Ready, Set, Go! 4.5 (Macintosh)
Illustrated Ventura 2.0
Ventura Troubleshooting Guide

General Advanced Topics
Consulting Handbook for the High-Tech Professional
Illustrated Dac Easy Accounting 3.0
Illustrated Dac Easy Accounting 4.0
Illustrated Harvard Graphics
Illustrated Novell NetWare 2.15
Novell NetWare: Advanced Techniques and
Applications

Programming Languages
Illustrated C Programming (ANSI) (2nd Ed.)
Illustrated Clipper 5.0
The FOCUS Developer's Handbook
Illustrated FoxBASE+ 2.01
Illustrated QuickBASIC 4.0
Illustrated Turbo C
Illustrated Turbo Debugger 1.0
Illustrated Turbo Pascal 4.0
Illustrated Turbo Pascal 5.5

Spreadsheet/Integrated
Illustrated Enable/OA
Illustrated Framework III
Illustrated Lotus 1-2-3 2.01
Illustrated Lotus 1-2-3 Rel. 3.0
Illustrated Lotus 1-2-3 2.2
Illustrated Microsoft Excel 2.10 (IBM)
Illustrated Microsoft Excel 1.5 (Macintosh)
Illustrated Microsoft Works 1.05
Illustrated Multiplan 2.0
Illustrated Q & A 3.0 (2nd Ed.)
Illustrated Quattro
Illustrated SuperCalc 5

Systems and Operating Guides
Illustrated Microsoft Windows 2.0
Illustrated MS/PC DOS 3.3
Illustrated MS/PC DOS 4.0 (6th Ed.)
Illustrated OS/2

Word Processing
Illustrated DisplayWrite 4
Illustrated Microsoft Word 5.0
Illustrated Microsoft Word for the Mac
Illustrated WordPerfect 1.0 (Macintosh)
Illustrated WordPerfect 4.2
Illustrated WordPerfect 5.0
Illustrated WordStar 3.3
Illustrated WordStar Professional (Rel. 5)
The New WordStar Customizing Guide 4.0
WordPerfect: Advanced Applications Handbook

Regional
This Dog'll Hunt
100 Days in Texas: The Alamo Letters
Exploring the Alamo Legends
Texas Wit and Wisdom
Forget the Alamo
Rainy Days in Texas Workbook

Call Wordware Publishing, Inc. for names of the bookstores in your area
(214) 423-0090